The Neighborhood Mint

Dahlonega in the Age of Jackson

Sylvia Head
Elizabeth W. Etheridge

GRG
GOLD RUSH GALLERY

ISBN 978-0-9679769-7

This volume was reproduced from a 1986 edition.
Reprinted with permission

The paper used in this publication meets
the minimum requirements of ANSI/NISO Z39.48-1992 (R1997),
Permanence of Paper for Publications and Documents
in Libraries and Archives
(revision and redesignation of ANSI Z39.48-1984).

Inquires to:
Gold Rush Gallery, Inc.
P.O. Box 38
Dahlonega, Georgia 30533
(404) 630-1861
www.goldrushgallery.com

Dedication to the Reprint Edition

This reprint edition of *The Neighborhood Mint* is dedicated to the memory of the following Georgians, who each had a love of the gold coinage produced in the United States Branch Mint at Dahlonega, Georgia.

Al C. Adams, Sr.

Joe M. Almand, Sr.

George Elliott

Pierce J. (Jack) Hancock, Jr.

William M. Lester

Acknowledgments to the Reprint Edition

The following individuals played a role in helping to bring this reprint of *The Neighborhood Mint* to fruition. The project was conceived and initiated by Al Adams of Gold Rush Gallery. Carl Lester of Gold Rush Gallery was responsible for preparing the new text and plates and for coordinating the project as publication neared. Permission to reprint the book was granted by co-authors Sylvia Gailey Head and Elizabeth W. Etheridge, as well as by the previous publisher, Mercer University Press. We especially want to thank Ms. Head for her patience and nurturing influence with this project. Anyone who knows her is aware of her boundless enthusiasm with the subject matter.

The source of the photograph of the Dahlonega Mint is the original photograph now residing in the archives of North Georgia College and State University, Dahlonega, Georgia. The drawing of the toggle-joint steam coining press was obtained from Don Taxay's *The U. S. Mint and Coinage, An Illustrated History from 1776 to the Present*. The color photographs of the Dahlonega gold coins were obtained through the courtesy of Gold Rush Gallery, the Carl Lester Collection, and Heritage Numismatic Auctions' sale of the North Georgia Collection. A special thanks is given to Greg Rohan of Heritage.

Thanks are also given to Randall Bollig of Buckhead Atlanta and Susan Tilley, Melanie Walz, and Don Dulin of Sheridan Books for their production assistance.

Foreword to the Reprint Edition

By Carl N. Lester

I remember how much I enjoyed reading *The Neighborhood Mint* when it was published in 1986. For those who may be unfamiliar with the work, it is a very readable, meticulously documented account of the day-to-day operations of the United States Branch Mint in Dahlonega, Georgia. The book traces the mint's genesis in the minds of the local miners (following discovery of gold in Georgia in 1828) to the mint's legal authorization via the United States Congress in 1835. Also covered are the mint's gold coinage years of 1838-1861 and its closure in 1861, brought on by the beginning of the Civil War. The treasure trove of information that forms the foundation of the book's research is the *Correspondence of the Mint of the United States at Philadelphia with the Branch Mint at Dahlonega, Georgia, 1835-1861*, obtained from the National Archives in Washington, D. C.

What makes *The Neighborhood Mint* so special are its flowing narrative, rich character studies of the mint personnel and townspeople of Dahlonega, and the "you are there" feeling that it imparts to the reader. One cannot help but gain a sympathetic understanding of the difficulties of the mint personnel, who were faced with all manner of uncertainty, both internal and external, not the least of which was the ever-changing political landscape. All of this is sure to delight history lovers, Dahlonega Mint aficionados, and anyone who likes a good story.

Gold Rush Gallery is having this volume reprinted because we feel that it is a very important historical work. At the same time, copies of this out-of-print book are extremely difficult to find in the numismatic and antiquarian literature markets. As the word "reprint" implies, we have left the original text and photographs unchanged. However, with the authors' permissions, we have taken the liberty of adding four high quality plates, to make this reprint edition special in its own right.

The first plate is the only-known, full-view photograph of the Dahlonega Mint, discovered in October 1997. Many dedicated numismatists and historians had searched for this breath-taking image during the twentieth century. Plates two and three consist of color photographs of a complete nine-piece type set of Dahlonega gold coins, illustrating all of the major design types produced at this historic mint. Plate four is a drawing of a toggle-joint steam coining press, of the type used at Dahlonega.

We hope that the reader enjoys this great book and that its reprinting will be a boon to present and future numismatists and historians.

The Neighborhood Mint

CONTENTS

PREFACE vii
ACKNOWLEDGMENTS xi

CHAPTER 1 1
CHAPTER 2 17
CHAPTER 3 47
CHAPTER 4 67
CHAPTER 5 87
CHAPTER 6 107
CHAPTER 7 131
CHAPTER 8 147
CHAPTER 9 163
CHAPTER 10 181

EPILOGUE 187

APPENDIX 191
GLOSSARY 193
BIBLIOGRAPHICAL NOTE 197
INDEX 199

PREFACE

In the 1830s the United States of America was a fascinating place to visit. Many foreign visitors came to America to witness the curious phenomenon of people governing themselves. The leader of the American people at that time was Andrew Jackson, a man controversial then as now; he was known variously as a backwoodsman, an Indian fighter, a murderer, the hero of New Orleans, defender of virtuous womanhood, and tribune of the people. Alexis de Tocqueville, perhaps the most astute foreign observer ever to come to America, met General Jackson, the walking symbol of democracy, at the White House and was not particularly impressed. What did impress de Tocqueville was the consuming interest of the American people in equality. They have a "passion for equality," he said. Mrs. Frances Trollope, an English woman and a contemporary of de Tocqueville's who spent many months in America traveling on the frontier, was not impressed with anything she saw except the horror of it all. She found Americans to be greedy and crass. They had dreadful manners, ate too fast, drank to excess, and settled their disputes with their fists.

Neither de Tocqueville nor Mrs. Trollope ever visited the little frontier settlement of Dahlonega, Georgia, but a visit there would not have changed their basic impressions of America. Dahlonega was a rough, brawling, frontier town, much affected by that great equalizer, gold fever. Dahlonega was, in fact, at the center of America's first gold rush. What set it apart from other frontier settlements of the 1830s was not only the fact that it was built on gold-bearing land, but that it was home for an institution of the federal government, a branch of the United States Mint. This was the heart and soul of the town.

The mint never served the purpose for which it was created. Although it coined more than $6 million in gold in its twenty-three-year history, this was hardly enough to alleviate the nation's chronic shortage of coins. As Dr. Robert Patterson, director of the United States Mint at Philadelphia, complained, the Dahlonega Branch Mint was a "neighborhood mint." Yet the mint's production never altered the monetary supply of Dahlonega and Lumpkin County. Gold rarely circulated in the area. It was much too valuable for that. The gold produced at the mint disappeared from the community almost as soon as it was issued. The people of Dahlonega used silver coins when they could get them, but most of the time they had only shinplasters, paper bank notes of uncertain value. The mint did not even serve the gold-mining interests of north Georgia, since the opening of the mint coincided almost exactly with the fading of the region's prospects as a great gold-producing area. The Dahlonega Branch Mint cost far more to run than its rather meager production of gold coins warranted. It survived for almost a quarter century not because it was efficient or served any really useful purpose but because it was politically popular.

The man who was largely responsible for the branch mint's existence was that courtly symbol of democracy, President Jackson. The president never visited Dahlonega, but his presence there was ubiquitous. It was his decision to remove the Cherokee Indians to territory west of the Mississippi River that made the existence of the town possible, located as it was in the heart of what had once been the Cherokee Nation. It was his obsession with sound money—gold and silver coins that would not fluctuate in value—and his determination to destroy the Second Bank of the United States that led directly to the establishment of a branch mint in the Georgia gold district. Although Jackson described the Bank of the United States as a "monster, complete with horns and a tail," he did not hate it any more than he did all other banks. He did not trust any bank nor the bank notes they issued, the value of which could change from day to day. But if he destroyed the Bank of the United States, which he considered to be a bastion of aristocracy, he had to provide a replacement for its services. He wanted more solid gold coins rushed into circulation as soon as possible to do battle with bank notes of doubtful worth.

It was also Jackson's obsession with the idea that all government jobs should be so simple that ordinary folk with ordinary intelligence could do them that led many a hopeful applicant to apply for work at the mint with no particular qualification for it and no excuse other than a need for money. And it was the Jacksonian spoils system, with its idea that to the victor went the spoils, that made the contest for office at the mint a lively one throughout its history in Whig as well as Democratic administrations. On President Jackson must also be laid some of the blame for the miserable roads that led to this distant frontier post. He refused to spend money for internal improvements that did not cross state lines, so Dahlonega and its mint were isolated.

Just as the mint owed its existence to national politics, its most important effect on the local community was political. Dahlonega was a town carved out of the woods where people competed for space with deer, turkey, and rattlesnakes, and with each other for life's prizes, among which were positions in the new branch mint. For more than twenty years, job hunting at the mint was a preoccupation of many of the citizens of Dahlonega. The local people did sometimes get jobs as workmen at the mint, but not one of them ever held the coveted post of superintendent. This always went to outsiders, or "foreigners," as the natives called them.

The Dahlonega Branch Mint represented Jacksonian democracy in action. It was a government institution close to the people, one whose operations were simple enough for ordinary people to perform. Those who lived there thought of it as their very own, and they apparently believed until the end that they had a voice in the appointment of the mint's officers and its daily operations. They were mistaken. But just as gold miners believed passionately that if they would but lift one more shovel of dirt or sift one more pan of gravel and riches would be theirs, so the citizens of Dahlonega kept the faith that one more petition would secure a post at the mint for one of their favorites. Hardly a year passed without some agitation in the community over the mint. Out of the sound and fury, however, came nothing. Shinplasters, not gold coins, circulated in Dahlonega, and appointment to the important offices there went in every instance to those favored by professional politicians. The tumult of American life which so impressed Alexis de Tocqueville was certainly present in Dahlonega, but the effective use of political power by the people to control their neighborhood mint was absent. Social, political, and economic equality was as elusive there as elsewhere. The story of the Dahlonega Mint and the men who worked there mirrors America in the age of the common man.

Acknowledgments

This book is the outgrowth of years of friendship with people in Dahlonega and our mutual curiosity about the branch mint that was such an important part of that community's early history. Chief among these is Madeleine Anthony, who almost a quarter-century ago asked a friend, the late Mardelle Lilly Reynolds, of Washington, D. C., to check the National Archives for material about the Dahlonega Mint. Mrs. Reynolds found a historical treasure, more than three thousand pages of letters. The samples she sent to Georgia were so lively and interesting that Mrs. Anthony and the first author of *The Neighborhood Mint* saw in them the basis of a book. We were encouraged by the late Garland Peyton, director of the Georgia Department of Mines and Mining.

Another Dahlonegan, the late Nina Head, requested Congressman Phil M. Landrum's aid in getting the materials from the National Archives put on microfilm. The research began. Elizabeth LaBoone, Leslie Kilgore, and the staff of the microfilm department at the University of Georgia Library were endlessly patient with the reader who, in time, became so indistinguishable from the machine that one Saturday she was completely overlooked and locked in the building. Porter Kellam, director of the library at that time, came to the rescue.

Coming to the rescue in a different way were John Bonner and Susan B. Tate, of the library's special collections staff, who gave much help especially during the search of the Howell Cobb Papers, permission to use which was given by the late Howell Erwin of Athens. Also of great help were Sidelle Ellis at the Clemson

University Library; Lilla Hawes, director of the Georgia Historical Society; Sammie S. Lackey, of the Augusta, Georgia, Library; Carroll Hart, Ruth Corry, and Pat Bryant of the Georgia State Archives; and Nelle Young, director of the Lumpkin County Library in Dahlonega.

For helpful suggestions in organizing the material, our appreciation goes to Susan B. Tate, Virginia Shields, Eliot Wigginton, and the late John Talmadge. Illustrations were obtained through the courtesy of Madeleine Anthony, Martha Hutcherson of Winder, and Sharon Johnson, superintendent of the Dahlonega Court House Gold Museum. We are especially indebted to Marc Cutright, director of media services of North Georgia College, who did the photography. Unstinting in their efforts to provide details about their ancestors were Marian G. Hammers, Madisonville, Kentucky, a descendant of James F. Cooper; Memma S. Kilgannon, Norristown, Pennsylvania, a descendant of David H. Mason; and Hart Shriver, Athens, Georgia, a descendant of Joseph J. Singleton.

For countless courtesies and excellent editorial help, we express our thanks to the staff of Mercer University Press.

To all those who have been patient and encouraging over the years while this book was in process or, for dozens of reasons, on hold, we give our thanks. This includes especially Charlotte Folk.

The Dahlonega Branch Mint, as it appeared originally
Taken from Lawton Bryan Evans, *A History of Georgia* (New York: American Book Co., 1908)

The mint building, after it was transferred to North Georgia Agricultural College
Taken from Andrew W. Cain, *History of Lumpkin County* (Atlanta: Stein Printing Co., 1932)

Present administration building of North Georgia College. After the mint was destroyed by fire in 1878, this building was constructed, using the same outline as the old mint and the same hand-hewn block walls in the basement rooms. Photograph and print by Marc Cutright

Joseph James Singleton, first superintendent of the Dahlonega Branch Mint, 1837-1841
Courtesy Dahlonega Court House Gold Museum

James Fairlie Cooper, third superintendent of the Dahlonega Branch Mint, 1843-1849
Courtesy Mrs. Marian G. Hammers and Atlanta Historical Society

Dr. Matthew Stephenson, amateur geologist and mineralogist, and assayer at the Dahlonega Branch Mint, 1850-1853. When the California gold rush threatened to make a ghost town out of Dahlonega, Stephenson mounted the courthouse steps, pointed toward Findlay Ridge, and cried, "Why go to California? In that ridge lies more gold than man ever dreamt of. There's millions in it." His plea was soon corrupted to the famous cry of many a hopeful miner, "Thar's gold in them thar hills."

Courtesy Madeleine Anthony

The Neighborhood Mint

CHAPTER 1

Four years after its founding, the little north Georgia village of Dahlonega presented a pleasing sight to an astute English visitor. George Featherstonhough, a geologist, liked the situation of the town, located as it was on a "fine knoll, sloping to the east, with the ground rising agreeably to the west." Nature had been lavish in its gifts to the area which but a short time before had been part of the Cherokee Nation. There was a backdrop of mountains, fine streams, large trees, and, in the village itself, two excellent springs of water. The settlers were on their way to making contributions to the area, too. By the time Featherstonhough visited there in the summer of 1837, they had erected what their visitor described as a "rather imposing looking granitic building, called the Mint," as well as a brick courthouse in the center of the square. In addition a few "tolerable-looking private buildings . . . gave the town an air of pretension."[1]

Featherstonhough was a critical observer. For the most part his praise stopped with his description of what God and nature had provided. As a geologist, he was most interested in the formation of the rocks and the soil on which the town was built. He noted that the courthouse stood on a broad vein of hornblende slate, and that the soil of the public square was impregnated with small specks of gold.[2] He, of course, was not the first to notice this.

---

[1]George W. Featherstonhough, *A Canoe Voyage Up the Minnay Sotor*, 2 vols. (London, 1847).

[2]Ibid., 2:303.

The Cherokees had called the area Talonega, which means yellow, and white men had driven the Cherokees out because they wanted the yellow stuff. The proper spelling of the Indian word was disputed for a time, until it eventually became Dahlonega,[3] but there never was any dispute about what it meant. It meant GOLD! with all of that word's economic and social consequences.

Featherstonhough stayed at a tavern in the village. He noted the manners of the people with a disapproval common to foreign visitors to America at that time. Such airs of pretension as the town had were "indifferently borne out by the inhabitants," he observed. The other guests at the tavern behaved in a manner incomprehensible to him. He cited the example of a pretty young lady, reputed to be an heir to a fortune, who had just married an itinerant doctor, "a vulgar man, probably without a dollar in the world," after an acquaintance of only three days. The groom had not even bothered to shave for the wedding; what was worse, in the view of this proper Victorian, he had taken her to the public supper table, where she sat "amongst stage drivers and all sorts of persons at that peculiar moment when women of refinement shrink from the gaze of their nearest friends."[4] Doubtless, Featherstonhough did not understand the "passion for equality" that Alexis de Tocqueville noted as the most distinctive characteristic of early nineteenth-century Americans.[5] And nothing would equalize a poor man faster than a good gold strike. With but one good strike, a failed physician might become an instant success as a miner.

As late as 1828 much of north Georgia had been the province of the Cherokees with only a few whites living here and there. Whites had moved into Nacoochee Valley east of Dahlonega in 1822, and for three decades missionaries had worked among the Cherokees, introducing them to Christianity and to the white man's civilization and trying to strengthen their resolve not to

---

[3]E. Merton Coulter, *Auraria* (Athens, 1956) 99-100. Featherstonhough spelled the Cherokee word "Tahlonekay."

[4]Featherstonhough, *A Canoe Voyage,* 2:302.

[5]Alexis de Tocqueville, *Democracy in America* (New York, 1966) 475.

move. But that was before the discovery of gold in the area. Late in the nineteenth century an old man, Benjamin Parks, remembered that early in 1828 when he was deer hunting on the Cherokee lands, he kicked up something that glinted. It was gold. When the word spread, fortune hunters came by the thousands.

The United States government was obligated by treaty to honor the rights of the Cherokees to this region, so troops were sent to protect them. Georgians were furious. They contended that the United States had an obligation to the state, too. In 1802, when Georgia ceded its western lands, the United States government promised to remove all Indians from the state. Georgia officials concluded that the time had come for the national government to honor its commitment. Within two years after the discovery of gold, the Cherokee Nation had become Cherokee County so far as the state of Georgia was concerned, and the state moved rapidly to consolidate its control of the region. The state legislature made it illegal to discourage Indians from moving. It put all people living there—Indians as well as whites—under the jurisdiction of the state. It forbade the meeting of all tribal organizations and councils and declared all Cherokee laws and customs null and void.

The new edicts of the state were stubbornly resisted by several missionaries living in the area. One of them, Samuel Worcester, was sentenced to the penitentiary for his refusal to obtain a permit to live in the territory and to take an oath to support the constitution of the state. The missionary's rights were upheld by the Supreme Court of the United States in the celebrated case of *Worcester vs. Georgia* (1832), a decision subsequently ignored by both the state of Georgia and President Andrew Jackson, who had no tender sentiments for the rights of Indians. In fact, President Jackson had already withdrawn the federal troops from the Cherokee Nation, and a band of Georgia Guards, never numbering more than sixty, had been given authority to keep order there. These sixty men were hardly a match for the motley thousands of gold hunters who subsequently poured into the region.[6]

---

[6]Coulter, *Auraria,* 2-5.

Auraria, located some five miles south of the Dahlonega site, was the first town settled in the gold country. At that point the Etowah and Chestatee Rivers are only a couple of miles apart, and their tributaries provided numerous opportunities for panning gold. At first the place was called Nuckollsville, after Nathaniel Nuckolls, the first innkeeper of the place, but the name was subsequently changed to the more elegant Latin one of Auraria, which means gold mine. It was a thriving town by the time Lumpkin County was carved out of the Cherokee territory by an act of the legislature on 3 December 1832, and was a likely site for the county's seat of government. Dahlonega did not then exist except as a place called "Licklog," so named because Benny Parks salted his livestock in log troughs there. Nevertheless, Licklog was chosen over Auraria as the county seat because it was more centrally located, and the boom town to the south was on its way to extinction. About the first of October 1833, when the Inferior Court of the county unanimously agreed on the name Talonega for the village, the *Western Herald* of Auraria admitted that the "village is improving with unprecedented rapidity."[7]

Dahlonega's first settlers moved into a thick forest. They had to contend with wild turkey and deer, and not so pleasantly with rattlesnakes. A single family killed 137 rattlers that first year. Gradually, however, the forest gave way to a respectable clearing, and in 1834 a good many houses were built. Harrison Riley erected the first store to supply the needs of an increasing number of miners, many of whom probably threw up pine pole cabins for shelter until they could do better. Because the town was to be the county seat, the citizens took great pains to clear the public square and get it ready for the new courthouse, but the streets of the town, especially the back streets, were in miserable enough condition for the grand jury to call them to the attention of the town commissioners. "Frequently," the grand jury reported in August 1834, "they are the repository of all manner of filth and garbage to the great annoyance of the citizens."[8]

---

[7]Quoted in Andrew W. Cain, *History of Lumpkin County for the First Hundred Years, 1832-1932* (Atlanta, 1932) 63.

[8]Ibid., 58-59, 66.

Two years later the two buildings in Dahlonega that most impressed Featherstonhough were the mint and the courthouse. If he had investigated either of these buildings on his visit, he would have found the saga of their construction less than exemplary. The yet unfinished mint building may have looked impressive, but a careful inspection would have revealed serious flaws in its construction. The courthouse had a distinguished air, too, but it had been built only after long delays. The first contractor, one John Humphries, was paid $2,000 to begin work on the building in February 1834 and another $500 the following July, but Humphries made not a move. Late in the summer the following year when still not a brick had been laid, the grand jury found that the "citizens of the county had been greatly and materially injured by the delay of said building." Not until October 1835, almost two years after work was supposed to have been started, did the law attempt action. It was then that the deputy sheriff tried to serve a writ on Humphries, who drew a pistol on the sheriff. As the sheriff went for a posse comitatus, Humphries hid himself. Later, as the deputy sheriff put it, he "absconded from the county of Lumpkin." The sureties on Humphries's bond were ordered to pay.[9]

The courthouse on the gold-flecked square which Featherstonhough admired was the work of Ephriam Clayton and was built largely in 1836. The foundation stone, the timber, and the sand for the mortar were found locally. The bricks were probably made in Lumpkin County, too, although they may have been hauled in by wagon from distant Augusta. The building itself was paid for, at least partly, in gold bullion, an appropriate enough medium of payment for a town built squarely on hopes for gold.[10]

The raucous life of the town's early inhabitants was surely a shock to the proper English visitor. But it was a harbinger of life styles of gold rush towns of the West two decades later. The county's first grand jury, meeting in the log courthouse which served until a better one could be built, indicted one man for the murder

---

[9]Ibid., 72.

[10]Ibid., 73-74.

of the Auraria postmaster, ordered several men tried for operating tables of chuckaluck, and recommended that a new jail be built as soon as possible. Indeed a new jail was a necessity. Within the bounds of the courtroom and while court was in session, fights broke out. As the months passed, more and more tippling shops opened in the county. There both whites and Negroes loitered, even on the Sabbath Day. Whisky brought in by wagon from Tennessee always enjoyed a ready sale, and if customers had not the cash to buy it, some had nerve enough to steal it. A kind of frontier justice was dispensed in some cases, but other offenders went to jail to await the due process of law.

The county's first jail cost a mere $127. As might be expected for such a modest cost, it was found to be useless because it was entirely insecure. The Inferior Court, therefore, in February 1834 contracted for another one to be built at a cost of $1,800, half of which was to be paid in advance. Significantly, the court ordered that the jail be built on the plan of the one in Hall County, which cost only $957.[11] This difference in cost is not without significance in a county where public buildings much larger than the jail were soon to be constructed.

If Featherstonhough knew about any graft in the construction of public buildings, he did not comment on it, but he did observe what the pursuit of gold did to the valleys around Dahlonega. He went to Cane Creek and Pigeon Roost and other streams where the search for gold was under way and climbed some of the picturesque hills and ridges to have a better look. These hills, wooded to the top, were separated by small valleys, often no more than fifty yards wide. From the hilltops the valleys looked to him like a series of brickyards, being all dug up with the washed gravel thrown in heaps. He found the miners so intent on the pursuit of gold that they were insensitive not only to the beauties of nature they were rapidly destroying, but also to the curiosities of nature they uncovered in their search for gold. On Pigeon Creek he was shown a remarkable thing—a large pine log buried twenty-one feet deep lying on a bed of slate. One end

---

[11]Ibid., 62-66, 75-76.

of the log was worn away in a crescent-like form. The side of the log next to the slate was clean, with the marks of the slate impressed on it, but the top was thickly indented with quartz gravel. Part of the outside of the log was carbonized, but the inside was still fresh. It had to have grown between the retreat of the ocean from that spot and the excavation by retrocession of the valley where it was found. It was a marvel to the geologist, but something of no interest at all to men with gold on their minds.[12]

Observing what had happened in those valleys where gold had already been mined, Featherstonhough wrote in his journal that he "could not but be sorry to see the destruction which awaited all these beautiful valleys." The trees would be rooted up, streams diverted from their courses, and places singularly beautiful turned into places of desolation.

> To obtain a small quantity of gold for the wants of the present generation, the most fertile bottoms are rendered barren for countless generations. And this must ever be the case in countries where the Government is not intelligent and strong enough to put the mining districts under regulations. By and by, when the gravel in the valleys is all dug out and washed, they will take to the hills, which will be violated and ransacked in a similar manner, and what was once a paradise will become a desert.[13]

Deposits of gold were found in the southern Appalachians along a line running from about Montgomery, Alabama, northeastward through northern Georgia and into North Carolina. The Georgia belt followed the same direction as the folds and ridges of the main Appalachian ranges, but a bit to the southeast. This gold belt was about two hundred miles long and some ten miles wide. A second band of gold was found in the South Mountain area of North Carolina, not a part of the Appalachian range, and a third east of the North Carolina mountains with Charlotte as the center. The predominant rock in all the Southern gold fields was gneiss mixed with mica, talcose slate, hornblende, and granite. The rock alternated in strata of various thickness from three

---

[12]Featherstonhough, *A Canoe Voyage,* 2:251-54.

[13]Ibid, 255.

inches to thirty feet. Much of the gold was found buried from one to four feet deep in the streams that crisscrossed the area. Sometimes a little gold was found in veins in the hills. While most of the finds were small—sometimes just dust to be carried about in a goose quill—some large chunks were found here and there. Featherstonhough knew of one piece weighing twenty-eight pounds that had been found in North Carolina and of heavy pieces found on Duke's Creek in Nacoochee Valley.[14]

The presence of gold in the mountains was known from earliest times. The Indians had certainly known of the existence of gold for centuries, for the miners in the 1830s found soapstone crucibles in the placers bearing the marks of Indian handicraft. Legend had it that the Cherokees jealously guarded the location of their mines and put to death one group of Spaniards who had located the mines lest they tell others. The earliest Spanish explorers were certainly interested in Georgia gold. In 1515 Ponce de Leon was told of a rich cacique in the interior who had much gold. Fifteen years later Panfilo de Narvaez was told more exactly that gold came from the interior Appalachians. In 1540 Hernando de Soto set out to explore the region for himself and to hunt personally for gold.[15]

The French knew of the existence of gold in the Appalachian area, too. René de Laudonnière's account told of the great mountains called "Apalatcy" in which "rise three great rivers sweeping down sand with which is mixed gold, silver, and copper. On this account the inhabitants of the region dig pits in the river so that the sand swept along by the water may fall into them by gravity." He said they then drew up the sand in a hollow cane reed until it was full, and shook and jarred it until they found the

---

[14]Ibid., 252-53; William Phillips, "Essay on Georgia Gold Mines," *American Journal of Science* 24(1833): 1-2; George F. Becker, *Gold Fields of the Southern Appalachians,* 54th Cong., 1st sess., 1895, House doc. 5, vol. 4, pt. 3, 252-53; "Gold Mining in Georgia," *Harper's New Monthly Magazine* 59 (Sept. 1879): 508.

[15]Fletcher M. Green, "Georgia's Forgotten Industry," *Georgia Historical Quarterly* 19 (1935): 96-98.

grains of metal.[16] The French map located the gold in the vicinity of Dahlonega.

What specific discovery set off the gold rush of the 1820s is a matter of dispute. Benny Parks said he was the first to find gold in the Cherokee country in 1828. He may have, but almost certainly gold had been found in the Appalachian regions earlier. Conrad Reed, a boy who lived in Cabarrus County, North Carolina, was said to have picked up a piece "large as a smoothing-iron" in 1799. Subsequent finds were made on a line running southward to the Cherokee territory of north Georgia. An Indian boy found a gold nugget in the Chestatee River not far from Auraria in 1815. In the late 1820s strikes were made on Duke's Creek near Nacoochee and at Ward's Creek near Dahlonega. One account said gold in Lumpkin County was found first on Pigeon Roost.[17] Accounts of the first strike were no more reliable than the tales of thousands of miners who flocked into the territory after 1828 to seek their fortunes. This was the great "intrusion." A departing major in the United States Army described one motley group of about two hundred whites, Indians, halfbreeds, Negroes, young boys, and old men in the region: "their occupations appeared to be as various as their complexions comprising diggers, sawyers, shopkeepers, pedlars, thieves, gamblers, etc., besides there were also found in the hopeful assemblage two colonels of Georgia Militia, two candidates for the legislature and two ministers of the Gospel, all no doubt attracted thither by the love of gold."[18]

It was estimated that by 1830 ten thousand intruders were taking out about $5 million in gold every year. The richest fields in the whole Appalachian area were found in Georgia and North Carolina, an area the engineers called the "real Potosi of Amer-

---

[16]Quoted in Becker, *Gold Fields of the Southern Appalachians*, 254-55.

[17]"Gold Mining in Georgia," 509; Walter R. Crane, *Gold and Silver* (New York, 1908) 71; Green, "Georgia's Forgotten Industry," 98-99; W. P. Morrell, *The Gold Rushes* (New York, 1941) 74-75.

[18]Quoted in Coulter, *Auraria*, 4-5.

ica." Some gold was gathered from the streams by shoveling gravel into a boat. Two men could take about five loads a day, and if they were lucky they would find a good bit of gold. The simplest way to get the gold, however, was by panning. A pan about fourteen inches in diameter was filled with gravel from the streams and washed and stirred until the lighter substances were carried off, leaving the gold on the bottom. Early observers described it as a "very tedious process," but one which would secure every particle of gold, however small. The first improvement on panning was the use of a hollow gum log about eight feet long and from twelve to twenty inches in diameter, hollowed into a semicylinder. Cleats or riffles fitted inside kept the gold from passing through. Gravel was thrown in at the upper end and stirred with a rake until water from a conductor washed off the dirt. The old gravel was taken out, a new supply put in, and the contents of the gum washed into a pan. This gum rocker saved labor, but it wasted gold. A writer for the *American Journal of Science* suggested an improvement on the hollow gum and other rockers: a revolving iron cylinder which would separate the larger gravel for discharge and sweep the gold and finer fragments of rock over a perforated plane. He thought more gold would be saved that way. When placer gold began to give out, the miners looked for it in veins. Those who were careless in the diggings paid with their lives when mines caved in. The luckier ones dug vein gold successfully, separating it from the rock by the use of a pounding mill and quicksilver. But as a visitor to the region in the 1840s noted, "in this particular department of their business the Dahlonega miners confess themselves to be comparatively ignorant; and what proves this to be the case is the fact that some of their ore has frequently been worked over a second time with considerable profit."[19]

The gold mined in Georgia was of excellent quality. In most of the state's gold areas it averaged 0.950 in fineness, higher than

---

[19]Green, "Georgia's Forgotten Industry," 94; Phillips, "Essay on Georgia Gold Mines," 14-17; Charles Lanman, *Adventures in the Wilds of the United States and British American Provinces,* 2 vols. (Philadelphia, 1856) 1:348-49.

that found in the South Mountain area or elsewhere in North Carolina. Some lumps found in the region were worth from $500 to $1,000 each. While large amounts of gold had been found in Virginia, the Carolinas, and Alabama, it was generally conceded that Georgia produced the largest quantity and decidedly the best quality.[20]

Not everyone was enthusiastic about gold mining in Georgia. The *Milledgeville Journal* once suggested that gold mining should be prohibited in Georgia, and no one disputed the fact that the lust for gold led to a "mania for speculation." But on the whole the prospects for mining looked good. The American mines might be worth the attention of an English company, the Englishman Godfrey T. Vigne observed in 1831. Mining even showed promise of improving the prospects for agriculture. Mining would create home markets for the farmer, Vigne said, and wise farmers would find it prudent to "stick to the plow and leave mining to miners." At a distant period, he predicted, less cotton would be grown in the gold districts giving way to bread stuffs and "farinaceous succulent vegetables."[21]

Certainly there was more than one way to cash in on Georgia's golden bonanza. Vigne's suggestion that farmers might find wealth in feeding hungry miners was perhaps the most difficult way to turn a dollar. Inventive minds were to think of many others in the years to come. In the immediate future the great land lottery afforded possibilities. A lucky man might draw a lot rich with gold; a luckier one might sell an unlikely lot to an unwary buyer. In the slightly more distant future, money-wise men of the community would seize fine opportunities for a good living—if not wealth—in the United States Branch Mint soon to be built in Dahlonega. For the man whose politics was right, turning gold dust into bright golden coins might be as lucrative if not as exciting as the search for a strike.

Whites who poured into the Cherokee country had no legal right to be there until the autumn of 1832, when the disposition

---

[20]Becker, *Gold Fields,* 258; Lanman, *Adventures,* 1:344-45.

[21]Green, "Georgia's Forgotten Industry," 150; Godfrey T. Vigne, *Six Months in America* (London, 1832) 237-40.

of all the lands in the territory was settled by lottery. Most of the country was divided into 160-acre lots, but the gold region was divided into prizes of 40 acres each. Under Georgia law all males who had resided in the state for four years were entitled to a draw, as were certain other classes of people, including widows and orphans of soldiers killed in war, the deaf, dumb, and blind. In all, some 130,000 citizens participated in the lottery with its 35,000 prizes. The choice lots were numbers 1031 and 1052. The latter was on the Yahoola River and was especially famous. It was within the bounds of the Indian reservation, but men were accustomed to creeping across the border at night to get a meal bag full of dirt which they panned the next day, finding, it was said, twenty to forty dollars in gold in each bag. When the lottery awarded this choice lot to a farmer in the middle of the state, speculators set off hurriedly to buy it from him.[22]

Some gold lots changed hands as many as twenty times by 1860. So much speculation, in fact, probably frightened real capital away from the region. Many attempts to take land away from an unsuspecting winner in the lottery were successful. Charles Lanman, an English visitor, told of the south Georgia man who won a plot in the lottery and came to look at it. He stopped at a farmer's house to get a guide and mentioned that he did not like rattlesnakes. The farmer, spotting an opportunity too good to miss, led the stranger to his lot across a ravine alive with rattlesnakes. So terrified was the would-be miner that he swapped his land for a horse on which to retreat south.[23]

The discovery of gold in the southern Appalachians had repercussions in Washington, D. C., where it led to an extended debate on the nation's currency. The sound money advocates argued that the rich strikes in the "new Eldorado" meant that prosperity was assured for the country if only the gold could be kept at home. Hardly any gold coins circulated in the United States during the 1820s despite the fact that the United States Mint at Philadel-

---

[22]Green, "Georgia's Forgotten Industry," 106-107; "Gold Mining in Georgia," 510.

[23]Lanman, *Adventures,* 1:346-47.

phia was busily coining them. The ratio of gold to silver was so much more favorable to gold in Europe than in America that the nation's gold supply was steadily drained for foreign trade. At the same time countries making remittances to the United States seldom paid in gold. The discovery of gold in the South, some thought, would surely mean an end to this situation, but not unless a more favorable ratio for gold could be obtained.

The debate on the proper ratio began in 1830 and was not finished until four years later. In that time it became entangled in President Jackson's war on the Bank of the United States. Gold was touted as the "National Currency," the "Sound Currency," by that bellwether of Jacksonian thought, the *Globe*. "Gold—the cherished currency of all nations—a currency banished from the United States for a whole generation by the power of bank legislation—this precious currency once more appears in our land, and in defiance of bank power, will diffuse and spread itself throughout the country, and become the familiar inmate of every industrious man's pocket." The glittering new coins, the *Globe* said, would dispense with the "danger of receiving, or the humiliation of offering to pass, the counterfeit imitation of a wretched paper currency."[24]

The gist of the long argument over gold versus silver was just what the ratio should be. The ratio that prevailed in England and France for more than a decade was 15.8:1 and was sufficiently accurate. Secretary of the Treasury Samuel D. Ingham suggested a ratio slightly less than this, but others held out for a ratio of 15.9:1 or even higher. "Gold goes where it finds its value, and that value is what the laws of great nations give it," Senator Thomas Hart Benton argued.

> In Mexico and South America, the countries which produce gold, and from which the United States must derive their chief supply, the value of gold is 16 to 1 over silver; in the West Indies, generally, it is the same. It is not to be supposed that gold will come from these countries to the United States if the importer is to lose one dollar in every sixteen that he brings in; or that our gold will

---

[24]Quoted in Don Taxay, *The U. S. Mint and Coinage: An Illustrated History from 1776 to the Present* (New York, 1966) 196-97.

> remain with us, when an exporter can gain a dollar upon every fifteen that he carries out. Such results would be contrary to the laws of trade, and therefore we must place the same value upon gold that other nations do, if we wish to gain any part of theirs, or to retain any part of our own.[25]

Not everyone was convinced that the bimetal system could be maintained, because constant adjustment of the ratio would be necessary. If they had to choose between gold and silver, these doubters said, they would take silver, the "ancient money of the United States." By 1834, however, gold fever reached such a pitch that Congress shifted its emphasis toward the high ratio of 16:1, which would surely keep gold at home, and just as surely, in time, drive out silver. The *Globe* was jubilant about the passage of the bill in late June 1834 which made official the "just and truly American ratio of 16 to 1." But the opposition press, the *Niles Weekly Register,* asked where the glorious gold was to come from. "The 'gold regions of Virginia,' and other States? Bah! It will require a Midas, with an ass's ears, to make a *long* bray about this!"[26]

Not one Midas, but several, with ears just the right length, soon began to press the issue. The gold country had to be outfitted with mints to turn bullion into gold coins. A private coiner, Templeton Reid, of Gainesville, Georgia, had made gold coins in 1830. He made quarter eagles, half eagles, and eagles—$2.50, $5, and $10 pieces—of such good quality that they were actually worth more than their face value. But neither miners nor politicians were content that a private coiner should process gold for which miners were often paid in bank notes of questionable value. Gold bullion varied so much in quality, and therefore in price, that it was difficult to use in commerce, and it took too long to send samples to Philadelphia to be assayed. A mint of their own would give miners "the real Jackson shiners," surely a great boon.[27]

---

[25]Quoted in A. Barton Hepburn, *History of Coins and Coinage in the United States* (New York, 1903) 38-39.

[26]Quoted in Taxay, *The U. S. Mint and Coinage,* 196, 197.

[27]*The Standard Catalogue of United States Coins from 1652 to Present* (New York, 1947) 114; Coulter, *Auraria,* 23-24.

The idea of building at least one branch mint was advanced as early as 1830. The *American Journal of Science* said one was needed in North Carolina, where gold cropped out on the surface and where "such treasures are obtained by slight movements of loose materials, as in some countries are collected at great depths."[28] Within six months after the passage of the bill establishing the ratio of gold to silver at 16:1, Senator George A. Waggamon of Louisiana introduced a bill for the establishment of branch mints. One was needed in New Orleans, he said, because of the great importation of gold and silver in that port which then had to be shipped to the mint at Philadelphia at great risk and expense. His bill was supported by Senator John C. Calhoun of South Carolina, who had mining interests in north Georgia, and by Senator Thomas Hart "Old Bullion" Benton of Missouri, who favored additional mints to provide "hard money." Senator Henry Clay of Kentucky led the forces opposed to the branch mints. Because the mints would be in the Cherokee country, he feared that their presence would bring added pressure for the early removal of the Cherokees. Besides, he said, it would save money to ship all the gold to Philadelphia for coining. The $5 million in gold imported in 1834 could all be shipped from New Orleans for a mere $375, a great savings over the cost of constructing a mint and maintaining it. But the advocates of building branch mints objected strongly to Clay's figures. Gold, they said, could never be shipped by the pound. Because of the risk involved, carriers demanded a percentage rate. It would cost at least $125,000 to ship such an amount of gold. The bill establishing three branch mints was passed 3 March 1835. One branch at New Orleans was for the coinage of gold and silver; the others at Charlotte, North Carolina, and "at or near Dahlonega in Lumpkin County, in the State of Georgia," for the coinage of gold only.[29]

The new mint at Dahlonega began to go up that very year. In the years of its operation it proved to be a more certain, if not a more ready source of wealth than the mines themselves. In 1838,

---

[28]"Miscellanies," *American Journal of Science* 20 (1831): 401-403.

[29]Taxay, *The U. S. Mint and Coinage,* 199-200.

when the branch mint issued its first gold coins with the imprint "D" for Dahlonega, the last of the Cherokees left for the Indian territory. Because the land was once theirs, and their language gave the town its name, it was ironic that the departure of the Cherokees coincided with the end of easy wealth. The deposit mines were nearly exhausted by then, and there was much doubt as to whether or not it would ever be profitable to work the vein mines.[30]

High hopes for the mint, jubilation at the departure of the Cherokees, and the speculators' eternal hope that vast wealth lay under the next rock masked the future. Dahlonega was not destined to become a great city. When it was about a dozen years old Charles Lanman found the village to be "uncommonly picturesque in form and location," snuggled up as it was against the mountains, but "antiquated" in appearance, consisting almost entirely of log houses. All of the watercourses about the town had been mutilated with spade and pickaxe and their water had turned a deep yellow. "All the streams in a circuit of many miles look that way. Large brooks and even an occasional river have been turned into a new channel and deprived of their beauty. All the hills in vicinity of Dahlonega are riddled with shafts and tunnels." Because several auriferous veins cut through the town itself, Lanman said, "it is common after a rain to see the inhabitants busily engaged in hunting for gold in the streets."[31]

If one of those inhabitants found as much as $100 worth of gold, he could take it at once to the "Mint Establishment," as the most prominent attraction at Dahlonega was called, and receive almost immediate attention. The nine employees of the mint would turn the gold into coins of uncommon beauty. They jingled in a man's pocket. The mint itself provided good livings for the long-eared Democrats, or when the political fortunes turned, to shorter-eared Whigs. It was only foreigners like Featherstonhough and Lanman who seemed to note or care what the price of these golden eagles was.

---

[30]"Miscellanies," *American Journal of Science* 34 (1838): 397.

[31]Lanman, *Adventures,* 1:343-44.

CHAPTER 2

A few weeks after the bill establishing the branch mint at Dahlonega was passed, the Reverend Ignatius Few, a lawyer and Methodist preacher, was appointed as commissioner to superintend the erection of the building. The appointment was made by Secretary of the Treasury Levi Woodbury, acting on orders from President Jackson. Few's qualifications for the post were as meager as the instructions he received from Washington, but he readily accepted the appointment and immediately fired off a dozen questions about selecting a site and making plans for the building. He wanted to advertise widely for possible builders because, he added in a masterpiece of understatement, "There are very few architects or master builders in the upper parts of Georgia who unite the requisite degrees of skill, capital, and honesty, for an undertaking of this sort."[1]

Plans for the building were to be drawn at the United States Mint in Philadelphia, but final decisions on both the plans and the site would be made in Washington. Secretary Woodbury urged Few to give "early and persevering attention" to this important business, a charge Few apparently took seriously, for in early May he left Athens, one of several towns he called home, to make the journey north to Dahlonega to select a site. Although the build-

---

[1]Few to Woodbury, 4 Apr. 1835, National Archives, RG 104, Letters from U. S. Mints and Branches to Secretary of Treasury, 1834-1861, hereafter cited as NA-lt.

ing plans Few hoped to receive from Philadelphia did not come, he decided to begin work anyway. In Dahlonega he found the residents annoyed at the delay in erecting the mint, a full two months having elapsed since passage of the bill authorizing its construction. They were losing from six to eight percent in exchanging their gold for currency, so to them time was of the essence. The delay in getting started, and the tension between citizens of Dahlonega and mint officials was an omen of things to come.

The first delay came with the selection of the site. Few described the village of Dahlonega to officials in Washington. It was located on forty acres of land, one of the original tracts in the gold country lottery. Streets ran diagonally across the tract, and the small town lots were laid off among the knobs and ravines of the mountainside on which it was located. No suitable site for the mint existed within the town itself, but an elevated ridge just north and west of the town provided some good tableland. Less desirable sites were available on the three remaining squares that bordered the town. Few selected six sites he thought would do, marked them A through F, and sent detailed descriptions to Washington. His first preference was for one of the three sites, A, B, or C, located just north of the town on land owned by a Mr. Cassidy of Savannah. These were on the "healthy" and respectable side of town and offered a fine view of the town and adjacent hills. The water supply was good and there was probably gold as well. Although any of these three would have been admirable, acquiring one of them required a long trip to Savannah to see Cassidy, a trip that might be useless if the rumors proved true that Cassidy's title to the land was not good. Few had no desire to go to Savannah but he persuaded Richard Persse, one of the citizens of the town, to go in his stead, authorizing him to offer $500 for ten acres.

If Cassidy would not sell—and this indeed turned out to be the case—Few had three alternative sites to offer. Of these, he preferred site E on a tract of land south of the town which belonged to William Worley. It, too, afforded a commanding view of the whole town and the country east, north, and west. Though a bit narrow at the top, it was probably big enough to contain all the buildings that would be needed. Some buildings were there already. A good well had been dug and the owner was willing to sell ten acres for $800 or the whole thirty-seven-acre tract for $1,500. The plot was heavily timbered, so there would be fuel enough for the mint; the soil was fertile, so gardens should flourish. Gold might be there, too. Unhappily, it was in that part of town where the "indigent and profligate" lived. But it would do, and the owner was willing to sell. The other two sites, D and F, were less desirable. One was on land too elevated for building; the other was level enough, but Few was afraid it was not a healthy spot. All the lands next to it were being worked for gold and were marked by "large and deep pits filled with rain water, generating miasmata, the fertile source of the endemic fever of the South."[2]

Not until early August was the matter finally settled. Cassidy refused to sell any of his land to the mint, despite repeated pleas, so Few paid Worley $1,050—a marked increase in the price he had quoted to officials in Washington and Philadelphia—for ten acres south of the town, complete with several small buildings. A possible contractor from Tennessee thought that brick could be made from clay found in the area, and Few had spotted a small mountain within a half-mile of the site with granite projecting from its sides. Lime could be shipped in from Gainesville, twenty-five miles away, for a modest price. After purchasing the lot, Few hired a surveyor to run the lines. By the end of the summer he was ready to advertise for bids on the building.[3]

A delay of five months between the passage of the bill authorizing the mint and the purchase of the site annoyed the impatient citizens of Dahlonega, and they looked for someone on whom to fix the blame. At a town meeting on 30 July the citizens drafted a vigorous protest to Secretary Woodbury, advising him of the "utter hopelessness of anything being done efficiently" by some one no more energetic than Few.

> [He] is labouring under permanent ill health from rupture of the lungs his case seems hopeless & he appears conscious of it himself which makes it the more surprising that he should hold on

---

[2]Few to Woodbury, 23 May 1835, NA-lt.

[3]Few to Woodbury, 23 May, 4 Aug. 1835, NA-lt.

> with so much tenacity to an office which he as well as every person at all acquainted with his situation must clearly see he cannot possibly fill be his intentions ever so good—all energy appears to have left him & his business habits *if ever he had any* has certainly escaped. he appears very laudibly & we may say entirely devoted to the affairs of another and better world & should be left quietly to their contemplation.

They reported that Few was living in Gainesville and had honored their town with but a single visit since his appointment. They assured the secretary that the interest of the community had "sorely suffered," and they hoped that some businessman on the spot would be appointed who could "give his constant and vigorous attention to the business."[4]

Col. Josiah Shaw presided at the town meeting that drafted the resolutions sent to Secretary Woodbury, President Andrew Jackson, and Dr. Robert Patterson, the director of the mint in Philadelphia. Among the seven members of the committee drafting the resolutions were Richard S. Persse, who had tried unsuccessfully to buy the land from Cassidy for the mint, and J. J. Singleton, who within two years was named its first superintendent. In their appeal to President Jackson the citizens pointed to the great wrongs they had suffered by the unconscionable delay, made the more irritating by the fact that the other two branch mints were "under contract and in a fair way to their completion." Dahlonega people thought there was a "total disregard of public duty" somewhere, and they called on the president "not only as Guardian of our liberties but of our private rights to exercise his constitutional powers in our behalf." The committee was hardly satisfied a few days later when Few arrived in town one afternoon, purchased a lot, and departed the next morning. They thought it likely he would resign, and if so, they very much hoped

---

[4]Dahlonega Committee to Woodbury, Jackson, and Patterson, 30 July 1835, National Archives, RG 104, Microcopy T 646, Correspondence of the Mint of the United States at Philadelphia with the Branch Mint at Dahlonega, Georgia, 1835-1861, hereafter cited as NA-c.

that someone from the community could be appointed in his place.[5]

The citizens of Dahlonega were certainly correct in their assessment of Few's health. Though only forty-six years old when he was appointed commissioner of the mint, he had been a victim of tuberculosis for eleven years. Within a year after he accepted his federal appointment, his health became so bad that he retired from the ministry and devoted his time and such energy as he had to the establishment of the new Methodist school, Emory College, near Covington. He did not, however, relinquish his commissioner's job as the Dahlonega citizens so fervently hoped, but continued to serve in his fashion until the mint, in an unfinished state, began operations three years later.

Methodist chroniclers remembered Few as a man of extraordinary abilities, known for his purity of heart and admired for the greatness of his mind, the soundness of his scholarship, and the dignity of his manners, but he was also remembered as a visionary, a man lacking in practical common sense, especially in financial affairs.[6] Certainly Few was not a greedy man. For years he received nothing at all for his services, although, as he reminded Secretary Woodbury, "in giving up my time to the control of the government, I have incurred both loss and expense." He just hoped he could be saved from the necessity of pledging his personal credit for debts incurred for the government.

He, too, was embarrassed by the delay in getting construction of the mint under way, but he was certain that he was in no way responsible. Did he not have to wait for the plans from Philadelphia? "I could do nothing," Few wrote to President Jackson.

> I had neither a plan of a building nor authority to obtain one in any other way than through the Director of the Mint, who ne-

---

[5]Dahlonega Committee to Woodbury, Jackson, and Patterson, 30 July 1835, NA-c; Josiah Shaw to Patterson, 5 Aug. 1835, National Archives, Records of the Bureau of the Mint, RG 104, "V" series, vol. 2, hereafter cited as RG 104, "V." The other members of the committee were Josiah Shaw, G. K. Cessna, Henry M. Clay, John Choice, and A. B. Holt.

[6]Alfred Mann Pierce, *Lest Faith Forget: Story of Methodism in Georgia* (Atlanta, 1951) 99.

> glected to furnish me with it. From the commencement I urged haste and prompt attention to the business, and whilst I experienced a painful anxiety . . . I sustained a pecuniary loss, because my compensation is only a commission on actual expenditures under my supervision & yet my time was obliged to be subjected to the exigencies of this business so as to preclude me from engaging in any other occupation.[7]

Dr. Samuel Moore, Dr. Patterson's predecessor as director of the mint at Philadelphia, offered a different account of the delay. Although he had no part in Few's appointment and had learned of it only from Few himself, Moore immediately invited the Georgian to visit Philadelphia so that he could see what a proper mint building looked like. Few had no intention of making such a tedious journey and did not even acknowledge the invitation. While he waited for Moore to send the plans, Moore waited in vain for Few's arrival in Philadelphia. Eventually, despairing of ever seeing Few, Moore forwarded a list of questions about the cost of labor and materials in Dahlonega, information he thought essential to the drawing of proper plans. Few ignored these questions. What did such mundane details have to do with dimensions, divisions, and the general outline of the building? As he wrote to Secretary Woodbury when another two months had elapsed, Dahlonega was "an obscure frontier village with only a few rude, and unskilful workmen, whose prices could not govern in estimating the cost of a building, which would attract competitors for its erection from the principal cities of the Union."[8]

Moore continued to press for answers even after he had left his post as director of the mint, and Woodbury wrote to Few regularly begging for information. Nothing but silence ensued from Georgia. Moore wanted practical information. What was the cost of the lot? Was enough water power available to run machinery of ten or fifteen horsepower? What were the transportation costs for machinery and other heavy items from the nearest port to Dahlonega? Were bricks, stone, and lumber available and at what

---

[7]Few to Jackson, 8 Sept. 1835, RG 104, "V," vol 2.

[8]Few to Woodbury, 23 May, 9 July 1835, NA-lt.

price? How much would labor cost? Did carpenters work by the day or by measure? What was the price of heavy blacksmith's work by the pound?

Perhaps Few was honest when he contended the questions were unimportant, but these were questions that could not be answered without making a trip to Dahlonega, and Few was not in the village from May until August. In early July he took up residence in Gainesville so that he would be near Dahlonega. There he waited, presumably in anxious suspense, for the mint plans to come and for Cassidy to change his mind about selling the lot. When he finally went to Dahlonega to purchase the land, he gathered information for Moore's questions. Since he was in town but a single day, the information must not have been too difficult to obtain.

The price and dimensions of the lot were easy enough, since he had just signed the papers. Water power was not available. Bricks could be easily made, the citizens of the town getting them for chimneys and underpinning at six to seven dollars per thousand delivered. Building stone was available, too, "but there are neither stone quarriers, cutters, nor masons in Dahlonega. Such work has never been done there," Few wrote. "Tis true, I was informed that there were two vagrant intemperate and irresponsible men, who were occasionally in Dahlonega, and were considered as stone masons, but they had done only a little job work amounting to a few dollars and could not be expected to fix the prices of such work." Lumber, too, was readily available: beams and joists at $25 per thousand; weatherboard, $20 per thousand; shingles at $3.50 to $4 per thousand, but prices would be lower for a large order.

A shortage of labor was the real problem in Dahlonega. Carpenters could be hired for $1.50 per day and they would board themselves, "but good workmen cannot be obtained for such a price." Since no brick structures existed in Dahlonega, Few could not find out how much bricklayers charged by the thousand, and they never furnished their own sand and lime as Moore seemed to think proper. "They build chimneys and underpin houses by the job, and the sand and lime are found them by the employer," Few wrote. Lime was available delivered on the site for 55 cents per bushel unslaked and 35 cents per bushel slaked. Dahlonega had no masons, and as for blacksmiths who worked by the pound, Few had never heard of such a thing. Blacksmiths worked for moderate wages and were paid by the month.

To answer Moore's questions on the cost of shipping machinery, Few probably had to get information from Savannah, the nearest seaport, and Augusta, the point up the Savannah River from which the overland trip to Dahlonega began. Freight charges from Savannah to Augusta for heavy articles like machinery were 40 cents per hundredweight. For bales and boxes the charge was $18^{3}/_{4}$ cents per square foot. From Augusta to Dahlonega the price for shipping goods was \$1.50 to \$1.75 per hundredweight, "depending on the state of the roads and the time of the year." Wharf, drayage, and storage expenses in Savannah and Augusta "may be assumed to be around \$30 to \$50." Few said insurance costs should be figured in Philadelphia.[9]

The same day that Few mailed his answers to Philadelphia he received in the mail a plan for the mint building. It was identical to that being built in Charlotte, having been prepared especially for the North Carolina site based on information received from the commissioner of that mint. But Director Patterson, in an effort to avoid further delay, decided to use the same plan for Dahlonega, "supposing that the circumstances of the two places might not be materially different." He found that Few's answers to the questions, while necessarily imperfect, conveyed very important information. "Permit me, Sir," Patterson continued, "to invite you to a full correspondence, hereafter, on the subject of the important business entrusted to your agency. You may depend upon my zealous cooperation; and I would most respectfully suggest, that a prompt attention to your communications with the Director might, considering the position in which he is placed, not only serve to aid you in advancing the work, but to relieve you, in part at least, from a painful responsibility. You have seen, no doubt, an account of the proceedings of a public meeting, held at Dahlonega, on the 30th of July."[10]

---

[9]Few to Patterson, 4 Aug. 1835, NA-c.

[10]Patterson to Few, 14 Aug. 1835, NA-c.

Few was testy in his reply. He denied neglecting either his duty or his correspondence. As for those questions, he still believed that if the answers to them were to be the basis of the estimate, "the consequence would be mischievous, as the prices which would be fixed by the contractor . . . would be different from those furnished by the answers."[11]

Few was not satisfied with the plans for the mint building. They were not specific enough. He had a dozen or more questions for Patterson. Had he waited a little, he could have saved himself trouble and spared the nerves of the exasperated Patterson, who was ordered by the Treasury Department to answer Few's questions before they had even been received in Philadelphia. Few's questions and Patterson's building specifications crossed in the mail. Few needed basic information: the depth of the cellar, the thickness of the foundation walls, the number of floors in the building exclusive of the cellar, the height of the ceilings, the thickness of outer and division walls. How were the vaults to be constructed and where? How were the fireproof apartments to be constructed? What special arrangements were needed for furnaces and for the steam engine? What order of architecture was the portico and the cast iron columns? What were the dimensions of the doors and windows? Would there be shutters?[12]

Within four days after Patterson received from Few the long sought information on the cost of supplies and labor in Dahlonega, he drew up a recommended advertisement for the mint contract. He suggested that Few run it as a circular letter in the newspaper, since that would be cheaper than an advertisement. He laid out some specifications:

> The building is to be 125 feet in front by 33½ feet in depth, with a projection in the rear of the centre of 53 by 35 ft., and to be two stories in height, with a basement story of five feet above the surface of the ground. The basement, in front, to be of hammer-dressed range work, the principal and attic stories of brick. The sills and heads of the windows to be of stone,—the cornice of

---

[11]Few to Patterson, 29 Aug. 1835, NA-c.

[12]Few to Patterson, 11 Aug. 1835, NA-c.

brick,—the roof covered with zinc. The basement and principal stories are to be arched, with groin arches, throughout the front building. The whole work is to be of the best materials, to be executed in a workmanlike and substantial manner and to be completed by the ____ of ________ in 183_.

A detailed description of the building with any information respecting it that may be required, will be given by the undersigned, on application made to him by letter.

Plans and elevations of the building may be seen on application to the undersigned at Dahlonega, or to the Director of the Mint at Philadelphia.[13]

Long before Patterson's suggested circular letter arrived, Few sent advertisements to the *Globe* in Washington, and the *New York Journal of Commerce,* and to papers in the Georgia towns of Athens, Augusta, Savannah, Milledgeville, and Columbus. He appointed 22 September as the day for letting out the contract. Small wonder he was anxious to get answers to his questions about the "technics of the art" to be employed in the construction. Without such specifications, he told Secretary of Treasury Woodbury, "I shall be liable to omit many things which ought to be inserted in the Bond, and to use terms in an erroneous sense, which may give a dangerous advantage to the Contractor."[14]

Fortunately, by the time the contractors made their bids, Few had further information from Patterson. The cellar was to be ten feet below the floor of the principal story. Partitions in the front building were to be of brick; partitions in the back building were to be omitted as this was to be a single large room. The vaults were to be barrel arched and doubled walled to make them drier and more fireproof. Furnaces should be left to a subsequent contract, but some provision should be made for them in the course of the building. More information would be sent later on the steam engine, the principal part of which was to go in the cellar of the back building. Carpenters were to follow the architect's drawings for the porch both as to style and proportions, but the cast iron pil-

---

[13]Patterson to Few, 17 Aug. 1835, NA-c.

[14]Few to Woodbury, 7 Aug., 12 Aug. 1835, RG 104, "V," vol. 2.

lars of the piazza were not intended to be formed in true architectural proportions. "Leave this to the taste and judgment of contractor with your aprobation."[15]

August 1835 was a busy month for Few. After purchasing the site for the mint early in the month, Few spent some time in Athens and Gainesville, writing letters on mint business from both towns. By month's end, after advertising for bids, he advised his correspondents to address him at Covington, to which he repaired often in the months ahead to look after the business of the fledgling Methodist school about to be established there.

The somewhat vague specifications for the mint forwarded by Patterson might not have created a problem for sophisticated contractors who read Few's advertisement in the Washington and New York papers, but none of these contractors made a bid for the job. Instead, all eight builders who journeyed to Dahlonega were from Georgia except two who came from the nearby states of North Carolina and Tennessee. Some of these contractors may have been experienced enough to build the mint even under the difficult conditions imposed by Dahlonega's frontier location, but the successful bidder found the work difficult indeed.

The would-be builders looked over the plans for the building, scouted the neighborhood for supplies, and made their bids. The lowest bidder was Benjamin Towns of Athens, who got the contract for $33,450. The agreement was signed 22 September 1835. Towns was required to finish the building within eighteen months—by 22 March 1837. He was to have two months longer to complete the work in case of accident, bad weather, or other unavoidable delay. The agreement was secured by a bond twice the amount of the bid by Col. John A. Cobb and Dr. James Tinsley, also of Athens. "Mr. Towns the Contractor is reported to be a skilful architect & a very respectable, honest man & Dr. James Tinsley of Athens, who is interested with him is a man of science, of great energy, and one who has also some practical acquaintance with architecture," Few wrote to Secretary Woodbury. He felt generally pleased with what he had done. The successful bid

---

[15]Patterson to Few, 24 Aug. 1835, NA-c.

was $263 less than the estimate made by the architect. The final agreement with Towns included exact specifications for the building, but Towns agreed to allow for alterations or modifications if these could be done without injury to him. Payment would be made in four installments, never exceeding the value of the work done up to that point.[16]

Dr. Tinsley, the signer of the bond, was actually a partner of Towns. If it was somewhat irregular for a partner to sign the bond, then it was no more irregular than much of Tinsley's life. Like many nineteenth-century Americans who knew a little something about many things, Tinsley did have skill in architecture, and he also knew a little Latin, Greek, and medicine. He studied the latter with a Wilkes County physician and attended some lectures in Philadelphia, but Dr. Tinsley's own practice of medicine was too unorthodox even for the lax standards of the day. He so defied the conventional rules of practice that his medical sponsor, probably to get him out of the way, secured an appointment for him as professor of chemistry and natural philosophy at Franklin College in Athens, a position for which he was remembered later as being "totally unqualified." Fortunately for the young scholars, Tinsley soon tired of the restraints of teaching and resigned within two years of his appointment.

An impressive-looking man with a large head, broad shoulders, black piercing eyes, and an equally black curling beard, Dr. Tinsley was a man of remarkable strength in spite of the fact that he suffered from hemorrhages of the lungs. To overcome this weakness he often went about in the coldest weather without an overcoat or hat. Though blessed with a good mind, Dr. Tinsley could never stick with anything very long. He built a number of buildings in Athens, including Demosthenian Hall on the Franklin College campus. He also established and edited the short-lived *Southern Cultivator*. And at one time he ran a tavern. All the while he practiced medicine in his fashion. It was an odd fashion. He never kept any medicines himself, but depended on whatever

---

[16]Articles of Agreement, I. S. Few, Agent, U. S., and Benjamin Towns, NA-c; Few to Woodbury, 28 Sept. 1835, RG 104, "V," vol. 2.

he found in the homes of families he visited. And though he sometimes performed surgery, he owned no surgical instruments, but used whatever was at hand, whether it was a borrowed pocket case of implements or a simple razor. Dr. Tinsley had little regard for the conventional rules of society, but he was a man of grace and charm. He married a woman of wealth, but as one of his contemporaries observed, "without extravagant living [he] gradually became poorer, until all his estate was gone."[17]

This was the man who went to Philadelphia to see exactly what a mint looked like so that the building in Dahlonega would be a proper one. Dr. Patterson insisted that the contractor make the long journey because so many explanations were necessary. The contractor for the branch mint at Charlotte had already made the trip and had declared that without having seen what a mint really was, he could not have executed his contract satisfactorily. So Dr. Tinsley traveled north in January 1836 to see a mint for himself.[18] He and Towns were launching a big project, one which, including the machinery, would cost more than $50,000.

Winter came early in the north Georgia mountains, so the making of bricks for the mint had to be delayed until spring, but work did get started after a fashion. A year after Few received his appointment as commissioner for the mint, the building consisted of a hole in the ground into which about two-thirds of the rubble foundation had been laid. Towns had hoped to be paid $8,000 to $10,000 on 1 April 1836, based on the amount of materials on hand, but Few insisted on paying only for work actually done, an amount he figured at $1,700. Writing to the Treasury Department for the money, Few reported that most of the principal story should be finished by the first week of June. In a burst of optimism, he added that enough of the building would be finished within the year so that mint operations could begin. He was wrong.

Few's hope for an early completion of the work may have been occasioned by the fact that he was so far away. After letting the

---

[17]Augustus Longstreet Hull, *Annals of Athens* (Athens, 1906) 57-60.

[18]Few to Patterson, 10 Dec. 1835; Patterson to Few, 30 Oct. 1835, 24 Jan. 1836, NA-c.

mint contract in September, Few left Dahlonega and went to Covington, where he busied himself with the new college. He subsequently wrote to Treasury officials in Washington and Philadelphia from Athens and Macon before taking up his residence in Columbus, more than two hundred miles away. After the first of June 1836 he had every intention of returning to Dahlonega and staying there, but he did not count on the Creek Indians going to war along the Georgia frontier. Those wars kept him in Columbus until late June, and they also prevented him from sending along official papers to Washington. When the wars broke out, Few's family retreated to the interior, taking all the official papers with them. The business of the mint had to wait until a measure of peace was restored.

The second payment was due the contractor in June, but the work had progressed so little by the time Few arrived there late in the month that he was reluctant to pay. He did give Towns $2,000 in July and another $5,000 in September to complete the second installment. Torrential rains fell in Dahlonega from April through much of the summer of 1836, slowing the work, Few explained. On the spot to assess the situation for himself, he was far less sanguine than he had been when he wrote from Columbus. "The Edifice . . . cannot be prepared to receive the machinery by the first of January next," he wrote to Woodbury. "I hope the Roof may be gotten on by that time, but I am very sure that it cannot be farther advanced." The "providential interruption" provided for in the contract had already occurred. The contractors could be expected to claim their extra two months.[19]

And claim it they did. When their third pay installment was due in February 1837, the work was so far short of the contractor's estimate that Few would pay him only $4,500. Just five days before the 22 May deadline, the "utmost limit allowed the [contractor] in the articles of agreement," Few wrote from the comfortably remote spot of Columbus that although "the work cannot be wholly accomplished before the first of August," the building

---

[19]Few to Woodbury, 25 May, 29 Sept. 1836, NA-lt; Few to Patterson, 26 Apr. 1836, NA-c.

was ready for the machinery. Few thought Towns had tried to fulfill his engagements punctually, and he expressed the wish that the government would not insist on forfeiture of his bond. Few completed the third installment of Towns's pay—another $6,600.[20]

The ineptitude of the contractors in reading building plans was part of the trouble. Dr. Tinsley had apparently understood little he had seen in Philadelphia, for when additional plans were sent south to make possible the installation of the machinery, neither Tinsley nor Few could understand them. Few could not distinguish vaults from arches, so he could not figure out what supported the walls and fireplaces. Neither he nor Tinsley could understand the need for two doors in each of the vaults, despite the fact that Dr. Tinsley had seen similar vaults in Philadelphia. Most puzzling to Few were the square black spots on one side of the kitchen fireplace in the basement and on the side of each of the three fireplaces in the in the second story. "What are they designed to represent?" he asked. Back came the reply. "The square black spots, as in all architectural drawings, represent *flues,*" Patterson wrote, and "what you term vaults are merely the arches that support the floors of the true vaults above, *and their walls,* including those which cross the arches." He went on to express his regret that the contractors found the designs so difficult to understand.[21]

Within a week after Congress voted to establish the branch mint at Dahlonega, the scramble for positions in it began. Applicants from Georgia abounded for any post the mint might have to offer—superintendent, assayer, melter, refiner, and coiner. Sometimes the applicants or their promoters got a bit confused and inquired about the posts of "assayist" or "smelter." One young man was warmly recommended for the post of refiner at the mint by his father, a recommendation subsequently endorsed by the Georgia congressional delegation, who added that "we still recommend him" even if the post of melter, refiner, and assayer be

---

[20]Few to Woodbury, 13 Mar., 17 May 1837, NA-lt.

[21]Few to Patterson, 26 June 1836; Patterson to Few, 5 Aug. 1836, NA-c.

combined into one. Often no attempt was made to disguise the reasons for seeking employment at the mint. One man was in a "peculiar situation," having loaned $70,000 to a New York house which proved insolvent. He would be satisfied with the job of superintendent at either Dahlonega or Charlotte.

"What are the requisite qualifications for the officers of the branch mint?" Josiah Shaw of Dahlonega wrote to the mint director in February 1836 when the building was scarcely more than a fair-sized hole. What did the superintendent, assayer, refiner, and fluxer need to know? Did the qualifications of the last three require their selection from the principal mint? Georgia's congressmen, beleaguered by their constituents, made similar inquiries of the secretary of the treasury. Congressman Jabez Jackson put the questions bluntly. "Is immediate practical knowledge *necessary* in the coiner; and in the assayer, and melter & the refiner?" If abstract science would avail for the position of coiner, he continued,

> I think that the Branch can have the benefit of the attainments of the Professor of Chemistry and Natural Philosophy at the University of Georgia. . . . A recommendation by the [Georgia congressional] Delegation for the threefold office of assayer, or melter & refiner, has been already made, but this individual has not much abstract scientific qualification, however worthy in general character, and the same may be said of the gentleman who having been nominated to the Senate will undoubtedly be confirmed as superintendent of the Establishment. I have supposed that the Government would be willing to avail itself of the circumstance of *one,* at least, of the three officers at Dahlonega being a man *professedly* of science.[22]

One man "professedly of science" did win an appointment to the Dahlonega Mint, but it was not Congressman Jackson's choice, his own brother James. Nor was it Dr. Asa Pond of Lexington, Georgia, who had also been recommended for the position of assayer. Dr. Pond should have the job, his sponsor said, be-

---

[22]Shaw to Patterson, 7 Feb. 1836, NA-c; Cong. C. E. Haynes to Woodbury, 8 Apr. 1836, RG 104, "V"; Cong. Jabez Jackson to Patterson, 20 Dec. 1836, NA-c.

cause many people had moved away from Dr. Pond's part of the state and those who remained were so healthy that "Dr. Pond's receipts from his profession [were] very small for the support of a charming family encreasing yearly in numbers." The lone scientist at the mint was to be Dr. Joseph W. Farnum, professor of chemistry and natural philosophy at Washington College in Lexington, Virginia. He was the choice of Director Patterson himself, and his appointment as assayer was the one in which the director felt "the most entire satisfaction."[23]

The position of coiner also went to a man of Patterson's choosing, David Hastings Mason, a wood engraver from Philadelphia. He was the inventor of a machine for engraving and stamping the borders and figures on bank notes, and he was making dies for the mint at Philadelphia when he was selected for the Dahlonega post.

The position of superintendent, however, was a political appointment. It went to Dr. Joseph J. Singleton of Athens, who had been both a state senator and legislator and was an unsuccessful candidate for Congress from the state at large in 1834. In that campaign, Singleton seemed certain to be elected despite the opposition of William E. Jones, editor of the *Athens Whig*. But Jones devised a scheme that would surely result in Singleton's defeat. He wrote an obituary for Dr. Singleton, arranged for it to appear shortly before election day in the *Augusta Sentinel,* and requested papers in Columbus, Macon, Milledgeville, and Savannah to copy. The notice of his death was, as Mark Twain would say, "greatly exaggerated," but it was too late for a correction to be published. Singleton's opponent won. Jones, fearing that Singleton's supporters would tar and feather him for his underhanded trick, wisely left for Texas. He came home only when Singleton's followers had been appeased by their hero's appointment as superintendent of the mint at Dahlonega.[24]

---

[23]Patterson to Woodbury, 23 Feb. 1837, NA-lt.

[24]Federal Writers Library Project, *Athens, Georgia, Guide Book* (1939-1941?) unpublished typescript in University of Georgia Library, Athens, 170.

The appointment was made in January 1837. Patterson assured Singleton that the appointment gave him "great satisfaction," and he urged the new branch mint superintendent to visit the mint at Philadelphia "as early as you can find it convenient." Go to Dahlonega first, he was advised, and then come on to Philadelphia. Singleton did not have to be urged. He expected the appointment and looked forward to the trip. Accompanied by Edward Wingfield, the young man who would be his clerk, Singleton had a fine time. He purchased stationery, carpeting, and an office table in Philadelphia, and then, before returning home, visited Washington.[25] He was there when Martin Van Buren was inaugurated as president of the United States.

Singleton attended to one important matter of business on this trip. He took the oath of office and signed his bond. Unfortunately, the oath was subsequently lost, so Singleton, in the spring of 1837, made the six-hundred-mile round trip from his home in north Georgia to Savannah, where the nearest federal judge was located, to take the oath again. That was bothersome enough, but what really worried him was the matter of his pay. He thought it ought to have started on the day he took the first oath, an opinion reinforced when the lost oath was subsequently found in the Treasury Department in Washington.

The next officer of the mint was anxious about his pay, too. No federal judge lived in Lexington, Virginia, where Dr. Joseph W. Farnum fulfilled his duties as a member of the faculty at Washington College. Farnum waited until he went to Philadelphia a month after he received his appointment before taking the oath of office, only to discover that the delay cost him a month's pay. He thought he should have been paid from the day he received notification of his appointment, and asked about it persistently enough until it was done.[26] Mason, the coiner who was on the spot

[25]Patterson to Singleton, 4 Jan. 1837, NA-c; Singleton to Patterson, 14 Jan., 9 Mar. 1837, NA-c.

[26]Singleton to Patterson, 11 May, 7 June 1837; Patterson to Singleton, 21 June 1837; Farnum to Patterson, 28 Mar. 1837; Patterson to Woodbury, 5 July 1837, NA-c.

in Philadelphia, took his oath and signed his bond promptly, and presumably was as promptly put on the payroll.

Meanwhile, plans were made to ship the mint machinery from Philadelphia. The peripatetic Few made arrangements from Columbus. Although he had not been in Dahlonega for more than six months, he assured authorities in Philadelphia that all would be ready to receive the machinery by mid-May. When Few gave the go-ahead signal, the building still did not even have a roof. Singleton, en route from Philadelphia, stopped in Augusta and made the necessary arrangements for the machinery to be shipped to that point. When he reached Dahlonega in late March he found the building, except for the roof, nearing completion, and he hoped the roof would be finished in a few days. Send the machinery, he advised. "Our anxiety to commence coining of our metal is fully equal to its value."[27]

Fifteen boxes of machinery valued at just over $15,000 were shipped on the brig *New Hanover* from Philadelphia to Savannah on 22 April 1837. Included in the shipment were cutting out presses, fly wheel, crank shaft, drawing frame, eighteen annealing pans, and a coining press. From Savannah, the machinery was shipped up river to Augusta, where Singleton ordered it loaded on ten wagons for the ten- or fifteen-day trip to Dahlonega. It arrived safely in late May, well before the mint building was ready for it. Singleton did not like the way the building was progressing, but was at a loss for a remedy, "as Col. Few is the Superintendent and lives three hundred miles off."[28]

Arrival of the mint machinery was occasion for considerable comment in town. "It is a much more complicated and massive concern than we had expected. The entire Machinery necessary for coining, weighs upwards of *fifty thousand pounds,* and cost the Gov-

---

[27]Few to Patterson, 13 Mar. 1837; Singleton to Patterson, 19 Mar., 27 Mar. 1837, NA-c.

[28]Bill of Lading, 22 Apr. 1837, NA-c; Singleton to Patterson, 11 May 1837, NA-c. Mint Director Patterson was paid a two and one-half percent commission on the machinery for Dahlonega, $379.81. Commissions of R. M. Patterson, n.d., NA-lt.

ernment for its transportation from Augusta to this place, upwards of one thousand dollars," the *Dahlonega Recorder* reported. That was a large sum for the depressed economy of 1837. The editor made excuses for the delay in completing the building—too much rain, early frosts, and freezing weather well into the spring—but he denied the persistent rumor that the mint would begin operations just as the gold supply in Georgia dwindled.

> This we assert, is erroneous. The mineral resources of this country never did hold out more flattering inducements to the industrious, than at the present important crisis in the monied world. . . . the whole amount of Gold bullion extracted from the Gold mines in the gold region of Georgia during the last year . . . is largely upwards of two hundred thousand pennyweights. . . . The labor of the present year will yield equally as much as that of the last. And as soon as the Mint shall go into operation, the Gold bullion will increase in value about 5 per cent. Under the present embarrassed condition of the country, would it not be the interest of the cotton planter, whose energies have been strained to the last extremity, for the last year or two in "making cotton to buy negroes with, and buying negroes to make cotton," to engage a portion of their slave labor in the Mines, where they can be assured it will yield them 80 cents per day to the hand at the lowest calculation?[29]

The lack of a roof on the building was but one of the problems. Just as crucial was the lack of a well to supply water for the engine. With the machinery ready to be installed, the well had not been started. Plans indicating where the well was to be placed had been sent to Few, who presumably still had them in Columbus. Singleton got started at once, however, and within the week he reported with satisfaction that the well was nearly finished. It was fifty-two feet deep with a water supply of about seven feet, and it could be deepened another three or four feet.[30]

The building progressed but slowly. Because iron was not available in north Georgia, Dr. Tinsley decided to substitute wood

---

[29] *Dahlonega Recorder,* quoted in unidentified clipping, NA-lt.

[30] Patterson to Singleton, 23 Mar., 19 Apr. 1837; Singleton to Patterson, 7 June, 5 July 1837, NA-c.

or brick columns for the cast iron ones specified. Far more serious, however, was the discovery that the walls of the mint were not strong enough to support the groin arches above the basement story. In fact, a large crack appeared in one wall. There was no alternative, Singleton said, but to "begin again and make new walls, support by *patch* work those already made, or dispense with the groin arches altogether above the basement story." Few was not available to give his advice. No one knew if he would come at all. Singleton did not believe the present contractors could make new walls satisfactorily nor did he think a patch job would do because "there will be eternal dread by the occupants of the building, so much so, that there is some doubt whether it will be occupied or not. I know of no better plan than to dispense with all the groin arches above the basement story, and substitute the common wooden floor protected by some preventive of fire." In Philadelphia, Patterson was irritated but not surprised. Few had not supervised the construction, and Patterson had heard from several sources that "the contract for the building had been executed in a most careless and slovenly manner." Obviously, inviting Georgians to Philadelphia for training had not worked. They either did not come, or if they came, they learned little. A reverse procedure seemed in order. Patterson decided to send Franklin Peale, the melter and refiner from the Philadelphia Mint, to Dahlonega to see what was wrong. The coiner, Mason, was finally on his way south, too, and he was a practical man who should know what to do about the groin arches.

It was very late summer before the skilled workmen, led by a Mr. Baker, arrived to install the mint machinery that had been on the grounds for more than three months. They came from Charlotte, where they had installed the machinery in the other gold mint. In Dahlonega they were handicapped because the irons and crosspipes they needed to support the boiler could not be obtained. They had barely started when Few arrived, after a year's absence, to check on the mint's progress. He did not stay long, but he was there long enough to disagree rather vigorously with Singleton's assessment of the quality of construction. That crack was nothing to worry about, no more than three or four feet in length in one of the partition walls. Singleton had already taken down the offending arches and erected substitutes of his own design.[31]

Few thought there was no need to change the plans for groined arches in the walls, but he urged the mint director to reconsider the zinc roof. "That metal is so sensible to temperature, that, in this climate it continually contracts and expands with the variations in heat, and it cannot be secured by nails, or soldering, because of its rapid oxidation when in contact with other metals." It had been tried in many cities in Georgia, he reported, and it is "generally, if not universally abandoned. Tin painted on both sides, seems to be in every respect preferable." For once Few was right, but Patterson would have none of it. He well remembered unfortunate experiences with tin roofs when he was a professor of natural philosophy at the University of Virginia, and he would not place any reliance in them. Zinc it was to be.[32]

Mason, a man of good common sense, arrived in Dahlonega in mid-September after a thirteen-day journey from Baltimore. He was not impressed by what he saw, and he described it with a minimum of periods. "The Village contains the mint, a court house, a bank, an academy, and about seventy five frame and log houses, about two thirds of the inhabitants are a disolute drinking set, there are a few respectable families, the weather is warm through the day, but rather cool in the night." He was unconcerned about the crack in the mint wall, since it was "not larger than would admit of a common sized quill." He and Singleton concluded that the arches on the first floor would be completed according to the contract, but that girders on either side of the chimney would be substituted on the second floor. The iron bars the contractor had put in the walls to strengthen them had been put in carelessly, and he thought them very probably useless.

The coiner's machinery could not be installed, because the equipment needed to install it was not there. Mason did not comment on this difficulty, perhaps because he had left that equip-

---

[31]Singleton to Patterson, 8 Aug., 1 Sept. 1837; Patterson to Woodbury, 18 Aug. 1837; Patterson to Singleton, 31 Aug. 1837, NA-c.

[32]Few to Woodbury, 9 Sept. 1837, NA-lt.

ment behind in Philadelphia, much to the chagrin of Patterson, who had to ship it later. "I am sorry to state,—but the blame must be laid where it belongs,—that you own this delay to Mr. Mason," Patterson wrote to Singleton. "I repeatedly told him that I depended entirely upon him to see to the procuring and *forwarding* of the articles wanted in his department. Indeed this was the reason, and the only excuse, for his remaining here."[33]

The first priority in installing the machinery was to get the pump working. Mason did not like the idea of a wooden pump, which he was supposed to make himself. Instead, he asked that an iron pump be sent to him. Without the pump, the engine could not be tried unless water was brought from a spring thirty rods distant to fill the boiler. He got his iron pump, but it was difficult to install, and the change in plans caused additional delay.

Other problems developed. The contract expressly called for a brick cornice around the building, but such a cornice was not to grace the mint at Dahlonega. The builders at Charlotte, working from identical plans, found that it was impossible to make a cornice of brick on the dimensions marked in the plans, so they used stone. "There is one thing certain," Singleton wrote to Patterson, "that our cornice is built of neither stone or brick, but simply of timber and mortar smoothed over by the deceptive art of plaistering." He thought the difference between the cornice specified and the one provided was so vast that it should cover any extra charges the contractors might make, though he did not think they would like such a settlement.[34]

It was not just the timber and mortar cornice that distinguished the Dahlonega mint from its sister mint in Charlotte. Franklin Peale, who had been sent to inspect them both, sent back a devastating report.

> The buildings at Charlotte have been faithfully executed according to the designes and contracts, made and furnished for that

---

[33]Mason to Patterson, 18 Sept. 1837; Patterson to Singleton, 18 Sept. 1837, NA-c.

[34]Mason to Patterson, 18 Sept. 1837; Patterson to Mason, 5 Oct. 1837; Patterson to Singleton, 22 Nov. 1837; Singleton to Patterson, 11 Dec. 1837, NA-c.

> purpose; the commissioner Maj. McComb, has been, and still continues in assiduous attendance and has carefully watched over the interests of the Government; the materials imployed have been the best that the country supplies, and the execution all that could be expected with the necessary allowances for the resources and habits of the neighbourhood. . . .
>
> I regret that I cannot report so favorably of the building at Dahlonega, it has not been executed with the care and skill which the contract calls for, and it appears from the details which follow that the commissioner Col. I. Few has not by his presence or attention, sufficiently protected the interests of the Government.
>
> It has been necessary to remove the groined aches in the principal story, and one of those in the basement, the iron straps, the materials and workmanship being deficient.
>
> The cornices, contrary to contract, have been made of lath and plaster.
>
> The brick of the whole building, is of bad manufacture.
>
> The roof, from bad workmanship, is decidedly insufficient to protect the interior from the weather.
>
> Nevertheless great allowances must be made on account of the remote situation of the mint, and the consequent difficulties from want of resources.[35]

Despite the building's obvious shortcomings, Peale recommended that it be received by the government, provided, of course, that a sufficient amount be retained to cover the cost of a new roof.

Peale did not exaggerate the remoteness of the situation nor the difficulty of getting materials. Before his arrival to inspect the building and put in the furnaces, he ordered a supply of hard burned brick, lime, sand, and iron. The only hard burned bricks available within fifty miles were some Singleton had prepared for his own use, but these he made available to the mint. Unable to get lime hauled from Gainesville, Singleton sent to his own plantation fifty-five miles away and had it hauled in his own wagons.

Nor did Peale exaggerate Few's lack of attention to the project. Singleton said Few had been in Dahlonega but three times since work on the building began, with each of his visits lasting

---

[35]Peale to Patterson, 23 Dec. 1837, NA-lt.

no longer than from late afternoon on the day of his arrival until just after an early breakfast the next morning. "I merely mention this to enable you to form only a tolerable estimate of the justice extended to the Government for her liberality to this section of [the] country," Singleton wrote to Secretary Woodbury in early February 1838. "Col. Few has not been here . . . since last summer, and it is very uncertain when he will come." The building was not quite finished, but even so, Singleton urged the government to accept it as it was "this building or none."[36]

It was not a simple matter to accept the building even with its faulty roof, for this was a job that only Few was empowered to do, and he was still absent. "Is it right that Col. Few should still be continued in his commission?" Patterson asked Woodbury. "Dr. Singleton is on the spot, is competent to the management of the business and is zealous for its early and faithful completion." Could he not be appointed as commissioner to succeed Few so that the work of the mint could commence?

Few was ordered to go to Dahlonega at once to turn over all the business to Singleton. It was one thing to order Few to do something, however, and quite another to get him to do it. The days dragged by. "Col. Few has not yet arrived," became a stock statement in all of Singleton's letters to his superiors. Of course, the building could not be received until Few made some move, and he made none. He was, as a matter of fact, giving little if any thought to affairs in Dahlonega. He was not even getting his mail, for he was in Covington looking after the new Methodist school, and his mail was still being sent to Columbus. "I am aware that the completion of the Branch Mint at Dahlonega has been unreasonably delayed," he finally replied, "but have hoped that the public service would not suffer, as the unfinished work for some time yet, consisted only of the ornamental parts of the building (except for some Iron doors, which were finished some weeks since.)" He did not mention the leaky roof but added that he would meet with the contractors on 10 March and he hoped that he could

---

[36]Singleton to Woodbury, 7 Feb. 1838, NA-lt; Singleton to Patterson, 7 Feb., 12 Feb. 1838, NA-c.

"report final tender of the building as completed." But March gave way to April and April to May before he arrived.

He came late in the afternoon of 29 May to inspect the building, leaving, as was his custom, early the next morning. Towns and Tinsley were not there, so Few could not receive the building, but he met with them later and they agreed to set a price for the extra work they had done and to take off the zinc roof and put it on anew. "I have required Mr. Towns to have that made tight before the work is received under the contract," Few wrote to Woodbury. "He is impelled by the strongest motives to do this immediately, as he has not received more than half the sum allowed for the Building, whilst the whole of the work has in fact been done."[37]

The contractors were anxious about their pay. They had put in two extra girders in place of the groin arches. At the insistence of mint officials, they had made many alterations so that the machinery could be installed. These included fifty feet of partitions in the rear building and a fair number of extra doors. They insisted that the cornice was a perfectly good one—as good and as expensive as a brick cornice. They defended the workmanship of their groined arches. Two of them were perfect, they maintained, and the third had been perfect, but was taken down at the suggestion of the chief coiner. They had been put to great expense with the additional joists for the straight ceilings, the second alteration in the construction of the floors over them, and the waste of lumber and labor in construction. Patterson was willing to go along with extra pay for some of the contractor's claims, but not for taking down those groined arches. They were defective.[38]

Few was anxious about his pay, too. He was too busy or too unwell to go to Dahlonega to receive the building or to check on

---

[37]Patterson to Woodbury, 28 Jan. 1838, NA-lt; Patterson to Singleton, 31 Jan. 1838, NA-c; Singleton to Woodbury, 7 Feb., 15 Feb. 1838, NA-lt; Few to Woodbury, 22 Feb. 1838; Singleton to Patterson, 14 Mar. 1838, NA-c; Few to Woodbury, 29 June 1838, NA-lt.

[38]Tinsley and Towns to Few, 2 Apr. 1838; Patterson to Woodbury, 20 Apr. 1838, NA-lt.

its many difficulties, but he had strength enough to ask for a higher commission. The two percent he had been promised was "so utterly inadequate to the duties imposed, the expense necessarily incurred, and the responsibility involved, that I should have resigned, as soon as I became aware of their nature and extent, but from the advice of [Secretary of State John] Forsyth, and the belief that you would enlarge the Salary whenever a proper representation was made to you." He denied any responsibility for delay of the building's completion. He supposed when he accepted the commission that the whole work would be completed in 1835. If the Treasury Department did not pay him more, "I shall sustain, what is to be a serious loss—the loss of time, which would have commanded the means of supporting my family, in other occupations, equally honorable, less vexatious & involving much less responsibility."

His plea was in vain. Woodbury would do nothing except to urge Few to complete his duties as soon as possible so that he could be relieved from "further trouble in the matter." Woodbury's tone was so sharp that Few's concern for money was preempted by a new concern to save his honor. Some misrepresentations must have been made to the department, Few protested. To protect himself in the future he would ask some "respectable gentleman" to help him make the examination and give his written opinion on the quality of the work. He insisted vigorously that he was entirely free from any fault. The contractors for the machinery and the officers of the mint were in possession of the building when he was there in September, and all that was left to do was a little painting and plastering. The work should have been finished in six weeks. "It has turned out otherwise . . . partly because of the alterations and additions made by order of the officers of the Mint."[39]

---

[39]Few to Woodbury, 6 Mar. 1838; Woodbury to Few, 16 Mar. 1838; Patterson to Woodbury, 20 Apr. 1838; Few to Woodbury, 6 Apr., 10 Apr. 1838, NA-lt. The commissioner of the mint at Charlotte, Samuel McComb, was awarded a higher compensation by Congress. See U. S., Congress, House, report 464, 25th Cong., 2d sess., 1838.

Overseeing the final completion of the "Mint Edifice" was but one of Singleton's concerns. He had to get his staff organized for the real work of the mint. It seemed to him that the number of workmen authorized by Congress would be entirely inadequate. The law establishing the branch mints specified the exact number of officers and their pay: a superintendent, $2,000; a chief coiner, $1,500; assayer-melter-refiner, $1,500; one clerk, $1,000; and five subordinate workmen and servants, to be paid wages customary to the place. Singleton did not see how the Dahlonega Branch Mint could get along with so few workmen. He wanted a doorkeeper to wait upon the many visitors who would surely come as well as a fireman "whose duties cannot be dispensed with." In addition, some funds were necessary for enclosing the mint. Charlotte got $7,500 for an enclosure, Singleton reminded the Georgia congressional delegation. "The plain question presenting itself; is Georgia entitled to the same?"

The officers of the mint needed suitable housing, too. At the time Singleton discovered the crack in the mint wall, he urged Patterson to have some suitable dwellings for the officers erected on the grounds. "Independent of the risk of imperfect walls, no decent and responsible man would like to seclude his family in such a place, and the salaries are not sufficient to enable a suitable Officer to furnish his own dwelling without some other consideration."[40]

Singleton was a bit worried that the mint might not be secure enough to protect the gold with which it would soon be filled, but he hoped this deficiency would be remedied by the addition of an iron vault he asked to be made in Philadelphia. Ready or not, secure or not, Singleton was anxious for the important work of the mint to begin. He set 1 February 1838 as the day operations would commence.[41]

The mint did go into operation that spring, the first coins being minted on 17 April 1838, but it did so amid persistent rumors—

---

[40]Singleton to Georgia congressional delegation, 4 Sept. 1837, NA-lt; Singleton to Patterson, 8 Aug. 1837, NA-c.

[41]Singleton to Patterson, 15 Jan. 1838, NA-c.

and vehement denials—that the gold supply of the region was dwindling. Franklin Peale observed that at both Charlotte and Dahlonega there was a "reaction in mining affairs," but that all that was needed to turn things around was skill and science, experience and capital. He was convinced that the gold region of the "u. States is entirely inexaustible." The press pointed out that the low price of cotton would surely lead to increased interest in mining and that as soon as the mint went into operation gold bullion would increase in value by five percent. Singleton reported optimistically to Woodbury that in the first six weeks of the mint's assay operations, it received more than 1,200 ounces of gold, and that twice that amount could be expected when coining began. "So soon as our Indians are removed, our soldiers returned to their homes, our Rail Roads completed, and all apprehensions of danger dispersed on account of the Indians, a new era of gold operations may be confidently expected."[42]

The time had come for the removal of the Cherokees. In May 1836 the New Echota Treaty, which provided for the cession of the Cherokee homeland and the removal of the Cherokee people within two years, was ratified. For two years the bulk of the Cherokee Nation tried to find a means to avoid the terms of the treaty agreed to by fewer than five hundred of their number. They were aided by people in liberal and intellectual circles of the North who showered Congress with memorials against the removal of the Cherokees. Ralph Waldo Emerson addressed a powerful open letter to President Martin Van Buren pressing upon him the moral implications of the Indian removal. But the president, if he had any doubts about the Indian policy he had inherited, was more moved by the warnings sent him by the Georgia governor and by Georgia's congressional delegation that any hesitancy in removing the Cherokees would precipitate a war. If there was anything the country did not need on the heels of the great economic panic of 1837, it was war. On 10 April, just one week before the branch mint at Dahlonega minted its first gold coins, President Van

---

[42]Peale to Patterson, 23 Dec. 1837, NA-lt; unidentified clipping in NA-lt; Singleton to Woodbury, 2 Apr. 1838, NA-lt.

Buren ordered Major General Winfield Scott to go to the Cherokee country and use whatever military force was required to compel the Cherokees to remove at once. General Scott took command of the military operation on 8 May. By 18 June it was all over. No Cherokee remained on Georgia soil except as a prisoner in a stockade. Thousands of Cherokees died on the "Trail of Tears," the eight-hundred-mile journey west to their new home beyond the western border of Arkansas, but the outrage that much of the country felt at the removal was not echoed in Georgia.

Georgians were glad the Indians were gone. Singleton had worried that the mint with its large amount of gold bullion might become the first object of attack. Three months after the departure of the last Indian, the Lumpkin County Grand Jury commented with satisfaction on the great change in population in the county; without shedding a drop of blood, all the Indians were removed. "We view the Cherokee country with emotions of unmixed pride and pleasure," the grand jury report continued. "This country is now thrown upon its own resources and if our citizens are not happy and prosperous for the future, the sin will be at their own door."[43]

[43]Dale Van Every, *Disinherited: The Lost Birthright of the American Indian* (New York, 1966) 206, 223, 235-250; Singleton to Gov. George Gilmer, 29 Jan. 1838, NA-c; Andrew W. Cain, *History of Lumpkin County for the First Hundred Years, 1832-1932* (Atlanta, 1932) 68-69.

CHAPTER 3

So eager was Singleton to begin work at the mint that he proclaimed in February 1838 that operations had begun. No one at all familiar with the situation could have taken him seriously. Copper and silver needed for coining were not available, the roof leaked, the contractor would not vacate the unfinished building, and, of course, Few was absent. But Singleton was anxious to put behind him the problems of construction. He did not yet realize that operating a unit of the United States government would increase the difficulties that had dogged him in the past. As director of the branch mint he had to bring supplies to a frontier outpost, get balky machinery to work, and settle petty quarrels among his employees, tasks that taxed his skills and his supervisor's patience. Every mail brought fresh complaints to Director Patterson at the mint in Philadelphia of something else gone wrong.[1]

Yet hopes were high in those first few weeks of the mint's operation. Gold came in fairly rapidly, almost a thousand ounces in the first two weeks. Singleton borrowed one thousand dollars to buy the silver needed for the separating process, and he sent his clerk, Edward Wingfield, to Charleston, South Carolina, to get the necessary copper for casting gold into ingots. When the pump

---

[1]An Act of Congress, passed 13 Feb. 1837, 5 Stat. 602, required that all business of the branch mints come under the control and regulation of the director of the mint at Philadelphia.

would not work, the staff hauled water for the steam engine that powered the presses. Their makeshift efforts produced a miracle of sorts. The first coins, eighty five-dollar gold pieces, were finished on 17 April.[2] Singleton thought they were beautiful.

Production of the first half eagles at Dahlonega was a saga of mishaps. Hardly anything went right. Machinery and supplies were on the road twenty-two days from Augusta, 150 miles distant, when a week should have sufficed. Equipment for the coiner, shipped from Philadelphia six months earlier, did not arrive at all. Fireproof bircks for the furnaces came, but not the necessary iron grates and lead pipes.[3]

The staff straggled in as irregularly as the supplies. Mason arrived in September in time to help install the machinery and to scour the countryside for substitute supplies, but Farnum did not get to Dahlonega until late November, having dallied in Philadelphia as long as he could. Such peace as Singleton enjoyed before they arrived vanished immediately afterward. Farnum, a fussy bachelor college professor, was a perfectionist ill-suited to frontier life. Mason, a more practical man, fared better, but he disliked Farnum on sight. They could not escape one another, not even after working hours, for both men—Mason with his family and Farnum in his bachelor quarters—were housed at the mint.

Although he arrived late Farnum set about his work promptly and so energetically that Singleton credited him with getting mint operations under way. His penchant for finding fault with everyone was less apparent in those early weeks of operation, but even then there were signs that this appointment in which both Patterson and Singleton took such pride was not without its difficulties. Farnum was a hard man to please. Long before he arrived in Georgia, he asked that none of the supplies and equipment meant for him be opened until he got there lest they be handled improperly. He was critical when Mason returned from a trip to Philadelphia and brought nothing with him but his family—no silver for refining, no

---

[2]Singleton to Patterson, 2 Mar., 14 Mar., 1 May 1838, NA-c.

[3]Singleton to Patterson, 5 Sept., 7 Nov. 1837, NA-c; Mason to Patterson, 26 Jan. 1838, NA-c.

copper for alloy, no ingot molds. He found fault with the mint's equipment and its staff. "Our furnaces draw but indifferently," he wrote to Patterson a week before the first coins were minted. "They are constructed of bad brick and mortar and after Mr. Peale left, the elder Barrett neglected his business."[4]

If the professional staff was difficult, so were the workmen. It was almost impossible to pay them enough. The first year's wages for the five laborers was estimated at $3,800, but that hardly began to cover the cost. Pay was high in a frontier outpost like Dahlonega, where "miserable mechanics" could command $2.50 a day. Mason brought three hands with him from Philadelphia—Charles Thomas, Charles Matlock, and Frederick Boartfield. He promised them twelve to fifteen dollars per week, but they complained so much that Singleton was obliged to pay the top price; one man got eighteen dollars per week. Farnum, stingy with himself, was parsimonious with his hands. The young apprentice, Isaac Todd, and the experienced melter, Charles Gilbert, who came with him, both agreed to work for a flat two dollars per day, but they soon demanded the higher wages paid Mason's men. Singleton reminded Director Patterson that the law "allows such wages as are customary and reasonable to their respective stations and occupations," and clothing, for instance, cost more in Dahlonega than it did in Philadelphia. Patterson nevertheless thought the demands "exorbitant."[5]

The workmen did not intend to work very hard for their pay, and Singleton could not force them. He did try, however. On 5 February 1838, just as the mint was beginning operations, he personally handed out this order to the workers:

> From and after Monday morning next the subordinate workmen of the Br. Mint at this place (To wit: Messrs Thomas, Bortfield, Matlock, and Todd) will be required to be at their respective posts

---

[4]Singleton to Patterson, 7 Feb. 1838; Farnum to Patterson, 8 Apr. 1838, NA-c.

[5]Singleton to Patterson, 7 Nov., 27 Nov. 1837; Patterson to Singleton, 22 Nov. 1837, NA-c; Branch at Dahlonega, Estimate of Expenses, 1838, NA-lt.

> of occupation by the hour of sun rise in the morning, for the purpose of being closely engaged in their business until the hour of sun set in the evening, allowing a reasonable time for breakfast and dinner. A strict observance of this order is expected, at the risk of a deduction of wages in proportion to the time served. It is to be regretted that this order is deemed necessary. Nothing but an ardent desire to fulfill public expectations produced it.
>
> Jos. J. Singleton,
> Supt.

The workmen paid little attention to the directive. Singleton was worried. What would happen if he tried to enforce his order and all the workmen quit?[6]

It was not a moot question. Farnum had been at his post but a month before he was complaining that Gilbert was "perfectly worthless," unwilling to take orders. He would not unload wagons, saying he did not come to Dahlonega "as a negro." He would not clean the rooms. Moreover, he was overly proud. He even introduced himself to Singleton as one of the officers, "melter and refiner." He was so obstreperous, in fact, that Farnum gave him a choice: take orders or leave. Gilbert left and set himself up as a jeweler in the town. Another melter, William Warwick, had to be sent from Philadelphia. He was an Englishman who, Director Patterson claimed, was "thoroughly bred to his business from boyhood . . . very industrious, good natured, and willing and never thinks of refusing to do anything which is asked of him." Unfortunately, Patterson confessed in describing this jewel to Farnum, "It is said that he will sometimes drink, and I fear it is true." So Warwick was sent off to the hard drinking town of Dahlonega, taking with him a few supplies.[7]

Gilbert did not last long as a jeweler in Dahlonega. Before his replacement could arrive in Georgia, Gilbert was back in Philadelphia demanding that the government pay the cost of his journey home. He thought as little of Farnum as the good professor thought of him. "As for Dr. Farnum," he complained to Patter-

---

[6]Singleton to Patterson, 12 Feb. 1838, NA-c.

[7]Farnum to Patterson, 29 Dec. 1837; Patterson to Farnum, 31 Jan. 1838; Patterson to Singleton, 10 Feb. 1838, NA-c.

son, "nothing but respect for my country and its institutions has kept me from making a public exposure of the whole transaction." The government refused to pay for Gilbert's trip home, having just had the expense of sending his replacement. Unfortunately, Warwick could not give up drinking, and within a year he was accused of "trafficking in gold," too. Nevertheless, he was a good workman, and for that Farnum was thankful.[8]

In addition to the five regular hands, Singleton hired one or two extras from time to time, a practice that bothered him a little since the number of employees was set by law. A doorkeeper was employed for a few days when the mint was first opened because the building was "thronged with visitors." On occasion Singleton hired a fireman because there was "an utter abhorence among the hands to act in that capacity."[9]

The balky pump caused the final delay in getting mint operations under way. Mason refused to make the wooden one the plans originally called for, and the substitute cast iron pump would not work. "The Messrs. Sellers palmed a deceptive article upon us," Singleton complained to Patterson, "and they, or their workmen must have known it." Mason and his hands worked on the pump for a week, and still it would not function. They took it up and found it full of holes, one of them larger than a man's thumb and a full six inches long. Another two weeks' work on the pump proved fruitless, so the branch mint began its operations with hauled water. That was preferable, Singleton thought, "to suffering our Bullion to accumulate on our hands." Mason substituted lead pipes for the cast iron ones. When this proved unsatisfactory he tried copper pipes instead. Miraculously, this worked. The pump required additional grinding, polishing, and packing and still another valve, but by early May, despair at the mint had turned to hope. The accomplished Mason had worked something of a miracle, and Singleton observed that the Georgia mint could enter into full competition with its sister branches.

---

[8]Gilbert to Patterson, 13 Feb. 1838, NA-c; Patterson to Gilbert, 15 Feb. 1838; Farnum to Patterson, 15 Mar. 1839, NA-c.

[9]Singleton to Patterson, 18 Apr., 17 June, 10 Aug. 1838, NA-c.

Unfortunately, there was also trouble with the rollers that rolled the ingots into sheets of gold just the thickness of coins. The rollers were too soft, a defect Mason thought could be remedied by occasional turning. Patterson warned against this. The rollers at Charlotte were too soft, too, but turning made them even softer. "The Messrs Sellers [the very same firm that had supplied the faulty pump] are now preparing to cast rolls for your mints in a chill, and as soon as they succeed, you shall be supplied with new ones."[10]

Meanwhile, everyone at Dahlonega took pride in a job well done. While Patterson found the half eagles from the first melt to be "perfectly well executed," Singleton thought them magnificent. "I believe our coin equal to any made in the world, both for its beauty and accuracy in its legal parts," he said. The Dahlonega coins met "a most cordial reception wherever [they were] carried." The first coins, made primarily from gold deposited by Singleton himself, were distributed in the community before approval came from Philadelphia. This premature circulation was the first of many mistakes Singleton made in handling the finer points of the superintendent's job.

The first coins had a slightly different color from those minted in Philadelphia, indicating that they approached the legal limit for silver alloy. Farnum attributed this to the faulty pump. It was so hard to carry water from the cellar to wash the gold and silver that Farnum had refined as little gold as he could, and sometimes he put in almost as much silver alloy as the law allowed. The coins were still of good quality, however. At the first annual assay of Dahlonega coins in February 1839 they exceeded the legal weight by only one part in 1,688, and when melted together and assayed, they exceeded the legal standard by only one part in 4,000.[11]

Farnum probably did not personally carry water from the cellar to wash the gold, but he was quick to complain that he was

---

[10]Singleton to Patterson, 28 Mar., 18 Apr., 1 May, 5 May 1838, NA-c; Patterson to Singleton, 28 Apr. 1838, NA-c.

[11]Singleton to Patterson, 1 May 1838; Patterson to Singleton, 12 May, 21 May 1838, 12 Feb. 1839; Farnum to Patterson, 17 June 1838, NA-c.

often overworked. He early decided that he was the only person at the mint who had very much to do, and he was working "day and night." Singleton was away from his post for six of the first twelve weeks that Farnum was on duty, and the coiner had to work but a few days each month. Farnum objected to being assayer, melter, and refiner. He suggested that the coiner assume the additional duties of melter, an idea that had little appeal for Mason. Besides, it was against the law. Farnum begged in vain for a lighter work load even though he warned that if he had to do everything, "I shall be obliged to forego the satisfaction of doing [my work] in the best manner."

One wonders what Farnum would have done with his time had he not been working. He lived alone in the mint, and such pleasures as the little village of Dahlonega afforded did not appeal to him. He spent little if any of his salary. Indeed, he refused to receive his wages, which were invested in Philadelphia, mostly in Lehigh Lines.[12]

Mason did not want to assume any duties that would put him into closer contact with Dr. Farnum. "[He] has not spoken to me since my return from Phil. except twice and only then in reply to my question," Mason wrote to Patterson shortly before the first coins were minted. Farnum's conduct was nearly always unpleasant, Mason explained in a single sentence embracing a variety of complaints, "especially when it leads to other acts rather hostile, for instance I received by Mr. Warwick the pan and one pair of scales with two setts of weights with this message, that Dr. Farnum had taken one pair of scales, that they were for himself and he has kept them ever since, and last week I wanted some lead pipe for the pump, and knowing he had spare pipe in the cellar, I sent to him to obtain it, he got into a passion and blustered declaring he would write to Dr. Patterson." Farnum also had all the carpenters and plasterers working on his apartment while Mason's was neglected. The carpenters were so busy working for

---

[12]Singleton to Patterson, 2 Apr., 1 June 1838; Farnum to Patterson, 8 Apr. 1838, 4 Mar., 15 Mar. 1839, NA-c. The law was not changed to transfer the duties of the melter and refiner at the branch mints to the coiner until 27 Feb. 1843.

Farnum that they had no time to complete the work about the engine. "The less I am brought into collision with such a man, I think the better for both," Mason concluded.[13]

Mason did not like his quarters in the mint, an attitude that shocked Singleton since the superintendent had turned over his entire apartment to the coiner except for one of the upper rooms which Wingfield, the clerk, used as a bed chamber. Mason wanted Singleton to fix up an extra room to take the place of that one. He asked that the cellar floor of his apartment be laid with plank, the walls and overhead plastered, and sash and glass be put into the windows. Without the cellar rooms Mason, his family, and servants had but four rooms "with the inconveniences of one room for a kitchen and dining room, and family and servants all mixed together, and when we retire to bed all mixed in the manner, and have to go through the Piazza with a light, frequently having it blown out by the wind, leaving us to feel our way in the dark." Since these improvements would cost three or four hundred dollars of the public's money, Singleton refused Mason's pleas. "Mr. Mason came into my office a few mornings ago very angry," Singleton wrote to Patterson, "and very imprudently made use of much abusive language, a description of which I do not deem necessary to trouble you with."

That description was about the only thing spared Patterson. A steady stream of letters detailed petty complaints. In the case of Mason's demands, Patterson served as a peacemaker. Mason was entitled to "a decent habitation," he wrote, and repairs of his apartment were well worth the money. Apartments were set aside in the building, he reminded Singleton, because it was such an advantage for the mint's security to have officers of the mint living there. When the money finally came through to enclose the grounds, there was also enough to complete Mason's apartment, so he was somewhat mollified.[14]

Constant friction marred the relationship between the "mechanic" Mason, as Farnum dubbed him, and the testy college pro-

---

[13]Mason to Patterson, 2 Apr. 1838, NA-c.

[14]Singleton to Patterson, 17 June, 30 June 1838; Mason to Patterson, 18 June 1838; Patterson to Singleton, 5 July 1838, NA-c.

fessor turned assayer. Farnum never ordered his men to help Mason when the coiner needed an extra hand with the rollers, even if there were nothing for them to do in the assaying department. He did not like Mason, refused even to speak to the Mason family when they were introduced, and asked Singleton to arrange it so that he would have no communication with Mason whatever. Farnum liked the clerk Wingfield no better, and for months would not speak to him.[15]

But animosities have a strange way turning. As soon as Farnum found there was trouble between Mason and Singleton over the apartment repairs, Farnum courted Mason's good will. Soon they were fast friends. They had a common cause: money. In a note written in pencil, dated 15 June 1838, they accused Singleton of misusing funds.

> Sir,
>
> BELIEVING THAT YOU HAVE HITHERTO WITHOUT our consent disposed of the funds transmitted for the payment of ourselves for a premium and which you have appropriated to your own use in defiance of the obvious intention of Congress that no perquisite should be allowed, as may be seen in Dr. Patterson's last report, we hereby inform you that we shall not submit hereafter to such injustice, and if again attempted we shall appeal to the proper authority for redress.
>
> Jos. W. Farnum.
> D. H. Mason.

Singleton's reply was equally terse. Ignoring the nature of the complaint, he commented only on its form.

> Sirs:
>
> As I am not in the habit of doing business with a pencil, you will therefore be pleased to say to me with ink and pen that what you intended to say with your pencil; and I will then bestow upon it that notice which I may deem it merits.
>
> Respectfully yours,
> Jos. J. Singleton[16]

---

[15]Singleton to Patterson, 17 June 1838, NA-c.

[16]Quoted in Singelton to Patterson, 17 June 1838, NA-c.

Singleton had reason to play for time. He had exchanged the treasury notes sent to him to meet the mint's payroll and operating expenses for smaller bills and pocketed the two percent premium the treasury notes brought. After the destruction of the Second Bank of the United States, bank notes fluctuated in value, and treasury notes were more valuable. The $5,000 in notes sent to Singleton in early December 1837 meant an extra $100 to him. When Farnum and Mason asked the superintendent about it, Singleton wrote defensively that "as good men as any in our county say that I am entitled to it upon the ground of my responsibility to the government for the whole amount received." Patterson resolved this dispute as he had so many others by suggesting a proportional distribution of the premiums, but the issue was not settled before Singleton had threatened to make Mason find lodgings out of the mint, and hinted that Farnum was saving gold from the melts for himself.

As victims of Singleton's attacks, Farnum and Mason joined forces to lay bare the superintendent's shortcomings. Among these was his lack of scientific expertise. Farnum reported to Philadelphia that Singleton had "assigned as a reason for a particular disposition of the [lightning] rods of the Mint, that lightning would descent more readily than ascent!"[17]

The mint superintendent had trouble not only with the men who worked for him, but with some of the citizens of the town as well. He publicly denounced some of Dahlonega's most prominent miners as "swindlers." They in turn issued printed circulars calling him a "slanderer," so he sued them for libel. This personal feud had repercussions at the mint, because one of Singleton's adversaries was the Dahlonega postmaster, G. K. Cessna. For six months during the mint's first year of operations Singleton adamantly refused to use the Dahlonega post office, insisting instead that all mint correspondence be handled at the Auraria post office five miles distant.

---

[17]Singleton to Patterson, 17 June 1838; Farnum to Patterson, 17 June 1838; Mason to Patterson, 18 June 1838; Patterson to Singleton, 5 July 1838, NA-c.

The mails were not safe, Singleton confided to Patterson, but he would give no reason except an oblique reference to the "peculiar and disagreeable relationship between the Post Master at this place and myself." He wrote an eight-page letter to the secretary of the treasury about it, because the secretary was more immediately connected with Amos Kendall, the postmaster general, than Patterson. Patterson was at a loss to understand it. Was not the use of the Auraria post office inconvenient? It took much longer for letters to arrive in Philadelphia. The delay and the inconvenience, Singleton replied, "weighed but a feather compared with my risk at the Post Office of this place." He could never use it for the important mint correspondence so long as Cessna was the incumbent.

Unfortunately, the use of the Auraria post office had serious drawbacks in addition to increasing the time it took for the mail to be delivered. Letters sent from Dahlonega containing slips of gold for assay at the mint in Philadelphia began to disappear. When this happened three times an exasperated Patterson wrote to Farnum instead of Singleton so that he could address the letter to Dahlonega. Was the messenger entrusted with the mail to and from Auraria a trustworthy person? he asked. Could the gold assay pieces have been stolen? Use the Dahlonega post office for sending the new assay pieces, he advised, "as the regularity, if not the security, of the other seems very doubtful."

It may have been local pressure that made Singleton give in and resume using the local post office. The depositors of gold at the mint were anxious for their coin, and none could be minted until the assay report had been received from Philadelphia. By September the mint had $50,000 in deposits for which owners made repeated requests. But it was probably the fact that Patterson wrote to Farnum on matters of important business that had the greatest effect on Singleton. He claimed to be shocked that Patterson wanted him to use the local mail facilities. But if it meant dealing with Patterson through Farnum, Singleton would use the Dahlonega post office "at all hazards." Before the end of the year the mystery of the missing assay pieces was solved. A deputy postmaster about twenty miles from Dahlonega was the culprit. A packet of letters from Singleton to Patterson, some of which contained assay slips, was recovered.[18]

Against this backdrop of quarrels both within and without the mint, of frustration with equipment that would not work, of constant delays in getting needed supplies, Colonel Few arrived to make his final inspection of the building. The roof leaked; the external walls were not dry; the rough coating put on the outside was breaking off. Few was certainly right about the inadequacies of a zinc roof. It was put on incorrectly, a development that irritated Patterson inasmuch as the mint had paid the expenses for one of the contractors to come to Philadelphia to get all the information necessary for construction, and his attention was particularly directed to the best manner of putting on zinc roofs. The contractors, however, had used a "long exploded method," so Patterson thought they ought to be responsible for the consequences. Few thought so, too. He directed the contractor to take off the roof and "lay it on anew on a different plan and by workmen more experienced." The work continued through the summer and into the fall. So did the leaks. Falling plaster was a hazard for workers and equipment alike. It was more than a year after the mint began operations before a third roof was put on the building. Finally the superintendent could say that though "our Edifice is not yet finished . . . at length I am happy in saying we can now work dry, and without dodging from room to room."[19]

A leaky roof was but one of the building's inadequacies. The mint was entirely too insecure to protect the gold bullion and coins. Singleton asked that an "iron clossett" be sent from Philadelphia, but when he found that it cost $500 he dropped the idea. Patterson thought a good watchman would be adequate to provide security for the mint, but Singleton protested that with wages

---

[18]Singleton to Patterson, 1 Mar., 21 Mar., 28 Mar., 18 Apr., 30 June, 13 Aug., 20 Sept., 26 Sept., 24 Oct., 2 Nov. 1838; Patterson to Singleton, 15 June, 13 Sept. 1838; Patterson to Farnum, 15 Sept. 1838, NA-c.

[19]Singleton to Patterson, 14 May, 4 Sept., 3 Oct., 9 Nov. 1838, 1 Mar., 1 May 1839; Patterson to Singleton, 21 May 1838, NA-c; Few to Woodbury, 29 June 1838, NA-lt.

costing two dollars per night, the price of two or three iron chests would soon be consumed. About the time the mint began to accept gold for coining, Singleton borrowed two small iron chests and chained them together in the vault in his office until he could get some of his own. These were not long in coming. Three iron chests, bought in Philadelphia for $180, were shipped in mid-April 1838. Two were for Singleton and one was for Farnum. The keys to all three were brought back to Dahlonega by one of the mint's first depositors, who was so impatient to get his coins that he went all the way to Philadelphia to get them.[20]

Of more pressing importance, because it was so visible, was the need for a suitable enclosure and outbuildings for the mint. The Charlotte Mint received a $7,500 appropriation for the purpose. At Singleton's insistence, the Georgia delegation in Congress was successful in getting the same amount for Dahlonega. Superintending the work was something Singleton thought one of the officers of the mint ought to do "without additional compensation, as the fund is barely sufficient for the purpose intended." What he did not add was that he had himself in mind for the job. "The common plan of letting out public works to the lowest bidder I think a bad one," Singleton confided to Patterson, "especially in the part of the country, where there are so many irresponsible persons always ready to grasp the funds of 'Uncle Sam' as they call it, and that without due regard to the fulfillment of stipulations however severe." Singleton himself was not averse to grasping Uncle Sam's funds. When he was given the authority to superintend the work, he found an opportunity to turn a profit. Patterson, who believed that anything was preferable to turning the task of supervision over to Few, approved of Singleton's new duties.[21]

Judging by the number of mistakes Singleton made in carrying out the responsibilities of his office, Singleton was ill

---

[20]Singleton to Patterson, 11 Dec. 1837, 7 Feb., 19 Feb., 14 Mar. 1838; Patterson to Singleton, 31 Jan., 11 Apr. 1838; Patterson to Farnum, 20 Apr. 1838, NA-c.

[21]Singleton to Patterson, 20 Nov. 1837, 1 June 1838; Patterson to Singleton, 15 June 1838, NA-c.

equipped to take on the additional task of overseeing the enclosure of the mint. He was a poor bookkeeper. Only with the greatest difficulty could he keep records straight. His account books were quite informal. He did not detail specifically how and where money was spent. He was confused about where accounts and vouchers should be sent, dispatching them to Philadelphia rather than to the Department of the Treasury in Washington where they belonged. By mid-summer of the first year, Patterson lost patience. "I had hoped that during your stay here in Philadelphia you had made yourself master of the system of keeping Mint accounts. As this seems, however, not to be the case, I will make out a set of specific instructions on the subject, and send them to you as soon as possible." Singleton was not an apt student. While his intentions were good, his ability to perform did not improve. About a year after he was first reprimanded for sending his accounts to the wrong place, a stern note came from a comptroller in the Treasury Department. "The auditor has felt it his duty to state, that your accounts have been rendered in such a manner that it is impossible to account for the differences satisfactorily, and he has therefore called my particular attention to the fact in order that steps may be taken to make you acquainted with the form in which they ought to be rendered." It took Singleton almost a month to do his report over.[22]

Farnum's attitude toward his work was exactly the reverse of Singleton's. Farnum was as meticulous as his superior officer was careless. His day and night attention to his duties resulted in a margin of error less than one-fifth that which the law allowed. During the first ten months that the mint accepted bullion for coining, Farnum received 77,083.767 ounces of gold from the treasurer and returned 77,077.424, losing only 4.545 ounces. His legal allowance would have been more than 22 ounces. "I have been able to save this much from *unnecessary* care," he reported to Patterson. "Indeed, I am confident, if the gold had been my own,

---

[22]Patterson to Woodbury, 23 Mar. 1838, NA-c; Singleton to Woodbury, 29 May, 22 June 1838, NA-lt; Patterson to Singleton, 12 July 1838, NA-c; Singleton to Patterson, 12 Oct. 1838, NA-c; J. N. Barker to Singleton, 4 Mar. 1839; Singleton to Barker, 4 Apr. 1839, NA-lt.

I should not have been so successful." He enjoyed checking his results with those of Adam Echfeldt, the assayer at Philadelphia. Only occasionally did they differ and that was only by a tiny fraction. Farnum was willing to accept Echfeldt's assay as more accurate, but he had an explanation. Perhaps the nitric acid Farnum used contained nitrous acid, and perhaps the water with which the acid was diluted contained a minute portion of common salt. That sometimes happened because it was so difficult to clean the glass perfectly. Or maybe it was because Farnum's assistant mistook the weak acid for the strong or boiled the cornet at too low a temperature. "I hope you will not permit my reputation for accuracy in your estimation to suffer," he said. In the first year he had not been obliged to recast a single ingot, although one that assayed $.900\frac{3}{4}$ he had recast voluntarily. The law required a uniform fineness of .900 for gold and silver coins, and that was sacred writ to the Dahlonega assayer.[23]

The operations of the branch mint that year were plagued not only by the peevishness of the personnel and the inadequacies of the still incomplete building, but by the perpetual problem of money and supplies. Singleton was supposed to get $30,000 from the secretary of the treasury to pay early depositors for their gold. That would finance certificates payable at the mint in Philadelphia. By the time this fund was exhausted the Dahlonega Mint would have $30,000 of its own gold coins available for the purchase of future deposits.

That was the way it was supposed to work, but the Dahlonega Mint never got the full $30,000, much to Singleton's chagrin. It was not so much that the mint needed the money as the fact that the Charlotte branch had the $30,000 deposit and the Dahlonega branch did not. In April 1838 the Treasury Department sent a draft for $20,000 to Philadelphia for the Dahlonega account with the notation that additional transfers would be made when necessary, but not even that amount was transferred to Georgia. On New Year's Day 1839 Singleton complained that only $12,842.62

---

[23]Farnum to Patterson, 2 Dec. 1838, 15 Mar., 22 Apr. 1839, NA-c; Don Taxay, *The U. S. Mint and Coinage: An Illustrated History from 1776 to the Present* (New York, 1966) 200.

had been sent to Dahlonega to pay depositors, so he was obliged to keep an account with them. This entailed bookkeeping, with duplicate receipts taken from depositors and vouchers to be sent to Washington. Such detail was anathema to Singleton. No account was kept with the depositors at the mint in Philadelphia, Singleton protested, begging for the rest of his money. If he could only get all the $20,000 sent to Philadelphia for his branch mint, "we shall too be enabled to pay Depositors without keeping an account with them." Better yet, if the Treasury Department would send along the extra $10,000 originally promised, Singleton could not only keep up with Charlotte, but satisfy the whim of Farnum, who had determined not to cast less than twenty-five ingots at each melt. If all the depositors applied for their money at the same time, there would not be enough funds to pay them without the additional money. His pleas came to naught. Patterson thought Singleton ought to have the money, but the funds simply were not available, either from the Treasury Department or from the mint in Philadelphia. The government had drawn so heavily on mint deposits, Patterson explained, that "even the trifling sum of $10,000 could not be spared."[24]

The Dahlonega Mint was as short on supplies and equipment as it was on money to pay depositors. The assay department always needed nitric acid and crucibles. In fact, the only things that department had in abundance were trouble and black pots. Black lead pots by the dozens arrived in Dahlonega. In mid-summer of the first year, three hogsheads of pots in various sizes arrived when crucibles had been expected. The larger pots could never be used, Farnum protested, and it would take years to use all the smaller ones. Meanwhile, they were nearly destitute for crucibles, and another three months would be required to get them. When that time elapsed, another hogshead of large black pots arrived, shipped to Dahlonega by mistake. Farnum, meanwhile, placed an order for black lead pot covers, but another mix-up kept them from being shipped. By the time they were available, win-

---

[24]Patterson to Singleton, 31 Jan. 1838; Woodbury to Patterson, 5 Apr. 1838, NA-c; Singleton to Woodbury, 1 Jan. 1839, NA-lt; Singleton to Patterson, 1 Mar. 1839; Patterson to Singleton 19 Mar. 1839, NA-c.

ter weather had closed the Delaware River. Why not carve some pot covers out of soapstone? asked the officials in Philadelphia.

The problem of getting crucibles was more acute. Farnum wanted round ones, but these were available only in Germany. Patterson promised to send triangular ones instead. They could be used by cutting away the inside rim of the black pots. But just as that order was executed, round crucibles arrived in New York. They were dispatched at once to Savannah. In due time two hogsheads arrived in Dahlonega, one with round sand crucibles, the other with black lead pots, already in abundant supply. Farnum returned these to Philadelphia, only to discover months later that crucibles of just the size he needed were in the hogshead. "I am fearful there has been a mistake elsewhere," Singleton explained, trying to shift the blame. Sometimes supplies meant for the Charlotte or New Orleans branches or even the Philadelphia Mint were sent to Dahlonega instead. Both Singleton and Farnum insisted they had opened the hogsheads and inspected them and they contained lead pots. Perhaps in dodging the falling plaster in the assay office and amidst the general chaos of the mint operations they had trouble telling the difference.[25]

The situation was as bad if not worse in the coiner's department. The rollers were so soft that it was almost impossible to use them and so rough that strips of gold could not be drawn smoothly enough to make handsome coins. Until rollers could be sent from Philadelphia, Mason tried turning his large roller to get a smooth surface, only to discover when he had taken off a half-inch that the metal got softer. By October it was doubtful if the rollers would last for even one more melt. Meanwhile, the coining press proved troublesome. Without consulting Mason, Singleton said that he wished the mint had a screw-driven press worked by hand. Fortunately for Mason, who preferred the power press, Patterson was not of a mind to put Dahlonega that much behind the times, frontier outpost though it was. The vast superiority of the power press over the screw press was no longer a matter of doubt, Patterson

---

[25]Singleton to Patterson, 24 July, 24 Oct. 1838, 11 Feb. 1839; Farnum to Patterson, 15 Oct. 1838; Patterson to Singleton, 11 Aug., 15 Nov. 1838; Patterson to Farnum, 17 Jan. 1839, NA-c.

advised. "I pray you not to think of using the screw press. This is not the age nor the country for going backwards."

They kept the power press even though it was so heavy that the floor began to collapse under it until large posts were brought in for support. A few months later the steam chest burst and a new one had to be ordered from Augusta. One of the two sets of dies had been kept in a damp vault and was too rusty to use. Besides, the dies bore the date 1838 and Mason "did not think it altogether right that our coin of 1839 should bear the date 1838." Having produced nothing but half eagles in the first year of coining, Mason busied himself preparing planchets for half eagles while waiting for the new dies to arrive. When they came they were for the smaller quarter eagles. Not until the middle of April 1839 did the much needed half eagle dies get to Dahlonega.

One year after the mint first began operations the rollers were still giving trouble. Singleton suggested that they get chilled rollers in Augusta, where there was a good foundry and where they would be quite as cheap and "quite as perfect as if from the Messrs. Sellers's." Since all the machinery secured from Philadelphia had been faulty, Singleton thought "we cannot be worsted in the change of manufacturers." Patterson agreed, but before this experiment could be tried the long anticipated chilled rollers from the Sellers firm were completed and shipped.[26]

In spite of the many troubles at the mint which meant that working there was, as Farnum put it, "no sinecure," still it was a job. Officers and workmen alike wanted to hang on to their security. Farnum and Mason were afraid of a plot to remove them from their posts late in 1838, but Patterson assured them that they had "no real cause of alarm from any intrigue that may be on foot." When officials considered the small amount of work being done at the mint, however, they had every reason to suspect that the government might not long sustain an operation so unprofitable. Though no specific goal was set for coinage at Dahlonega, the budget for 1838 had allowed for $2,000 wastage in gold, an

---

[26]Singleton to Patterson, 17 June, 24 Oct., 1 Dec., 19 Dec. 1838, 1 Mar. 1839; Patterson to Singleton, 5 July, 3 Aug. 1838, 13 Mar. 1839; Mason to Patterson, 18 June 1838, NA-c.

amount ample enough to cover a half-million dollars in coinage. The final report for that year showed that the Dahlonega Mint had receipts of $141,763.41 and had minted from that 20,583 golden half eagles.

This was a great deal more than Farnum had anticipated six months earlier, when he gloomily reported that prospects were anything but "golden" in Dahlonega, and that the deposit mines were nearly exhausted. Singleton had a good explanation for the relatively small amount of gold presented at the mint. It was "occasioned by Indians, Soldiers, Railroad Competition &c. &c." The first two distractions to the important business of mining had been removed by early 1839, "but the latter remains with all its alluring inducements to call off our miners with their numerous trains of Laborers." As soon as the "thirst for Rail Road wages"—about twenty dollars per month—was over, Singleton thought the mint could get more of "the precious article."

But Farnum thought the mint's days were numbered. Much of the gold brought to the mint in 1838 had been accumulating in banks for some time. During some months, like January 1839, not a single coin was minted. It behooved a far-sighted man like Farnum to look for opportunities elsewhere. When a resignation at the Philadelphia Mint left open the job of melter and refiner there, Patterson recommended Farnum for it, but President Martin Van Buren "deemed it expedient . . . to select a Pennsylvanian for the place." It was after all the year before an election. That opportunity closed, Farnum suggested the possibility that if the Dahlonega Mint were closed, its assay offices might remain open. The deposits could still be purchased, and every six months or so the bullion could be taken to Philadelphia at small expense. The public would still benefit. "Under any circumstances," he wrote, "some one will be required to superintend the public property—and this could be done by the Assayer while in the discharge of the duties of his office."[27]

---

[27]Farnum and Mason to Patterson, 17 Dec. 1838; Patterson to Farnum, 17 Jan. 1839; Farnum to Patterson, 17 June 1838, 15 Mar., 15 Apr. 1839, NA-c; Singleton to Patterson, 31 Dec. 1838, NA-c; Singleton to Woodbury, 11 Jan. 1839, NA-lt; Reports of Superintendent of Mint, n.d., NA-c.

Farnum's anxieties were as groundless as his hopes for advancement. The branch mint at Dahlonega did not close. Although it contributed little to solving the problem of supplying the country with sound money, keeping it open was sound politics. The mint survived.

CHAPTER 4

Both gold and tempers were short at the mint in 1839 and 1840. The amount of gold presented for coining dropped from the low figure of the mint's first year, and all pretense to harmony among the mint's personnel vanished. "I wish we had more to do," Singleton observed, a wish fervently seconded by his superior officer in Philadelphia, who dubbed the Dahlonega establishment a "neighborhood mint" which little served the function for which it was intended.

While President Van Buren struggled to provide the country with a stable money supply in the aftermath of the destruction of the Second Bank of the United States, the branch mint was only secondarily concerned with minting gold coins. Of much more immediate concern was the intensely personal campaign by the mint's officers and workmen to satisfy their own needs. If Farnum had lived after Sigmund Freud did his work, his driving ambitions, his compulsion to achieve perfection and recognition, and his penury might have been given a proper psychological name, but Singleton described his assayer simply as a man with "a multitude of frailties peculiar to our nature." Mason, a far more practical man, was easier to understand. He wanted security for himself and his family and a bit of autonomy. He thought nepotism a fine thing, although he probably did not know the word. Singleton was motivated mainly by money. He liked the perquisites of office, a weakness that got him into a great deal of trouble. These conflicting ambitions clashed under the roof—such as it was—of the still unfinished mint building. By the time the final drama of completing the building was over, the principal actor, the long absent parson, the Reverend Mr. Few, emerged for a curtain call of sorts to protest his shabby treatment. To all of them the mint was important. They did not enjoy their work when they had any to do, and they certainly did not like each other. Nevertheless, they vigorously protested the merest hint that the mint might not be a permanent fixture. After all, it provided livings, and they were entitled to that.

Dr. Farnum was probably the most irascible of all the mint's officers. Almost nothing pleased him. He jealousy guarded his equipment and would let nobody help him with his work, but he complained when he had more to do than the others. He took pride in the accuracy of his assays, and when his skill excelled that of the assayers at the main mint in Philadelphia he expected suitable recognition. Singleton had nothing but praise for Farnum as an assayer. "The discharge of this duty speaks for itself," he said; "all I could wish of him is that he was a more agreeable companion."[1]

Not even the prospect of a leave brightened Farnum's disposition. Two years after coming to Dahlonega, Farnum requested permission to spend a month visiting friends in the North. "Since we commenced operations, I can say with great confidence, that I have not been absent from the Mint, in a single instance, two hours at any one time." The leave was granted. Farnum made certain that the mint could operate while he was away by casting enough ingots for coining, but he refused to take half of the annual assay coins to Philadelphia with him because he did not want the responsibility. Ever vigilant to protect his interests, when Farnum arrived in Philadelphia he asked to see Singleton's letters on which he took notes.

While he was on leave one of Farnum's main concerns, if not his principal one, was to invest properly the salary that he had accumulated, more than $4,000 by 1839. Savings of that magnitude on a salary of $1,500 a year could be amassed only by parsimony, to which Farnum admitted in explaining the necessity

---

[1]Patterson to Farnum, 13 Feb. 1840; Singleton to Patterson, 25 Feb. 1840, NA-c.

for another leave a year later. Trips to Philadelphia were long, tedious, and expensive, he explained, "but living as I do in perfect exile, compelled to forego almost everything for which life is worth possessing, and unable to procure many things necessary for my comfort, it is in a measure, unavoidable."[2]

In Dahlonega Farnum prided himself on his good relationship with the men who worked with him, Todd and Warwick. Despite talk from time to time about getting rid of one or the other of them since there was not enough business to keep them both busy, Singleton could never get Farnum to decide between them, and Patterson wisely advised Singleton not to take unilateral action in dismissing anyone on Farnum's staff. "Warwick is never actuated by any principle but whiskey and the spirit of kindness," Farnum wrote to Patterson in what was probably as kind a remark as he ever made. "Todd knows that if he leaves, his place would not be supplied." When paid leave for Todd was denied, Farnum did not protest, even though he thought Todd deserved it on the basis of his "faithful and efficient service." Farnum explained that he got along with his men while Mason did not because "Mr. Mason treats his men as companions, I keep mine at a distance. His men know that they are indispensable to him, and that he could not immediately supply their place. Mine understand perfectly, that should they leave, my operations would not be suspended one hour."[3]

David Mason, the coiner, was Dr. Farnum's opposite. He was quick to take offense when he thought his authority had been infringed, and he was certainly eager to get as much out of his job as he could, but he did not express his dissatisfactions in icy silences or in formal calls on the superintendent as Farnum was wont to do. Rather, he engaged in heated exchanges in language too strong for Singleton to commit to paper, perhaps accompanied by physical threats as well. "And it would astonish you," Single-

---

[2]Farnum to Patterson, 4 Aug. 1839, 12 Aug. 1840; Singleton to Patterson, 8 Sept., 1 Oct. 1840, NA-c.

[3]Farnum to Patterson, 30 June, 12 July 1840; Singleton to Patterson, 7 Oct. 1840; Patterson to Singleton, 6 July 1840; NA-c.

ton wrote to Patterson after one such encounter, "were I to relate what immediately followed in my own office. I forbear to mention it, and I assure you that I would not now trouble you with this, but for my apprehensions of its repeated occurance." The occasion of this outburst was the fee Singleton paid Frederick Boartfield, a member of Mason's work force, and two of his sons for hauling firewood and water for the mint. Mason did not object to the work being done or even to the fee paid, but rather to the fact that Singleton had overstepped the bounds of his job into Mason's domain.[4]

Although Farnum charged Mason with the "fault" of treating his men as companions, the fact was that the coiner did not get along well with his men. The most important man on Mason's staff was Charles Thomas, the engineer, who at eighteen dollars per week was also the highest paid workman at the mint. He complained of the "tyranicble" oppression of the chief coiner, who never finished ordering him around. Thomas was promised that he would have little to do at the mint and that he could work much of the time for himself. It seemed, however, that he never had any spare time, because Mason always had some experiments for him to work on, so many in fact that he had no time to complete the tools necessary for the repairs of the machinery. When Mason set Thomas to making scales, Thomas concluded that Mason was trying to drive him off, for he did not know how to make scales. He contended that they did not need an extra pair. He believed that Mason wanted to show his "authority" and perhaps drive him off so that he could hire his son Zelotes instead. Thomas reported that Mason offered him $100 to give up his situation soon after his son arrived for a visit. "I had an Idea he wanted to get me away by Mr. Masons actions previous to this offer, but was not sattisfyed untill by conversation with his son I made a proposal to the affect & Mr. Mason coming in at the time said he would give it & with the sincerity he spoke I knew it is true."[5] The next day Mason gave Thomas an ultimatum: either do the work requested or

---

[4]Singleton to Patterson, 30 Jan. 1840, NA-c

[5]Thomas to Patterson, 12 May 1839, NA-c.

be discharged. So Thomas left the mint. Mason thought he would have no trouble filling Thomas's place. Mr. Boartfield's son was available, and his own son as well, although Mason repeatedly disclaimed any intention of hiring someone in his family.

Others at the mint were little mollified by Mason's disclaimer. Thomas called Mason's son a drunk and promised that the rest of the mint staff would "publish him" as such if Thomas would but consent. Instead, in stilted prose that must have been Farnum's, the staff sent Thomas off with a recommendation. Thomas's dismissal, they said, "was not occasioned by any want of capasity in Mr. Thomas for the discharge of any duty required of him in said Department—nor was it occasioned by the slightest doubt in the integrity or sobriety of Mr. Thomas. Hence we must regret the loss of Mr. Thomas from amongst us, not only as a superior mechanic, but as an obliging and honorable man." The recommendation was signed by all the mint's officers and workmen except, of course, Mason. No one was sadder to see Thomas go than Singleton, who described him as a "perfect machinest" whose services were very important to the coiner's department.[6]

Despite Mason's protests that he would under no circumstances hire his son, within a year rumors circulated about the mint that Mason was determined to have his son employed. Singleton was distraught. The mint already had an intemperate man on its staff, he said. "I allude to poor Warwick; and but for his humble and obliging disposition I should have dismissed him long since." Young Mason, on the other hand, not only drank to excess when he visited Dahlonega the previous year, but "while intoxicated, his behavior was such that I could not put up with were he connected with this branch of the Mint." Singleton was sympathetic to the "parental regard of a father for his son," but the mint needed a machinist. If Mason got his way with his son, would it end there? "He has a son-in-law now an inmate of the mint Edifice, who would no doubt be as much pleased with any of our situations in the Mint as it would be gratifying to the Father-in-law

---

[6]Mason to Patterson, 13 May 1839; Thomas to Patterson, 21 May 1839, NA-c. The recommendation, dated 15 May 1839, was included in Thomas's letter.

to place him in one of them." Despite Singleton's misgivings, Mason's son was on the way by the time Singleton wrote his letter. Although Patterson assured him that all he had to do was to refuse to hire him, Singleton lacked the nerve to interfere. Mason wanted to hire his son so that he would have at least one man whom he could trust, one who would not be a "tool" of the superintendent. In the interest of harmony, young Mason was retained. He was soon "snugly fixed with his birth at the Mint," as Singleton put it. Much to the superintendent's amazement, things worked out far better than he expected. "I am happy to say to you that we are now getting along more harmoniously than ever," Singleton wrote to Patterson four months after the young Mason joined the staff. "Mr. Mason gives much more of his personal attention to business since the appointment of his son than formerly, consequently all things work together much smoother."[7]

Some of the problems of the mint could surely be laid to Singleton, whose shortcomings became more obvious as the years went by. Both Farnum and Mason frequently complained that Singleton tried to turn the workmen against their immediate superior officers and to "conciliate and retain them as his dependents." Farnum said Singleton's principal object was "to swell the list of his retainers, to back him in his broils, at the expense of the government." To illustrate his point, he recounted Singleton's tough stance on Mason's cow. Mason wanted to buy a cow. At his own expense, he put up bars at the entrance of the lane to the mint to keep the cow from straying. "While engaged in the work, the Dr. came down surrounded by some of his retainers, and brandishing his cane, swore that he would let down the bars, and leave them down, which his men have, accordingly since done." Mason had to forgo the purchase of the cow, but apparently not for long. A couple of months later Mason himself complained that Singleton and others through him continually left the bars to the cow yard down and hogs got in and damaged the garden. "If this passage was essential to Dr. Singleton I should have been more in-

[7]Singleton to Patterson, 17 Apr., 8 Sept., 28 Nov. 1840; Mason to Patterson, 14 July 1840, NA-c.

clined to be silent on the subject," Mason protested.[8] Whether the fault was Mason's or Singleton's, it is clear that Mason and Farnum thought that Singleton was using mint employees to extend his authority over them in inappropriate ways.

Farnum, who never hesitated to express his opinion on any subject, questioned not only Singleton's intellectual fitness for the post but his moral qualities a well. He found these "lamentably deficient," and insisted that he for one had "not the least reliance upon his word, having repeatedly detected in him in the most unblushing falsehood." Furthermore, he was stingy, an odd criticism coming from anyone as frugal as Farnum. He accused Singleton of paying a poor collier with shinplasters instead of gold although he had gold in his pockets.[9]

But the most serious charge made against Singleton grew out of his supervision of the enclosure of the mint. Congress, at his insistence, had appropriated $7,500 for the project. Singleton took an active part in the work himself. The contractor for the brick work engaged him to make the brick, and his own shop did the blacksmith's work.

This was not a situation that the job-hungry citizens of Dahlonega were likely to overlook, especially if any of them had a grudge against the mint superintendent, as the postmaster G. K. Cessna did. In the summer of 1839 Cessna reported Singleton to Secretary of Treasury Woodbury for corruption in office:

> Charge 1st. Disbursement of public monies to officers and laborers (Branch Mint) in depreciated paper not known as payment by your department.
>
> Charge 2nd. For contracting public work (at Mint) in a private manner for three Thousand dollars above mechanical rates of this country & strongly suspected of collusion and pecuniary Interest.

---

[8]Farnum to Patterson, 12 July 1840; Mason to Patterson, 12 Sept. 1840, NA-c.

[9]Farnum to Patterson, 12 July 1840, NA-c.

Charge 3'd. For selling contingent funds at a premium and paying the claimants of the government in depreciated paper. All of which I submit to your consideration.[10]

The first charge was the one Farnum and Mason had made, namely that Singleton pocketed the premium he got for Treasury notes. The third was the same except that it referred to the payment of the mint's creditors. The second charge was the most serious.

When Singleton assumed responsibility for supervising the enclosure of the mint, he consulted the contractor, Benjamin Towns, and the coiner, Mason. Towns said the work would cost $9,000. Mason set the price at $7,500. Towns expected to get the work himself. As he later remarked to Singleton, "you could not expect me to give a rigid estimate: I now tell you that you ought not to have given more than $3,500." Singleton made the contracts "in a private manner," not to the lowest bidder. He divided the work into two contracts—$4,750 for brick work and $2,500 for woodwork. These came from workmen in Dahlonega. When he found no lower offers in Athens, he closed the agreement. Singleton protested that this did not add to his pecuniary interest.

Cessna called for a full-scale investigation of the business of the mint, and Singleton was equally loud in calling for a full-scale investigation of Cessna's character. Patterson thought that the charge of gross corruption in public office was unproved, but he observed that the superintendent's "disposition . . . to add to his income from the Mint by jobs and perquisites proves him to be deficient in that delicate sense of propriety which alone can screen a public officer from reproach." President Martin Van Buren finally determined that it was best to do nothing, although Singleton was advised to be more cautious in avoiding not only real wrong but the appearance of it as well. Private emoluments must be kept separate from the public business with "scrupulous care."[11]

The charges against Singleton were made amidst persistent reports that the two branch mints could not survive. Patterson did

---

[10]Cessna to Woodbury, 22 Aug. 1839, NA-c.

[11]Singleton to Patterson, 12 Sept. 1839; Patterson to Woodbury, 24 Oct., 2 Nov. 1839; Woodbury to Patterson, 6 Nov. 1839, NA-c.

not see how it was possible to sustain the one at Dahlonega since the amount of gold deposited there in the first nine months of 1839 was but $77,659, while the cost of maintaining it for the year was $13,900. Even if deposits should reach the anticipated level of $100,000, to continue coinage at an annual cost of fourteen percent was "too extravagant a proposition to be successfully defended." But the uncertain future of the mint posed a problem of what to do with Singleton. "If the Dahlonega Mint is to fall," Patterson confided to Woodbury, "it becomes a question whether it is necessary to remove the present superintendent, even though he is not the kind of man that ought to occupy that station: and it is a still more serious question, whether such an individual as should be in all respects desirable for the place, ought to be asked to change his residence and occupation to assume an office of so precarious a nature."[12]

The cost of maintaining the mint was, of course, over and above the cost of the mint building itself, which, four years after its construction began, the government had neither accepted nor paid for. Understandably, the contractors were anxious. The wooden cornice was the issue. Patterson's objections to it were as strong as ever, but he was willing to withdraw them if Commissioner Few was satisfied. The contractors insisted that a brick cornice was "palpably impracticable, unless they expected the contractor to make Bricks four ft. in length." They wanted their money so that they could pay the men who had done the work. Surely this was a matter to take up with representatives in Washington.

Commissioner Few had not been heard from in almost a year and a half when he finally wrote to the secretary of the treasury that the building ought to be accepted. He thought the wooden cornice was perfectly acceptable, since a brick one "*could not* have been made of full proportion, without using bricks of a size never made, or supporting those of ordinary size with beams of wood or bars of iron, which so far as I can learn has never been done." With the charge for extra work of $1,569.50, Few said that Towns and Tinsley were due $19,719.50 from the government.

---

[12]Patterson to Woodbury, 2 Nov. 1839, NA-c.

When two months passed and still no payment had been made to the contractors, Senator Wilson Lumpkin of Georgia made some inquiries. Both Tinsley and Towns were from his home town of Athens and so were many of the unpaid laborers who brought suit against the contractors. The senator thought that some fault was doubtless chargeable to Few. He suggested that Singleton be asked to disburse the money. "Singleton may be relied upon for integrity," he wrote.

Funds to pay for the building were not immediately available. Because of the long delay in completing it, funds originally appropriated for the mint's construction but not spent reverted to the surplus. Senator Lumpkin had great difficulty explaining this to men long unpaid. Woodbury assumed the responsibility for finding the money. He wrote to Few, who still had about $5,000 in his account, to pay Tinsley and Towns $4,000 at once. Another $2,000 in the building fund which had not reverted to the surplus was forwarded to Singleton with an order to pay it to the contractors as well. The Senate Finance Committee and the House Ways and Means Committee were asked to check into the matter of the surplus funds. A little more than a week after Senator Lumpkin first wrote to the secretary of the treasury, the treasurer of the United States sent Singleton a draft for $11,094.17 to be given to the contractors. This did not cover the extra work, but it paid for everything else. Singleton accepted this new responsibility reluctantly, but early in January 1840 he met with the contractors and paid them. Weeks went by, however, before Few also got around to paying Tinsley and Towns.[13]

When Few took the commissioner's job he expected to receive two percent of the amount spent for the erection of the buildings and purchase of the site. The government claimed that he was en-

---

[13]Few to Woodbury, 14 Oct. 1839; Towns and Tinsley to Woodbury, 12 Nov. 1839; Patterson to Woodbury, 31 Oct. 1839; Lumpkin to Woodbury, 14 Dec., 17 Dec., 19 Dec. 1839, NA-lt; Woodbury to Singleton, 19 Dec. 1839; Woodbury to Few, 20 Dec. 1839; Woodbury to Singleton, 23 Dec. 1839, NA-Treasury Letterbook; Singleton to Patterson, 2 Jan. 1840, NA-c; Singleton to Woodbury, 7 Jan. 1840, NA-lt; Few to Woodbury, 20 Jan. 1840, NA-lt.

titled only to two percent of the funds actually paid out by him, a sum so small that Few was shocked. "Without further reference to the parsimonious allowance made to me by stipulation, I can only express my surprise that there should be any attempt made to defeat my claim to it, after I have performed all the duties, onerous & vexatious as they were, and I will say it, & defy refutation, performed them well." The government was willing to allow him only $414.79 for his work. Few insisted on at least $729.16 and thought he should get more. A year after the final bills were paid, Few wrote to his fellow Georgian, Secretary of State John Forsyth, for help. It was February 1841, and the current administration was about to go out of office. Few did not want to have to explain the situation again to those "not acquainted with the business and who perhaps may seek occasion to find errors where none exist." He could not understand why the secretary of the treasury was depriving him of his just compensation. "I might ask cui bono it cannot profit him, and why he should wish to injure, unjustly, a private citizen, for the purpose of putting this trifling amount into the Treasury I cannot conceive." Few maintained, apparently without any effect, that his expenses of fulfilling the job were more than the commission. If justice was impossible, he added, "I only hope that I may never again hold *any office of profit* under the government."[14]

No more than a month after the mint building was accepted from the contractor, a letter bearing a familiar complaint was sent from Dahlonega to Philadelphia. The roof of the branch mint will not do, Singleton sadly reported. "It has again given way by contraction or expansion or both in such a way to leak intolerable, so much so, that the Building will soon be materially injured, if it is not recovered with other material besides that of zink; and I am at a loss to know what is best to substitute in its place." Singleton and Mason thought that in a climate like Dahlonega's with sudden changes from heat to cold a lasting tight roof could never be made from "zink." Singleton suggested that shingles, made tight

---

[14]Few to Woodbury, 25 Apr. 1840; Few to Forsyth, 18 Feb. 1841; Statement of Few's disbursements, n.d., NA-lt.

with "one or two coats of paint and Rawsin" might work fairly well. It would cost a modest five or six hundred dollars, and should last a quarter century or more. Farnum was sure that a shingle roof would be a fire hazard, so officials toyed briefly with the idea of a leaded iron roof put on by workmen sent from Philadelphia, but the expense was too great. Patterson explained to Woodbury the need for this additional expense. "Like all the rest of the job there, [the zinc roof] seems to have been wretchedly executed," he said. So shingles it was. Within a matter of months, the work was done. "For the first time . . . we have a tight and durable roof over our heads," Singleton reported as the New Year began, "at a cost of about $900 to the Government."[15] Considering the generally high cost of everything in Dahlonega and Singleton's penchant for underestimating expenses, a mere fifty percent increase in the anticipated price tag was probably not too bad.

As perennial a problem as the roof was that of paying the depositors for gold bullion. One-third of the $30,000 appropriation for a bullion fund was never sent to Dahlonega, so the mint was always a bit short. The problem was complicated by the fact that Farnum, in an attempt to keep wastage to a minimum, would not cast fewer than twenty-five ingots at a time. If all the depositors applied at once for their coin, the mint could not pay them. At least those were the arguments Singleton advanced in his perennial quest for the extra $10,000. Patterson was not impressed. He insisted that the mint must have as its first duty the accommodation of its depositors. If this could best be done by casting fewer than twenty-five ingots at a time, he was sure that Farnum would "cheerfully concur." The present state of public money matters insofar as specie was concerned did not permit the government to send the $10,000, so it was vain to ask. Singleton blamed the small amount of deposits coming into the mint—a total of only eighteen deposits valued at $5,724.85 in March 1840—on the fact that the depositors had to wait as much as a month for their coin. In March there was no coinage at all. Patterson would not accept this ar-

[15]Singleton to Patterson, 8 Feb., 1 Mar., 30 Mar. 1840, 3 Jan. 1841; Patterson to Singleton, 19 Feb., 11 Mar. 1840; Patterson to Woodbury, 14 Apr. 1840, NA-c.

gument. A $20,000 fund was certainly ample to pay that number of depositors. He asked pointedly for a report on the condition of the government deposits.[16]

Another reason Singleton advanced for the decline in gold deposits was the presence in the community of a man named Pinchback, who purchased gold bullion at a premium of six percent over its mint evaluation, alloyed it with a large amount of silver, and shipped it out to regions unknown whenever he had a melt of $40,000 to $50,000. Such fraud in the sale of mixed metals so close to the branch mint was anathema to Singleton, who "cried loud and spared not." He attributed the ready market for Pinchback gold to the high price of exchange in the North, and the universal depression caused by the "ruinous system of tolerated Bank suspensions." Some of the bogus gold found its way to the mint in Philadelphia, where it assayed from 594 to 605 parts gold per thousand with silver making up 332 to 346 parts.[17]

Financial trouble rained on the mint. As soon as the competition from Pinchback gold abated, terrible news came from Washington. The treasury of the United States was so low on funds that it might be necessary to draw on the mint's bullion account—the inadequate $20,000 that Singleton had tried for so long to supplement. How much could the mint spare without interfering with coining operations? Not any, was the response from Dahlonega. Nevertheless, the word came that the treasury would probably call for half of the fund to be returned. With extreme reluctance, Singleton set about getting the money ready. He thought it a ruinous course, "blasting the prospects of this branch of the Mint," an institution so important to the miners of the gold region. Even if the government never called for the money, having to hold it in reserve was equivalent to withdrawal because the mint could not use the money. The only course Singleton could suggest to allay the difficulties caused by this decision was to melt

---

[16]Singleton to Patterson, 19 June 1839, 1 Apr. 1840; Patterson to Singleton, 29 June 1839, 9 Apr. 1840, NA-c.

[17]Singleton to Patterson, 10 Oct. 1839, 20 Apr., 2 May, 20 May 1840; Patterson to Singleton, 29 May 1840, NA-c.

ingots more frequently. Every time they had $5,000 in bullion and clippings, they would melt, he said. Not surprisingly, he expected opposition from one of the departments at least.[18]

Occasionally, good news came from the mint: the new rollers for the coining press were fine; much of the time Farnum had enough crucibles, nitric acid, and other items needs for his multiple duties as assayer, melter, and refiner; and the mint's record for wastage was always superior. The Dahlonega branch rivaled the Philadelphia Mint in keeping its level of wastage low, and it far excelled the other two branches. In 1840 the Senate passed a bill enabling the Dahlonega Mint to coin silver parted from gold, but this was never done. The extremely high quality of Georgia gold meant that there was little silver in the deposits. Also, Farnum routinely used silver for nearly half the alloy needed because nitric acid, used to part silver from gold, was so difficult to obtain. Nor was it likely that the mint could readily get a supply of silver, which commanded a premium of eight percent in the Dahlonega area. Even small coins could not compete with shinplasters. For more than one reason Farnum wished it were possible for the Dahlonega Mint to coin silver. It would relieve the mint personnel from the "imputation (too true), of being an 'idle set of pensioners.' "[19]

In the first years of the mint's operations, only half eagles and quarter eagles were coined. The smaller coins were not popular; eighteen months after the first ones were coined, not a single call had been made for them. They were more difficult to mint than the half eagles, too. Their dies cracked often, and a machinist was required just to turn these dies. Singleton asked that the minting of quarter eagles be discontinued, but his request may have been motivated by purely personal reasons. "We are getting on well

---

[18]Woodbury to Singleton, 27 July 1840, NA-Treasury Letterbook; Singleton to Woodbury, 10 Aug. 1840, 16 Jan., 13 Feb. 1841, NA-lt; Singleton to Patterson, 21 Mar. 1841, NA-c.

[19]Singleton to Patterson, 29 May, 17 June 1839; Patterson to Singleton, 26 Jan. 1841; Patterson to Farnum, 27 Apr. 1840; Farnum to Patterson, 5 May 1840, NA-c.

with three hands, and if Mr. Mason would only consent to turn our Quarter eagle Dies, we should not want the machinist." Young Mason, the machinist whom Singleton did not like, had been employed for just over a month at that time. But Patterson would not give his consent. "Unfavorable remarks would be made if this coinage were altogether neglected by you," he said.[20]

The most frequent problem at the mint was that of cracked dies. It seemed that all the difficulties the coiner once had with the rollers were transferred to the coining press, which destroyed dies with abandon. Almost every letter from Dahlonega mentioned dies, and most of the time the news was bad. Dies cracked regularly, sometimes in being prepared for use, sometimes the first time they were used. Often they were cracked so badly that they could not be used again. If the defect was small, the imperfect ones were used anyway. "I do not know where the fault lies in this unfortunate cracking of dies," Singleton wrote. "Mr. Mason thinks it to be in the quality of the steel." Actually, the blame for the cracked dies probably lay in a defect in the construction of the coining press, which had an arch fastened to an iron table. There was too much vibration for dies to withstand. When the Philadelphia press was remodeled and rebuilt some years later, cracked dies posed less of a problem.

More dies came from Philadelphia, but they would hardly last the day. On one expected return of $10,000 in quarter eagles, only six hundred pieces were coined before both pairs of quarter eagle dies were ruined. The dies cracked, perhaps ominously, when they coined the money to cover the Treasury Department's expected call for $10,000. The staff tried to meet the drafts with all possible dispatch, Singleton explained. But for this unfortunate occurrence they would have been ready "however deleterious its consequences would be in blasting the prosperity of this branch of the mint." New dies arrived in mid-February 1841. Singleton thought they had enough to last "to the end of our minting existence," an event he expected momentarily on account of the out-

---

[20]Singleton to Patterson, 29 Aug. 1840; Patterson to Singleton, 9 Sept. 1840, NA-c.

rageous demands of the government for its $10,000. But not so. The new half eagle head die cracked within the week. It was so bad it would not have been used except in case of an emergency like the present one of preparing for the government draft.[21]

Irregular coins were not infrequently produced at Dahlonega. Perhaps it was appropriate that the government got its money in defective coins. Between the time that the machinist Thomas left and the younger Mason was hired, the under die slipped a quarter turn so that the head of Liberty was not precisely opposite the tail of the Eagle on a few of the 1,817 half eagles coined that day, 10 June 1840. Mason said it happened while he was at dinner and the "men through neglect or otherwise, let the under Die be turned in its position so that the heads of the devices stand quartering." Singleton described this as some irregularity in the impressions, but after consulting with Farnum decided to receive them because he found the law silent on the relative position of the two figures. Patterson agreed that it would be all right if the coins were otherwise unexceptional.[22]

Unfortunate as defective coins might be, a more serious cause for concern was the limited amount of bullion brought to the Dahlonega Mint and consequently, the limited number of coins minted. In 1839 only 6,051 ounces of gold was received, and $128,880 in coins minted—13,674 quarter eagles and 18,939 half eagles. Singleton was sure that receipts at the mint would increase in 1840 because "the exceeding low price of cotton" combined with improvements in mining would lure men back to the mines. In fact, he predicted that receipts would double, but he was mistaken. Only slightly more bullion was received that year than in 1839—6,549 ounces—and coinage dropped to $123,310. The unpopular quarter eagles, difficult to coin under any circumstances because the dies cracked so often, and impossible to coin without the services of a machinist, composed only $8,830 of this amount. There were just 3,532 of these

---

[21]Singleton to Patterson, 19 Sept. 1840, 12 Jan., 19 Jan., 20 Feb., 27 Mar. 1841, NA-c.; *Coins and Coinage* (Philadelphia, 1884) 12, 13.

[22]Singleton to Patterson, 11 June 1840; Patterson to Singleton, 26 June 1840; Mason to Patterson, 14 July 1840, NA-c.

coins and more than seven times as many half eagles—22,896. The bullion that came to the mint was almost always in small amounts, so that Farnum, who had to assay each deposit separately, was far busier than Mason.[23]

The branch mint at Charlotte was doing little better than the one at Dahlonega. It was inevitable that sooner or later Congress would begin to ask questions. How much gold is mined in the United States? the Senate asked the secretary of the treasury, who asked Patterson, who in turn asked the superintendents of the mints at Dahlonega and Charlotte. Patterson did not hope for an accurate estimate, but he wanted something "nearer the truth than the vague and exaggerated guesses heretofore presented." He especially wanted to know what proportion of the gold mined was brought to the mint, and what proportion was sold to manufacturers. His hope for more precise information was in vain at least so far as Singleton was concerned. Singleton replied immediately that he thought the "greater part is coined." But in the very next sentence he cited a conversation with a miner from the western part of the state who said that nine-tenths of the bullion from that section went to Augusta, where it was sold to brokers and merchants for the purpose of northern exchange, then shipped to New York where it was made into jewelry. "Compare this with other sections of our gold Region remote from our Mints, and it is reasonable to suppose that the greater part of our gold Bullion is sold to manufacturers." He gave no explanation for this diametrical shift in views within the space of a single paragraph. With equal vagueness he suggested that a turnabout in the amount of gold brought to the mint could be expected, for "just in proportion to our progress in civilization our reformation is hoped for."

The Georgia delegation in Congress also asked for precise information on the mint and its prospects, a request Singleton honored with his usual imprecision. The reasons he cited for the decrease in mining activity were the removal of the Indians, requiring mounted volunteers at high wages; the building of the

---

[23]Singleton to Patterson, 2 Jan. 1840, 3 Jan. 1841; Patterson to Singleton, 11 Aug. 1840, NA-c.

Western and Atlantic Railroad, which required much labor; and the temporary rise in the price of cotton. But things were sure to improve. "The increased success in raising the precious metals from their beds of obscurity, guaranties a safety in embarking in the enterprise which no one can doubt. . . . our gold veins . . . are daily opening new sources of immence profit to the miner and the farther we penetrate them, the richer they appear to get." He described the Southern gold region as "one of the best . . . hitherto discovered upon the face of the earth." If this was not a persuasive enough argument, he suggested that the mint ought to be saved because it had been so expensive. The grounds, buildings, tools, chemical apparatus, and so forth, had cost at least $75,000. If such a vast pile of expensive articles had to be sold at public outcry, they would not bring $10,000.[24]

Farnum was far less sanguine. He had predicted for some time that the mines were failing, and he had not changed his mind. "There is no avocation in which one can embark with so poor a prospect of success as mining in this country," he wrote to Patterson in the spring of 1840. "Where one man has made, ten have lost money. No part of the Union is filled with a poorer and more depraved population." Having disposed summarily of the people, Farnum then spoke candidly about the utter uselessness of the branch mints. "No man of judgement, or candour, will say, that the Branch Mints are of use at all commensurate with the expense of their support; some support them from motives of state pride, others from pecuniary considerations, not connected with the object of their establishment." He concluded his verbal assault on the institution that provided him a living with the charge that the mints did not even serve the purpose of providing the country with a stable currency. "Gold coin forms no part of the circulation of this region." he said, "The banks when compelled to pay specie, pay silver or foreign gold coin, very rarely domestic coin." Singleton, he said, was so blinded by his fears that the mints

---

[24]Patterson to Singleton, 8 Jan. 1840; Singleton to Patterson, 23 Jan. 1840; Singleton to Georgia delegation, printed in *Southern Banner*, undated clipping, NA-c.

would be discontinued that he entertained "the most extravagant expectations of the produce of the mines."[25]

Singleton had every reason to fear for the security of his own job. The Democrats who had provided him with his appointment were defeated in the election of 1840. Singleton was in trouble and he knew it. Still, he continued to hope for the best. He did not flag in his correspondence to Philadelphia detailing the small triumphs of the mint: the amount of deposits was up, the "notorious swindlers" had been broken up, the price of cotton was going down, and the railroad was hiring fewer men. Even Farnum, who so often declaimed on the utter uselessness of the branch mints, was worried after the inauguration of President William Henry Harrison. "I have reason to believe that strenuous efforts are making to remove us from office, on the ostensible ground of our friendship for the late administration, but really to secure our places for themselves," he wrote. Would Patterson address the secretary of the treasury on their behalf?[26]

Moves were indeed under way to remove Singleton. In January 1841, as President Van Buren's term drew to a close, eighty-eight citizens of Dahlonega and neighboring counties sent a petition to the Georgia delegation in Congress requesting the removal of Singleton from office on the grounds that "General Harrison and his friends had pledged to follow the example set by Thomas Jefferson. Our first reason for removal is that he meddles in every election from constable to President of the United States contrary to the rule laid down by Mr. Jefferson. He patronized that dirty sheet the extra Globe which print we consider a disgrace to any civilized community." The *Extra Globe* was a broadside supporting Van Buren, edited by former Postmaster General Amos Kendall. He promised "to take care" of those who helped the cause. Subscription to such papers was a common form of assessment for officeholders. Singleton was further charged

---

[25]Farnum to Patterson, 18 Apr. 1840, NA-c.

[26]Singleton to Patterson, 28 Nov. 1840, 3 Jan. 1841; Farnum to Patterson, 8 Mar. 1841, NA-c.; Leonard White, *The Jacksonians* (New York, 1954) 333-34.

with being incompetent to the duties assigned him, and with running public business for private profit. The fourth charge of the petitioners was that "numbers of persons that deal largely in gold" would not deposit gold at the mint so long as Singleton presided over the institution.

Singleton, of course, denied the charges he learned of only two days before Van Buren left office. He had not interfered in "all elections," although he admitted he felt "that kind of interest in the late Presidential so common through our whole country." He thought the whole petition was marked by a malicious design, one delayed in its presentation until Singleton's friends would be out of Washington. He distributed circulars to the principal depositors asking if they had any cause to complain. The Lumpkin County Grand Jury vindicated Singleton. It studied the charges brought to remove him from office and found them unfounded, "gotten up for malicious and selfish purposes and perhaps both."[27]

But Singleton could not save himself. He was replaced by Paul Rossignol, a man who probably knew no more about running a mint than Singleton but one whose politics was right. Singleton did not leave gladly. It seemed unfair that just as he was finding himself qualified for the complicated duties of his office he was "hurled from office for the single cause of exercising the ordinary rights of an American citizen in the late Presidential Election." These were "rights solemnly consecrated to me by the Blood of my Revolutionary Father," he reminded Patterson. "Frederick the great lost his all, yet exulted in the retention of his honor. My office is gone, still my honor mingles with the warm blood of a Republican, where it cannot be touched and in comparison of which, offices are mere trash."[28] Offices at the mint may have been trash, but even so, they were enthusiastically pursued by dozens of people in the years to come.

---

[27]Singleton to secretary of treasury, 2 Mar. 1841, NA-lt; Singleton to secretary of treasury, 6 Mar. 1841, NA-c; Lumpkin County Grand Jury Report, Mar. 1841, copy in NA-lt.

[28]Singleton to Patterson, 3 Apr. 1841, NA-c.

CHAPTER 5

Paul Rossignol. The name had a peculiar ring. It did not sound like that of a man who really belonged in those mountains—names like Riley and Varnum, Adams and Awtry. French it was. Even if the people of Dahlonega did not know that the name at one time had been "Roth de Laing Royal"—Roth of Royal Blood—they knew that yet another "foreigner" was in charge of the mint, and they were not happy about it. "Old Soaptail" Singleton was a foreigner imported from his plantation near Athens; Rossignol came from the nearby county of Habersham, but he had not been there long enough for the foreign taint to be removed. With a name like Rossignol and a rather elegant family who spoke French, he was almost sure to have trouble in a rough and tumble place like Dahlonega.

Besides, as mint superintendent, he had the choicest political plum in all of north Georgia, so every man who coveted the job for himself or for a friend was set to dislike Rossignol from the start. Singleton knew it and Rossignol would find out soon enough. In defending his own position which was so rudely snatched away from him, Singleton explained the difficulties of an honest, well-meaning outsider: "Be pleased to imagine to yourself an honest man, coming in contact with a community principally composed of every other description of characters, such as had no other object in coming to a gold region but speedy acquisition (not from 'sweat of the brow') of the precious stuff, disappointed, bankrupt, desperate, resorting to every species of stratagem ever invoked by man."[1] That was the situation Singleton faced, and the new superintendent had to come to terms with it as well.

Several petitions from the local community pushed a favorite son for the post of mint superintendent, and some individuals applied for the office on their own. The office was of some importance; as one hopeful candidate observed, "its respectability and liberal salary for the services *now required* will no doubt call forth many applicants of respectability." It was a Whig year, and a man's politics had to be right. A group of Dahlonega citizens put forward the name of a man who seemed to possess unexcelled qualifications: he was right politically and he was one of them. "We have suffered much disadvantage already by foreigners and persons from a distance being placed over this branch mint, who are stiff in their manners and hardly to be approached by the people."[2]

Nevertheless, it was the "foreigner" Rossignol who got the appointment. He was born in Santo Domingo into a family that originally came from the south of France. The various branches of the family were distinguished by the names of the island plantations on which they lived. The future mint superintendent's family was Rossignol de Belle Anse. In 1792, when Rossignol was six years old, his family fled the slave uprising in Santo Domingo, settling first in Charleston, later in Savannah, and still later in Augusta. It was there that Rossignol married into the distinguished Dugas family and became cashier in a bank. He inherited some land in Habersham County and later acquired some additional land there which he owned and operated with his brother-in-law. He called his farm on the Soquee River "Sans Souci."[3] It was from nearby Habersham that Rossignol at age fifty-

---

[1]Singleton to Thomas Ewing, 23 Mar. 1841, Record Group 56, General Records of the Secretary of the Treasury, National Archives, hereafter cited as RG 56.

[2]Reuben Thompson to R. W. Habersham, 3 Jan. 1841; Petition to Daniel Webster, 12 Mar. 1841, RG 56.

[3]Background on the Rossignol family is taken from a letter to Sylvia Head from John I. Coddington, National Genealogical Society, 20 Sept. 1962.

five came to Dahlonega to assume his duties as mint superintendent, but it was from faraway Augusta that the support for his candidacy for the post came. The only petition asking for his appointment came from Augusta. It bore but eighteen signatures, but it had the endorsement of Georgia's Whig congressman, William Dawson.[4]

Rossignol had been in office but a month or so when he made his first big mistake. He appointed Samuel S. Blair, a schoolteacher from Habersham, as his clerk, that envied post that paid $1,000 per year. Like Rossignol, Blair was a "foreigner." He had come south from Pennsylvania. That fact did not seem significant to the politically naive Rossignol, who described his new assistant as "a very fine young man and of good moral character." Not surprisingly, the appointment was an affront to the disappointed office-seekers of Lumpkin County. Rosignol had turned down twelve applicants for the clerkship because none of them possessed the necessary qualifications. One of the disappointed men immediately got up a petition to abolish the mint and sent it to Congress. Ostensibly, the reason was that the cost of coining gold at Dahlonega was so high—12½ percent—but Rossignol was convinced that the idea had occurred to the would-be clerk as an afterthought. A counter-petition by friends of the mint was forwarded to Congress, too, but the new superintendent did not think it would have much effect. "If Congress have determined to abolish the three Branch Mints, it will do so, notwithstanding all the petitions which might be presented for their continuance."[5]

The possibility of closing the mint dogged Rossignol throughout his tenure as mint superintendent. Of more immediate concern, however, was the problem of paying depositors quickly for the gold they brought in. With the possibility that the Treasury Department might call at any moment for its $10,000, Rossignol had a reserve of only $10,000 on hand with which to pay depositors. This was not enough. Sometimes miners had to wait a month or more for their coin. This intolerable situation, one irate miner

---

[4]Petition for Paul Rossignol, 1841, RG 56.

[5]Rossignol to Patterson, 20 July, 1 June 1841, NA-c.

complained to the secretary of the treasury, "threw [the miners] into the hands of brokers who did not fail to shave off from 5 to 10% of earnings." Besides, this particular complaint continued, the mint would not make a melt until there was about $10,000 on hand, and all the while the officers drew their "fat salaries." Or do their salaries stop while they wait for a melting? he asked. "If so I apprehend they would soon discover they could melt & coin less than $10,000 at a time." Patterson urged Rossignol to pay the depositors whatever funds he had on hand—even from the $10,000 held in reserve for the Government—and to make more frequent smaller melts if necessary.[6]

Under these trying circumstances Rossignol tried very hard to please. He had to get along not only with the depositors whose demands seemed insatiable, but with his staff whose dispositions had not improved. It was one thing for Patterson in Philadelphia to direct Rossignol in Dahlonega to make more frequent melts; it was another for Rossignol to give that order to Dr. Farnum. "I do not wish to interfere in anything that does not belong to my office," Rossignol wrote cautiously to Patterson. Were deposits to be melted only when he desired it or whenever the assayer wished it? How far did he have to go to please depositors? If a depositor wanted his deposit melted before him, must his wish be complied with, exclusive of other business? What about mint hours? Was it all right to open at eight in the morning and close between five and six in the evening with an hour off at midday for dinner? Was that long enough? Patterson agreed to the hours Rossignol designated, told him to accommodate depositors whenever possible by melting their deposits in their presence but at a time fixed by the mint. As for making melts when Rossignol wanted them or when Farnum wanted them, Patterson wisely cautioned Rossignol to take the assayer's advice. "The propriety of this practice is manifest," he said.[7]

---

[6]John A. Jones to secretary of the treasury, 30 May 1841, NA-lt; Patterson to Rossignol, 18 June 1841, NA-c; Patterson to Walter Forward, 23 Sept. 1841, NA-lt; Rossignol to Patterson, 5 Oct. 1841, NA-c.

[7]Rossignol to Patterson, 14 Aug. 1841; Patterson to Rossignol, 25 Aug. 1841, NA-c.

The lingering suspicion that the mint's days were numbered was reinforced in the fall of 1841 when the House of Representatives asked for a report on operations of the mint with an eye to retrenchment. A questionnaire arrived in Dahlonega for mint officers to fill out. Rossignol did not have any real difficulty with his questions. He said he gave all his time to the duties of his office, not that he was always busy (if all deposits were made in the course of two or three days, he could perform all his duties in one-third of the time) but as it was, he had to be constantly at the office. The clerk, Blair, was a necessity, too, because if Rossignol were sick, Blair would be on hand to keep the office open. Mason reported that he had already retrenched by cutting the number of hands in the coiner's department from three to two and that further cuts could not be made. Dr. Farnum's answers to the questionnaire were so devious that Rossignol avowed that "if it had not been handed to me by Mr. Mason, I should not have known that it was his answer to my letter." To the query on retrenchment and reform in the assayer's office, Farnum wrote, "Abolish the office and divide the duties between other officers of the Mint. Dispense moreover with one of the hands and thus effect a saving of $2200 per annum." A few weeks earlier he had written to Patterson that "this mint should be abolished, and the building converted into an arsenal for the deposite of arms."[8]

At least one citizen of Dahlonega fervently hoped the mint would be closed because this would provide him with an opportunity for office. James J. Field, whose name in future years would show up on many a petition recommending some change or other at the mint, thought the mint's closing would afford him the chance to become caretaker for the property "at perhaps a handsome salary." Even if the salary were small, he would like to have the job anyway, times being hard.[9]

But the mint did not close. Instead, business increased appreciably during 1841 and 1842, so much so that Mint Director Pat-

---

[8]Rossignol to Patterson, 22 Oct. 1841; Mason to Rossignol, 21 Oct. 1841; Farnum to Rossignol, 19 Oct. 1841; Farnum to Patterson, 4 Oct. 1841, NA-c.

[9]J. J. Field to Capt. A. R. Hertzel, 27 Mar. 1842, RG 56.

terson was very pleased. The amount of gold deposited at the Dahlonega branch increased steadily almost from the time Rossignol took office, and the amount of coinage, of course, increased as well. There was a marked rise during the first eight months of 1841 from the rather slow returns of the same period the year before, up from $57,334.54 to $95,498.49. The situation was even better the following year, when the value of deposits doubled. May 1842 was a very big month; the mint received 98 deposits for a total of $36,055.47 and coined 6,339 half eagles with a value of $31,695. August 1842 was another successful month; 91 deposits worth $30,100 were made and 9,445 half eagles—$47,215—were coined. In each of those months, there were three coining days.[10]

Such an increase in business was not without its problems. The mint needed more money for wastage and contingent expenses than it had in the past, up from $400 to $900 a year, and there was a constant need for more and more supplies: a carboy of sulfuric acid, three dozen dipping pots, three assay cups, three dozen black lead covers, one hundred coupelles, ten carboys of nitric acid, five hundred slips of rolled lead for assaying, three dozen more black lead covers ("those sent before were too small"), one cask of sand crucibles, six quires of red blotting paper, one large anvil, and "in case Congress should not abolish the Branch Mints," one copy of Ure's *Dictionary of Arts and Manufactures*. Not everything ordered came as soon as it was needed. A delay of two to three months on the road was common. In spite of the greatly increased coinage, Mason apparently had much better luck with his dies than he had had before. Frantic requests for new ones were few, and when the head dies for 1841 were defaced, the mint still had left three half eagle tail dies and four quarter eagle tails for 1841 as well as the new dies for 1842. In the midst of this prosperity boom, the iron safe in Rossignol's office gave way, the lock falling down between iron plates, the wood to which it was fastened having rotted away. Rossignol asked permission to construct a strong box "the thickness of two planks with a sheet of

---

[10]Rossignol to [secretary of the treasury?], 9 Sept. 1841, NA-lt; May and August 1842 reports of branch mint, Dahlonega, NA-c; Patterson to Rossignol, 16 Sept. 1842, NA-c.

iron between them, the whole secure with iron bars and big enough to hold the present safe." Patterson approved this forty-dollar investment.[11]

Increased activity at the mint may be attributed directly to greatly increased mining activity in the Dahlonega area in 1842 and 1843. A fabulously rich strike was made in May 1842 at the O'Bar Mine, which belonged to Senator John C. Calhoun of South Carolina. The tract was on a high steep hill overlooking the Chestatee River about three miles from town and was crossed by an old Indian trail. A boy passing along the path picked up a specimen that led to the discovery of a vein so rich that Calhoun was told he must come at once. The senator could not leave Washington immediately, so he sent his son-in-law, Thomas Green Clemson, an engineer of considerable skill. The rumors of great wealth proved true. Clemson arrived about a month after the discovery. Although he had no way of estimating how much had been taken from the mine in that time, May 1842 was one of the busiest months the branch mint ever enjoyed. Ninety-eight deposits were made averaging $368 each. Some of these came from the O'Bar Mine.

Clemson found heaps of ore at the mine that had been rapidly culled over. Since only the richest portions had been selected, the mounds were still rich in visible gold. In the three months he stayed at the mine, working with only two men, he extracted many thousands of dollars of gold. "I have often taken from two to five hundred dollars from a single pan of ore," Clemson wrote years later. He considered that the amount of gold taken from a comparatively small piece of ground made this "among the richest gold mines ever discovered."[12] During a congressional lull Calhoun himself visited the mine for a few days in June 1842 and

---

[11]Cong. Richard W. Habersham to Walter Forward, 28 July 1842, RG 104, "V"; Rossignol to Patterson, 8 Dec., 21 Dec. 1841, 15 Jan., 12 Mar., 14 May, 10 June, 28 June, 6 Aug., 27 Aug., 13 Dec. 1842, NA-c; Patterson to Rossignol, 20 Aug. 1842, NA-c.

[12]Clemson to Patrick Calhoun, 12 Oct. 1856, quoted in Alester G. Holmes and George R. Sherrill, *Thomas Green Clemson, His Life and Work* (Richmond, 1937) 67.

discovered that the vein continued to produce rich yields. "It would excite you to see it," Clemson wrote to his wife; "really if it continues there is no telling to what extent it may yield."[13] Even though Clemson thought the mine would continue to pay richly, he left after three months because the rock had become harder and some water had entered the mine, temporarily preventing operations. He advised Calhoun that it would be unwise for him to pursue extensive mining activities, because he would have to trust to the judgment and honesty of other men, and the profits already realized might be lost.[14]

Director of the Mint Patterson got a firsthand account of the Calhoun mine and its prospects when Samuel Blair resigned his post as clerk of the Dahlonega Mint and went home to Pennsylvania in August 1842. Blair told Patterson that Calhoun had leased the mine for a month in May-June for one-fourth of the product and that gold deposited at the branch mint from that working amounted to about $10,500, coming from two deposits, one for about $6,000 and the other for $4,500. Calhoun stopped the lease, he said, and Clemson was working the mine. It was Blair's opinion that Calhoun had spent a great deal of money on mining speculations, most of it unprofitable, and that every dollar produced in gold cost two in labor. "There is something enticing, however, in gold hunting which still keeps numbers engaged in it. As in lotteries, the general view is turned to the prizes and the blanks are forgotten."[15]

Within a year the hopes for prizes had drawn nearly twelve thousand laborers to the Lumpkin County gold mines, and more thousands were expected, according to the Athens paper, the

---

[13]Quoted in Charles M. Wiltse, *John C. Calhoun, Sectionalist, 1840-1850* (Indianapolis, 1951) 128. Wiltse differs in the number of workers at O'Bar Mine: "With only 8 workmen and no machinery $8000 worth of gold had been taken from the mine in two weeks not counting ore still unrefined" (127).

[14]Holmes and Sherrill, *Thomas Green Clemson*, 67-68.

[15]Notes on visit of Samuel Blair with Robert Patterson, 10 Aug. 1842, NA-c.

Southern Banner. A writer for that paper advised the state's farmer-miners that there was no better cure for the low price of cotton. "Let them raise everything for their own consumption, live within their means, and dig, dig, dig, as long as a grain of gold is to be found among our hills."[16]

While in Philadelphia, Blair told Patterson the other news from Dahlonega. Mason had formed a company or partnership to go into the tanning business. He had contrived a new apparatus for hastening the tanning process and eventually intended to connect a shoe factory to the tannery. The new enterprise, along with his duties as a coiner at the mint and his church work—he was a Presbyterian minister—must have kept him fairly busy. Blair said nothing of Farnum, but reported that the unfortunate Warwick had "fallen into such habits of intemperance that his dismissal from the Mint became necessary." Blair was mistaken in this, for Warwick, however intemperate, stayed on the mint payroll for another nine years.

Blair's resignation created a vacancy on the mint staff, and office-seekers abhor a vacuum. Immediately Superintendent Rossignol was besieged with applications. At first he decided he would do the clerk's work himself, apparently coming to the conclusion that some retrenchment at the mint was possible after all. But he reckoned without the hungry hordes who saw in the clerk's post better prospects than they found in mining. To get rid of them, most of whom Rossignol did not consider qualified for the job, he appointed Major William E. Derrick, "an old soldier who formerly served . . . as captain in the United States Army and afterwards as Major under General Jackson. He is believed and respected by all who know him and I sincerely believe [him] to be a man of strict honor and integrity." Rossignol described the appointment as "an act of justice towards a man who has served his country faithfully. His appointment has given satisfaction here, and if you knew him, you would approve my choice."[17]

There was one drawback, however, which Director Patterson was quick to note as soon as Derrick's bond arrived in Philadel-

[16]Athens (Georgia) *Southern Banner,* 7 Apr. 1843.

[17]Rossignol to Patterson, 1 Oct. 1842, NA-c.

phia for approval. Derrick's handwriting was virtually illegible. "I must be permitted to express my apprehension that an individual who writes so bad a hand as is exhibited in the two signatures of Mr. Derrick cannot be capable of keeping your books and accounts in a satisfactory manner," Patterson complained. He regretted that Rossignol had overlooked "so essential a qualification in a clerk as his being able to write at least a tolerable hand." But Rossignol had a remedy for this apparent flaw. He would do all the writing in the office himself, and Derrick would receive the deposits and attend to the melting. Besides, Derrick was so willing that Rossignol had no doubt that given time he would do nearly all the writing as well as any other who could have been chosen.[18]

Some months later when Rossignol tried to determine the reason for the trouble that had befallen him, he concluded that it all began with the hiring of Derrick. Those who wanted the job and did not get it were determined to have their revenge. That may have been part of the problem, but almost certainly the difficulties that cost Rossignol his job had deeper roots. He probably tried too hard. The boom in Georgia mining prospects in the summer of 1842 that vastly increased deposits at the mint made it quite difficult to pay depositors promptly in coin, since the amount of deposits for any one month far exceeded the cash reserve the mint had on hand. Also, Rossignol's long years in banking and his willingness to accommodate his old banking associates who wanted to buy the Georgia gold caused him to make a mistake that men hungry for office were quick to seize upon.

When depositors brought their gold to the mint to be turned into coin, they had to wait a week and sometimes as much as a month before their coin was ready. To assist those who did not want to wait, Rossignol agreed to exchange bank notes on the Insurance and Banking Company of Augusta for mint certificates issued to depositors. Certificates were discounted by one-fourth of one percent per week for up to four weeks. Rossignol thought

---

[18]Patterson to Rossignol, 17 Sept. 1842; Rossignol to Patterson, 1 Oct. 1842, NA-c.

he was doing a favor to the Augusta bank, which was a specie-paying bank, and to the depositors who wanted immediate cash. He saw no impropriety in it.

Perhaps nothing was wrong, but a mint superintendent could not be too prudent. Inevitably charges were filed against Rossignol. They came from three Dahlonega citizens, whom Rossignol described as disappointed office-seekers. They claimed that the superintendent had purchased mint certificates for less than their true value, paying for them in "depreciated bank bills . . . for *profit to himself*." They added that it was within the superintendent's power to delay the coinage, thus improving his chance for personal gain. That was the principal charge against Rossignol, but there was a second: that the superintendent was not accommodating enough. He closed the office every Saturday about one o'clock and would not transact business after that "to the great inconvenience of citizens generally." The charges were filed by John D. Field, Adam Peck, and William M. Varnum.[19] Soon three more depositors swore affidavits that they had received bank bills for their bullion, affidavits sent on to Washington. Petitions asking for Rossignol's removal began to circulate in the area. The clerk William Derrick claimed that these petitions were kept only in grog shops patronized by a "transient population . . . that would sign anything," but these, too, found their way to the capital.[20]

Rossignol was ready to defend himself, first stating the reasons for paying depositors in bank notes, and then assessing his critics. Over a period of three weeks in August 1842 he bought only eight certificates, totaling $1,588.54, on which the premium was but $10.25. The small premium of one-quarter of one percent per week was much less than the two percent charged by brokers, one of whom, incidentally, accepted bank notes for bullion and then filed an affidavit against Rossignol. The superintendent de-

---

[19]John D. Field, Adam Peck, and William Varnum to secretary of the treasury, 1 Sept. 1842, NA-c.

[20]Affidavits of Allen E. Matthews, F. I. Sullivan, and James Sanford, 9 Sept. 1842, NA-c; William Derrick to Capt. A. R. Hertzel, 29 Dec. 1842, RG 56.

nied that he had ever delayed coining; indeed, "all the town knows when we coin and very frequently if not always, before I have received the coin from the Coiner, depositors are in my office waiting to receive theirs." He also denied ever receiving any profit. On the contrary, he sometimes advanced gold coin of his own to individuals of Dahlonega, charging them no interest and waiting two or three weeks before getting his money. As for the mint's hours, these were long enough. He often stayed open until four or five o'clock on Saturdays and until 8:00 P.M. on weekdays.

Rossignol's character was good. He cited his impeccable record of sixteen years as a teller in the Bank of Augusta. During that time not a single complaint had ever been filed against him. He pointed out that the mint's first clerk, Wingfield, bought gold and that nobody complained. "No sir, and those three men would not have made charges against me if J. J. Field had been appointed clerk and if I had not left the house of John Choice."

Here was the nub of the matter. Rossignol claimed that James J. Field, a disappointed office-seeker and brother of one of the two men in Dahlonega named John D. Field, was the man behind the whole scheme. The year before, when he was not appointed mint clerk, "[he] became my enemy. . . . he made petitions to abolish the Mint. I understand that he wrote near two hundred letters to members of the Congress, for that purpose." John Choice ran a tavern where the Rossignol family lived before they moved to a competing establishment.

Rossignol then assessed each of the three men who had filed charges against him. The John D. Field who was James's brother was also Mason's son-in-law. Rossignol believed that he was the one who had signed the letter, for earlier Mason had applied for the office of clerk for J. D. Field, "wishing thereby . . . to people the Mint with his own family. I refused the office because neither he nor his brother suited me." Adam Peck, the next man on the list, had wanted to be superintendent himself but was friendly as long as Rossignol and his family remained at the hotel of his friend, John Choice, but as soon as Rossignol moved, Peck became his enemy. W. M. Varnum, the third man to sign the complaint, was a man to whom Rossignol had hired some Negroes belonging to different persons. When Varnum's account fell behind and Rossignol asked for money, Varnum was offended. The account was placed in the hands of a lawyer for collection. Rossignol insisted that he did nothing wrong.[21]

The Rossignol family lived at John Choice's hotel from the time Rossignol became mint superintendent until the summer of 1842. Then they moved to Harrison Riley's hotel on the village square. Riley's hotel was not only more pleasant but less expensive. At Choice's they paid fifty dollars per month for three people and had to pay for the domestics. At Riley's the cost was only thirty-two dollars, and they could bring their own servants. Rossignol's daughter Emily wrote to her uncle a few months earlier that the new quarters were "always crowded with gentlemen. It is a treat to sit at this table after having staid so long at Choice's." It was obvious, however, that the Rossignols remained aloof from the community. They felt themselves to be better than the people of Dahlonega, and the people were aware of that feeling. "None of the folks about here comes to see us," Emily wrote to her uncle. About the time Rossignol was defending himself against the charges of Field and his associates, he was moving his family once again, this time to a private house where they would do their own housekeeping and escape the confinement of "boarding out" in two rooms. Mrs. Rossignol was tired of boarding and weary of the torment inflicted on her husband. "We have had enough of all these devils who are in this ugly village and their devilment. I think that here is the worst of the human race and if my poor Paul didn't need this job he would leave immediately."[22]

Field, Peck, and Varnum hoped to get the other officers of the mint to support their charges against Rossignol. They had good reason to hope for Mason's support, since the coiner was trying to get the clerkship for his son-in-law, and they were almost as hopeful of securing Farnum's support as well. The assayer had

---

[21]Rossignol to Patterson, 13 Oct. 1842, NA-c.

[22]Emily Rossignol to L. F. E. Dugas, 18 July, 25 Sept. 1842; Adrienne Rossignol to Louis Charles Dugas, 13 May 1842 (translated from French), Dugas Papers, Georgia Historical Society, Savannah.

abetted James J. Field, Peck, and Varnum in their efforts the year before to get the branch mint downgraded to an assay office. Many times they claimed that Farnum protested against Rossignol, saying that "it was too bad to suffer a foreigner to preside over this branch Mint at a salary of two thousand dollars per annum when there were plenty of old soldiers who had fought and bled for their country and deserved promotion at their country's hand and . . . that any man what could keep the books of a grog shop was competent to discharge the duties required of the superintendent of this branch mint."[23] But Farnum, once so anxious to get rid of Rossignol, now became one of his defenders.

The purchase of mint certificates was simply a service to depositors anxious to get their money immediately, the meticulous assayer explained to Patterson. Depositors often paid the shopkeepers of Dahlonega a two percent premium for immediate payment of their certificates; in fact, the charges against Rossignol would never have been filed if "the deponent [had not] lamented the loss of their two per cent premium," and if "John D. Field, the murderer" had been named clerk, and if the Rossignols had not left Choice's.[24] It was this combination of things that made Rossignol vulnerable.

Farnum was extremely critical of all of Rossignol's enemies. Not even the judge, Milton H. Gathright, before whom the three unhappy depositors made their affidavits about having sold mint certificates at a discount, escaped. Gathright, Farnum maintained, is a "pettyfogging lawyer, formerly candidate for Clerkship in the Mint, believed to be hostile to Mr. Rossignol because he thought to remove, with his family to the tavern of G's deadly enemy." He dismissed Adam Peck as another "disappointed office seeker" and said that William Varnum was "hostile on account of some negroes hired of Mr. Rossignol." He saved his strongest invective for John D. Field, Mason's son-in-law. "A few years since, a Negro trader; and three years since, in attempting to shoot his enemy, murdered a poor widow woman in the streets

---

[23]J. J. Field to Farnum, 11 Sept. 1842, NA-c.

[24]Farnum to Patterson, 13 Oct. 1842, NA-c.

of Dahlonega." He, too, was disappointed because he did not obtain the clerkship.[25]

The faithful clerk Derrick also came to Rossignol's defense. "I believe a more industrious caplable or gentlemany men dont live than Paul Rossignol," he wrote. To underscore the difference between Rossignol and James J. Field, Derrick swore an affidavit as to the "true character" of the latter, with whom he had served in the army for nine months. "He [Field] is extremely dissipated, his intellect and attainments are far below mediocrity and his temper of the most vindicative and revengeful character," he charged. Derrick's predecessor, Blair, praised Rossignol, too, more eloquently than Derrick but not more clearly. "There does not live on the soil of Georgia a more honest and worthy man than Mr. R.," he wrote; "his undeviating rectitude and well known particularity in the conduct of business render him an invaluable officer."[26]

The explanations apparently satisfied Patterson and Secretary of the Treasury Walter Forward, but President John Tyler was not so sure. "The conduct charged upon the Superintendent is greatly censurable. Let the charges be immediately investigated by bringing them to the notice of Mr. Rossignol. If true however innocent in purpose, he will have to be substituted."[27] It was just a matter of time.

The whole problem would never have arisen if it had been possible to pay depositors as soon as their bullion was assayed. But there was never enough money for this, and no amount of overtime work by the mint staff would make up the difference. Farnum was not aware that coinage had ever been delayed by the coiner and certainly not by the treasurer, who was "most importunate for the speedy conversion of bullion into coin." As for himself, Farnum said, just look at the record. Could anyone do more? "For two years I have not been absent from the Mint a day, and hardly an hour. I keep no Holy days, and work on Sundays as usual." The business of the mint

---

[25]Farnum to Patterson, 11 Oct. 1842, NA-c.

[26]Derrick to Hertzel, 29 Dec. 1842, RG 56; Derrick Affidavit, 14 Oct. 1842, NA-c; Blair to Patterson, 4 Nov. 1842, NA-c.

[27]President J[ohn] Tyler to [Walter Forward?], 21 Nov. 1842, RG 56.

had grown so much that there was no way of judging its needs. The number of depositors had grown from 170 per year to more than a thousand, and sometimes a single deposit would require more acid in refining than the mint had previously used in a year. When gold was coined, only about half the value of bullion was returned in coins, the rest being in clippings, so the means of paying the depositors was quite limited.[28]

The reform that might have saved Rossignol's job came late in 1842, when Secretary of the Treasury Walter Forward agreed that in order to make it possible to pay depositors more promptly the treasurer's deposit for that purpose should be increased by $10,000. Subsequently, in February and March of 1843 two drafts for $5,000 each on New York banks were sent to Dahlonega to be added to the mint treasury.[29]

Another reform that Farnum had long advocated was also made in the spring of 1843. The duties of melter and refiner were shifted from the assayer to the coiner. Rossignol, perhaps pushed by Farnum a bit, outlined the proposal to Patterson. The duties of the assayer are "too onerous," while the coiner was free half the time. Could not the law be changed to shift the duties of melter and refiner from one to the other? Patterson was aware that such a shift had some advantages, but it was also studded with difficulties. The assayer was a man of science and always competent to perform the duties of melter and refiner. The coiner ought to be a mechanic. He wondered if such a man were competent to perform chemical operations—refining base metal, toughening those that were brittle, parting gold and silver when combined, and mixing metals of different fineness so that when cast they formed ingots of standard gold. There would be bookkeeping problems, too, in that the melter/refiner and coiner had different wastage allowances; this would be confusing if the offices were combined in one person. Moreover, was it possible to find a coiner who would

---

[28]Farnum to Patterson, 10 Oct. 1842, NA-c; Farnum to Forward, 17 Oct. 1842, RG 56.

[29]Forward to Rossignol, 28 Dec. 1842, 7 Feb., 22 Mar. 1843, RG 104, "V."

The United States Branch Mint at Dahlonega, Georgia, Circa 1877
Source: North Georgia College and State University, Dahlonega, Georgia

Nine-Piece Type Set of Dahlonega Gold Coins

Illustrating All of the Major Design Types Produced at the United States Branch Mint in Dahlonega, Georgia, 1838-1861

Type I Gold Dollar
Minted 1849-1854

1849-D, from the Carl Lester Collection, ex Louis Eliasberg, North Georgia Collections

Type II Gold Dollar
Minted 1855 Only

1855-D, from Heritage Numismatic Auctions, ex North Georgia Collection

Type III Gold Dollar
Minted 1856-1861

1859-D, from Gold Rush Gallery, ex North Georgia Collection

Classic Head Quarter Eagle
Minted 1839 Only

1839-D, from Heritage Numismatic Auctions, ex North Georgia Collection

Coronet Quarter Eagle
Minted 1840-1857, 1859

1846-D, from the Carl Lester Collection, ex R. Henry Norweb Collection

Three Dollar Gold Piece
Minted 1854 Only

1854-D, from Heritage Numismatic Auctions, ex North Georgia Collection

Coronet Half Eagle (Obverse Mintmark)
Minted 1839 Only

1839-D, from the Carl Lester Collection, ex Doug Winter, 1986 GNA Sale

Classic Head Half Eagle
Minted 1838 Only

1838-D, from Gold Rush Gallery, ex North Georgia Collection

Coronet Half Eagle (Reverse Mintmark)
Minted 1840-1861

1850-D, from the Carl Lester Collection, ex Larry Jackson

Toggle-Joint Steam Coining Press of the Type Used at the Dahlonega Mint
Source: Taxay, Don. *The U. S. Mint and Coinage, An Illustrated History from 1776 to the Present.* New York, NY: Arco Publishing Company, 1966, page 168.

take both jobs? Specifically, would Mason consent to take on both tasks? He had not even been consulted. Patterson was sure that the proposed change came too late for Congress to act at its current session, but that perhaps something could be done later to relieve the assayer. Almost as Patterson was writing, however, the bill authorizing the change was introduced by Congressman Mark A. Cooper of Georgia. He had not consulted Patterson, but within a week it was the law.[30]

The shift of duties of melter and refiner from Farnum to Mason, along with the precious metals, materials, machinery, and workmen, took place on 31 March 1843. Before the end of the following month Farnum left for a month's vacation, well deserved, he maintained, because he had for so long carried such a great burden. It seemed like a good time for him to be away, since most of the miners were busy planting crops and there was less activity at the mint. Farnum had spent part of the winter training Rossignol as melter and refiner and Isaac Todd as assayer. He reported that Rossignol had become "quite as expert as myself, and without his assistance it would be impossible for me to discharge my duties," and that Todd could assay to within a half-millieme. Assay slips from ingots were to be double-checked in Philadelphia before being coined, and slips from several deposits would be reserved. Any mistakes could be corrected after Farnum's return.[31] So Farnum left for the north, little knowing he would not be back. It was a far different vacation from the one he took a few years before, when he fretted so much about his stocks. This time he had no stocks to worry about. The market had dropped and he had sold them at a great loss a few months before. The meager $670.50 that they brought was held for him in a vault at the Philadelphia Mint.[32] There would be little joy in this trip.

---

[30]Rossignol to Patterson, 3 Jan. 1843; Patterson to Rossignol, 23 Jan. 1843; Patterson to Sen. John M. Berrien, 3 Feb. 1843, NA-c; Act Combining Duties of Melter-Refiner & Coiner, H.R. 767, 27th Cong., 3d sess. (passed 27 Feb. 1843, 5 Stat. 147).

[31]Farnum to Patterson, 1 Mar. 1843, NA-c.

[32]Patterson to Farnum, 23 Dec. 1842, NA-c.

On 1 May John A. Spencer, the new secretary of the treasury, notified Patterson that James F. Cooper had been appointed by President Tyler as superintendent of the Dahlonega Mint. When Farnum arrived in Philadelphia and heard the news, he was shocked. He took the only course of action he thought was open to him, resigning his position as assayer "to take effect on the present day [10 May] or if it be deemed desirable, on the appointment of my successor." He added that he would do anything to prevent even a temporary suspension of operations "provided that I be not required to return to Dahlonega." He told Patterson he felt a great repugnance to returning.[33] Patterson pleaded with Farnum not to do anything hasty. Perhaps if he talked to Cooper he would find he could work with him very well. But Farnum was adamant. He would not change his mind. He would not go back.

His resignation threw the mint operation at Dahlonega into vast confusion. Todd could do satisfactory assays, but as Patterson explained to the secretary of the treasury, "he is a man without education—wholly ignorant of chemistry—merely acquainted with the routine of an ordinary assay—and likely to be entirely baulked if any new combination of metals should be presented to him." If Farnum's resignation were accepted, Todd did not have the legal authority to continue his assays, and the work at Dahlonega would have to be suspended. Then there was the problem of finding a suitable successor to Farnum, whom Patterson described as "unexcelled for skill and accuracy." Whoever succeeded him should be a man of science with an opportunity of practicing in Philadelphia before he began his duties.[34] The only activity at Dahlonega that could be legally conducted until a successor could be named was the acceptance of deposits if individuals were disposed to leave them.

It seemed strange that a man so exacting in his devotion to duty should leave the mint in such disarray. Farnum was indeed

---

[33]Farnum to President Tyler, 10 May 1843, RG 56; Farnum to Patterson, 10 May 1843, NA-c.

[34]Patterson to Secretary of the Treasury John C. Spencer, 11 May 1843, RG 104, "V"; Patterson to Rossignol, 24 May 1843, NA-c.

"painfully anxious" about the dangers of responsibility, so anxious that if his resignation were not to be accepted immediately, he hoped that some new regulation might be adopted for his protection. Patterson tried to persuade him to return to Dahlonega, at least until a successor could be appointed, but Farnum refused because of his "extreme sensitiveness as to what he considers the *disgrace* of being removed from office. He says he has the same enemies as Rossignol, and that he knows they would be doubly active to procure his dismissal." Nothing Patterson could say could reassure him.

Farnum's resignation was accepted, since the government had no power to compel a civil officer to serve. Farnum had few things left to do: he asked Derrick to clean out his vault and give the keys to the superintendent; he asked Todd to deliver the silver he had received as assayer to the superintendent; and he asked for his salary. He had it figured out exactly: "April 1 to May 10 = 40 days = 40/91 of $375 = $164.83. From which subtracting $70 (advanced before leaving Dahlonega) there is left for the amount of the draft, $94.83."[35]

Meanwhile, in Dahlonega all was confusion. Todd had no real authority to do assays after 10 May, the day of Farnum's resignation, yet miners continued to bring their gold to the mint. There were 125 deposits made during the remainder of that month. Rossignol had no doubt that he had been removed, although he had heard nothing officially. He was anxious to leave this "abominable place" and go home to Habersham. Not until the middle of June did the official word come that the assays done by Todd through the end of May would be acceptable provided that they were all cast into standard plugs and sent to Philadelphia for assay. So careful a man as Farnum would take no chances that any error might be made for which he would be blamed.

With the new superintendent already appointed, it was pointless for Georgians to put forward the names of their favorites, and for once there was unusual unanimity about the only post left va-

---

[35]Patterson to Spencer, 19 May 1843; Patterson to Rossignol, 12 June 1843, NA-c.

cant—that of assayer. This was a position heretofore unaffected by politics, and for a while longer that situation would prevail. A petition containing 117 signatures asked for Todd's appointment as assayer. The only two men left in Dahlonega who really knew anything about the job, former superintendent Singleton and the coiner Mason, both recommended him. Mason cited Todd's two months of lessons in assaying with Farnum, and he praised Todd's personal characteristics. He is "a correct, industrious, moral man," and is "married and settled among us." Singleton, who had had his bad moments with the irascible Farnum, nevertheless regretted his departure and thought the post would never again "be so ably filled." But Todd was a suitable person to fill the assayer's department "as near in the character of Dr. Farnum as it is possible for any other person to do." As for Rossignol, Singleton hated to see him go to be replaced by an unknown. "If this odious system of proscription is continued," he warned, "none but the sycophantic bankrupts in the end will hold our public offices."[36] Singleton was almost a prophet, and in the years to come none would be a more eager supplicant than he.

---

[36]Mason to Patterson, 27 May 1843; Singleton to Patterson, 27 May 1843, NA-c.

CHAPTER 6

"Our people are . . . clamorous for coin," wrote James Fairlie Cooper, the brand new superintendent of the Dahlonega Branch Mint, to his superior officer in Philadelphia in early July 1843. It had been almost three months since Farnum had left for the vacation from which he never returned and more than a month since anyone at the mint had had authority to assay gold. Cooper, though inexperienced in mint operations, had a natural feel for politics, and he knew the situation as it then existed in Dahlonega would not do for long. Deposits for June at the mint were less than half what they had been in May, as miners sent their gold to Augusta and Charleston for sale. The delay in sending an assayer "is certainly very unaccountable in these office seeking days," Cooper observed. "I believe that all the functionaries at Washington have been written to upon the subject—and as yet there is no answer." Could not Farnum authorize Todd to sign through 30 June as well as through 31 May? "If it depends solely upon his saying so he will surely grant us another month."[1]

Patterson was as anxious as Cooper for a new assayer to be appointed at once, and just as incredulous at the long delay. He knew that "great injury" was caused by the vacancy. Although he thought Todd's training to be somewhat deficient, Patterson believed he would be appointed. Todd had the definite advantage of being available and ready to go on with assay operations. To

---

[1]Cooper to Patterson, 5 July, 15 July 1843, NA-c.

look for another candidate would mean additional delay at a time when a larger amount of gold than ever before was being mined in the South. This argument was persuasive enough for President Tyler, who ordered Todd's commission to be sent up at once. By the end of July Todd was diligently at work, and the people of the Georgia gold country were "most gratified" by the resumption of business at the mint.[2]

Cooper and Todd were commissioned as officers in the greatest era of prosperity the mint had ever known. Deposits came in unprecedented numbers and size. All of the officers, including the new clerk, Augustus M. Russell, were so busy that it must have been an annoyance for all three new appointees to have to make the three-hundred-mile trip to Savannah and back to subscribe their oaths before a federal judge. Cooper and Russell took their oaths before a state judge in May, and they sent in their bonds. Unfortunately, the bonds were not accepted in Philadelphia, so in relays Cooper, then Russell, and finally Todd set out for Savannah, where the nearest federal judge lived, to do it over again.[3]

Cooper assumed his duties as mint superintendent on 19 June 1843. Receipts at the mint were light that month because of the absence of an assayer, but in July deposits in excess of $50,000 were made, and in August 201 deposits totaled $75,443.71. "We are getting along quite bravely now," Cooper reported to the director. By year's end the mint had coined more than a half-million dollars. Its business had nearly doubled.[4]

---

[2]Patterson to Cooper, 26 June, 8 July 1843; Patterson to Secretary of the Treasury John C. Spencer, 7 July 1843; Cooper to Patterson, 30 July 1843, NA-c.

[3]Cooper to Spencer, 29 May, 7 July 1843, RG 104 "V," vol. 6; Spencer to Cooper, 2 July 1843; Cooper to Spencer, 24 Aug. 1843, NA-c. The Mint Act of 1835 required oaths to be taken before a federal judge. The Mint Act of 1837 authorized officers and clerks to take their oaths before any judge, but the Act of 1835 was enforced for the branch mint at Dahlonega.

[4]Reports of Deposits, Coinage for 1843, NA-c; Cooper to Patterson, 26 Aug., 14 Oct. 1843, NA-c. In 1843 the mint coined 98,452 half eagles and 36,209 quarter eagles with a value of $582,782.50.

Included in these coins were almost nine times as many quarter eagles as the mint had coined the year before. It was not that Mason, who continued as coiner, had lost his aversion to coining the smaller pieces nor that there was more demand for them, but the mint had an order from the secretary of the treasury. His reason was clear enough: it would benefit the country. "I have been unable to perceive the peculiar advantage of a mint which merely coined as all other mints in the world coined," Secretary Spencer wrote to Patterson. "The country is entitled to some benefit from such an expensive establishment, and that benefit will be found chiefly in the coinage of such pieces as will be most likely to remain in circulation and are least useful for exportation."[5] Farnum long before had observed that little of the gold minted at Dahlonega remained in circulation in the community. Bank notes, depreciated or not, and shinplasters were a far more common form of currency.

The vastly increased business at the Dahlonega Mint was recorded in a register that Cooper ordered the first week he was in office, each page folio of which was marked "Register of Gold Bullion Received from the Depositors and Coins Paid Out at the Treasury of the Mint."[6] Doubtless the new register gave some pleasure to Cooper and to the clerk Russell, but not half as much as the establishment of a regular schedule for payment of coins brought to the miners. Cooper's efficiency, the greatly increased deposits, and the extra $10,000 that was put in the mint's fund from the Treasury solved the problem that brought Rossignol down. In November area newspapers ran this announcement:[7]

MINT NOTICE

> Depositors and others interested, may rely upon the observance of the following arrangement, regulating the receipt and payment of Gold Deposites at this Mint, viz.:

---

[5]Secretary of the Treasury [Spencer] to Patterson, 25 May 1843, RG 104, "V," vol. 1.

[6]Cooper to Patterson, 28 June 1843, NA-c.

[7][Athens] *Southern Banner,* 16 Nov. 1843.

Day of deposite	Day of Payment	
Monday	Thurs.	following
Tuesday	Fri.	"
Wed.	Sat.	"
Thurs.	Tues.	"
Fri.	Tues.	"
Sat.	Wed.	"

James F. Cooper, Supt.
U. S. Branch Mint

The new mint superintendent was twenty-eight years old—just half the age of his predecessor—intelligent, and well educated. He was born in New York into a talented and celebrated family. His father, Thomas A. Cooper, was a famous Shakespearean actor, one of America's first stars who performed in all the states of the union. Thomas had a taste for the good life. Handsome, strong, and a fine horseman, he was also lucky at cards. He wagered huge sums with reckless abandon not only at the gaming table but on almost anything from the outcome of an election to the height of a room. Once he bet $1,200, the proceeds of a benefit performance, that he could pull the longest straw from a passing wagon. When he lost he laughed it off. "It's only two hours acting," he said. The new mint superintendent's mother was as beautiful as his father was charming, and she had the advantage of being a member of an aristocratic family. She was Mary Fairlie, an acknowledged belle of New York society. Her lifelong friend, Washington Irving, made her into a celebrity as "Sophie Sparkle" in the Salamagundi Papers. Amidst a host of six daughters, James was the only son of Thomas and Mary.

"My next child, my only son, James Fairlie Cooper is a cadet at West Point—and a noble youth he is," Mary Fairlie Cooper wrote to Irving in the fall of 1830. "[He] stands very high there already, although only entered there last June." Cooper's appointment to West Point, from which he graduated in 1834 standing seventeenth in a class of thirty-four, was secured for him by another of his mother's old friends, Martin Van Buren, who was then secretary of state in the Jackson administration. When Irving met the young West Point cadet, he described him as "a tall stripling . . . who had much of his mother's countenance."

In the 1830s, after Mrs. Cooper's death, the family experienced financial disaster brought about by a combination of the elder Cooper's improvidence and the nation's banking disasters. The son, James, lived out these years in the army. In 1837 he got a position as a civil engineer building the Georgia-owned Western and Atlantic Railroad. It was from that post that he came to Dahlonega.

Cooper probably had his father's charm, for although he was another foreigner, he soon captivated the populace of Dahlonega as much as his father had charmed his audiences. He fit into the community as Rossignol never had. Cooper's natural assets and abilities were soon obvious, but perhaps more important were his political connections. Cooper had a personal spokesman within the White House. His favorite sister Priscilla was the president's daughter-in-law and official White House hostess. She was probably responsible for the appointments of her talented but extravagant father as keeper of the arsenal at Frankford, and her brother James as superintendent of the branch mint.[8]

Anyway, Cooper was soon quite popular in Dahlonega. He kept business at the mint running smoothly, he got along well with his fellow officers and workmen, and he attended to all mint business with the promptness and exactitude one might expect from a West Point graduate. If he did fall behind, he explained his failures without self-serving excuses. When the reports for October 1846 were late getting to Philadelphia, he explained that he had been attending a meeting of the Grand Lodge of Georgia and the sessions lasted longer than he had anticipated. He did not return home until the seventh, and the first mail did not go out until the eleventh. "The omission of my signature & dates when I did return, is a piece of negligence that cannot be charged even to my *Masonic* obligations, nor to the irregularities of the mail." He was not self-righteous himself, and he had little patience with those

---

[8]This synopsis of Cooper's background is based largely on Elizabeth Tyler Coleman, *Priscilla Cooper Tyler and the American Scene* (University AL, 1955) 1-9, 24.

who were. He was miffed when Dr. Farnum appealed to the secretary of the treasury for his back pay. He called the former assayer's conduct "exceedingly gratuitous and discourteous."[9]

But Cooper had little time to waste on trivia like this. Instead, he looked forward eagerly to the time when the mint would coin a million dollars per year. Pursuit of this goal was not easy. Business was slower in 1844, when the mint coined only $488,600, but Cooper was not discouraged. He thought they needed a new machinest for the coiner's department, and he made so many requests that Patterson employed one in Philadelphia. Valentine Hodgson, a man with a reputation for both skill and good character, arrived in October 1845.[10]

No amount of zeal, however, could solve the continuing problem of getting supplies to Dahlonega. Materials ordered did not arrive on time or not at all, while items for which the mint had no use came pouring in. Good quality copper was especially hard to come by; that secured by the mint's agent in Charleston was so impure that it could not be used at all. Sulfuric acid needed to reduce silver was also impure. The assayer requested that nitric acid essential to his work be purified by distillation before shipment. If the quality of items was uncertain, transportation of them to the frontier post was even more so. Supplies ordered weeks or even months in advance of need failed to arrive on time, and mint operations had to be suspended. Whenever possible, important supplies were brought back by a mint laborer like Valentine Hodgson, who returned to his home in Pennsylvania occasionally. More often they were sent by public carrier. There was always the possibility—indeed the probability—that fragile items would be broken in transit. "Please have purchased, well packed with great care & sent to this branch 3 or 4 retorts, one tube about $1\frac{1}{2}$ or $1\frac{3}{4}$ in. diameter etc.," the Dahlonega clerk wrote to Patterson. "Several of the last items of this description were broke before they

---

[9]Cooper to Patterson, 26 Nov. 1846, NA-c; Farnum to Spencer, 17 Aug. 1843; Cooper to Patterson, 7 Sept. 1843, NA-c.

[10]Cooper to Patterson, 6 Dec. 1843, 2 Jan., 4 Oct. 1845; Patterson to Cooper, 4 Aug. 1845; Report Summary for 1844, NA-c.

came here, we suppose for want of packing." Most often goods were shipped to Charleston and then overland by wagon, a journey on which no time schedule could be set. Sometimes the worst fears were confirmed, and goods for Dahlonega were aboard vessels that shipwrecked.

Transportation costs were high. To save freight on one order of crucibles, Cooper suggested that someone in Philadelphia throw out the largest and smallest sizes from each nest since these were never used. Little could be done to reduce shipping costs on other items. The toll was four dollars to ship one carboy of nitric acid from Philadelphia because it had to be marked "extra hazardous." No economy could be effected there. Dies for coining generally came by mail, and postage charges were "enormous." The postage on one box of half eagle dies was $6.30, for two boxes of quarter eagle dies, $9.30. Fortunately, the coiner did not crack as many dies as he had in the past, but occasionally accidents did occur. Of course, new dies had to be sent for each year. Sometimes authorities in Philadelphia forgot to send these. Then, with the new year, the branch mint had to suspend operations until they arrived. As an economy measure Cooper suggested that the Philadelphia Mint need not bother to send the "usual complement of tail dies. . . . it is an unnecessary addition to postage."[11]

Cooper had a rather casual attitude toward the dies, perhaps because he was belatedly informed that an annual defacement of dies was necessary. He had been superintendent of the branch mint for more than three years before this oversight was called to his attention. "We have received no report of the defacement of your rejected dies, since that made by Mr. Rossignol, dated 7th January 1843," Patterson wrote to Cooper in November 1846. "Let me pray you attend to this matter at the termination of the present year." Cooper reported that he had defaced twenty dies in January 1845. Two months after receiving Patterson's reminder, he defaced another twenty-two dies. He listed what he had on hand:

---

[11]Cooper to Patterson, 3 May, 6 Dec. 1843, 23 Jan. 1846, 24 Aug. 1847, 4 Jan., 2 Mar., 1 July, 4 Oct. 1848, 2 June 1849; William Grisham to Patterson, 12 Feb., 20 Feb. 1845; Patterson to Cooper, 19 Dec. 1845, 13 Jan. 1847, 4 Jan., 15 Apr. 1848, NA-c.

three heads and five tails each for half eagles and quarter eagles. Patterson checked Cooper's report with his own and discovered that there should be another set of quarter eagle dies in Dahlonega, but Cooper knew nothing about it and could not account for the missing set. "I never before perfectly appreciated the importance which is attached to this portion of my duty. . . . We have not even kept a memorandum of the dies received, so that great accuracy could scarcely have been expected. It does not seem improbable that under such an irregular mode of proceeding a pair of dies might have been overlooked, without being absolutely lost." He did not mention the fact that they might have been stolen, but, in fact, in 1844 the newspapers reported that Dahlonega's quarter eagles had been counterfeited.[12]

The most difficult coining job undertaken at the mint while Cooper was superintendent was the coining of gold dollars. The mint's officers and workmen set to work on this task in the spring of 1849. Cooper explained that everything could be done at Dahlonega except the milling; the milling machine they had could not be adapted for a coin so small. The experts in Philadelphia disagreed. They sent detailed instructions on making the necessary modifications. By June the preparations for the new coinage were complete and the dollar dies were sent from Philadelphia. "Your coiner will please to polish them with great caution and tenderness," Patterson warned. Patterson also sent by steamer a set of gold dollar molds, a small mill for making collars, and a milling press, which appeared to have been made for milling eagles, not dollars. Cooper hired another machinest and a blacksmith to get the extra work done, but "by the most unwearied exertions of officers and men" Georgia's first gold dollars were issued in July. They were among the last coins minted while Cooper was superintendent, for he was replaced two months later. "As usual in similar cases there was more work to be done than was anticipated," he wrote to Patterson, "but all were desirous of giving me

---

[12]Patterson to Cooper, 24 June 1844, 17 Nov. 1846; Cooper to Patterson, 4 Jan., 4 Mar. 1847, NA-c.

the honor of issuing the first Gold Dollars in Georgia before the arrival of my successor in this office."[13]

The gold dollars were not perfect. One of the specimens sent to Philadelphia was $^1/_{32}$ of a grain too light and the other was $^5/_{32}$ of a grain too heavy. The milling on the coin was too slight, the reverse blurred and out of center. In spite of these defects, however, Patterson said the gold dollars did the branch mint credit, and most of the imperfections were remedied in the second coining. Cooper hoped the new coins would be popular, and he advertised their availability in the *Dahlonega Watchman:* "GOLD DOLLARS. Depositors of gold bullion requiring payments in these coins can now & hereafter be accommodated."[14] That year they made 21,588 of the tiny coins.

Clippings from the coining room were routinely melted, cast into ingots, and turned into more coins, but some waste in the coining process was more difficult to recover. Some gold was left in the sweeps, broken crucibles, and remnants of black lead pots in which it was melted. Almost four tons of sweeps accumulated at Dahlonega by 1845. Patterson suggested to Cooper that the time had come to sell. He offered his services for the transaction "because I have the facilities in executing it that you cannot be supposed to possess." Dr. Joseph Farnum wished to make a bid on them. Patterson ordered that a sample of the sweeps be sent to Philadelphia for assay, and that the bulk of the sweeps be dried, put in barrels, weighed, marked, and shipped to Charleston. The sweeps filled twenty-one barrels and weighed 7,944 pounds. In the remarkably short time of one month, they were on their way.

Assay of the Dahlonega sweeps showed them to be "so rich as to alarm the smelter to whom we expected to sell it," Patterson reported. The assay showed gold worth \$55.46$^1/_2$ per hundredweight and silver worth \$2.76$^1/_2$ per hundredweight, for a total of

---

[13]Cooper to Patterson, 5 Apr., 3 July, 12 July 1849, NA-c; Misc. Treas. Acct. 102130, RG 217, Records of the United States General Accounting Office, National Archives.

[14]Patterson to Cooper, 20 July 1849; Cooper to Patterson, 4 Aug. 1849, NA-c; Bills Paid, 31 Aug. 1849, RG 217.

$58.23. This was so much above the assay for sweeps at other mints that the buyer was wary that it was not a representative sample. Farnum wanted another sample taken from the barrels at Charleston. This second sample did not allay his fears. Two more assays made from the keg of sweeps sent to Philadelphia from Charleston showed as much as $52.76 in gold and silver per hundredweight, so Farnum's cautious offer of $35 per hundredweight was turned down. Patterson wrote to Farnum that it was inadvisable "both for you and me, that your offer be accepted." It was considerably below the usual rate if the assays could be relied upon, and that would be the ground of judgment of the propriety of the contract. "You know that there are not wanting at Dahlonega, those who would scan this matter closely, and probably not in a friendly spirit." The sweeps were sold in London. They brought just over £521s.—$2,521.36—after expenses were paid. Cooper, always short of money for maintenance, used the proceeds to pay for repairs to the mint wall.[15]

Cooper was the first superintendent to live in the mint. To secure the quarters that had been built for the superintendent but never occupied by him required great delicacy, for since the mint opened its doors, the coiner David Mason and his family had lived there. The fact that Cooper was able to edge Mason gently out of the mint without any apparent difficulty or resentment was testimony to the fact that harmony prevailed among its officers and workmen.

Cooper's reasons for wanting to move into the mint were excellent and urgent. "My family is on the point of increase and it is out of the question for my wife and three young children any longer to be confined to a room in a hotel," he wrote to Patterson. "I do not feel authorized to build a dwelling house, because I hold an office which is regarded as the legitimate prey of the Monster 'reform'—and as I came in under his auspices I can not murmur at his dispensations—not so with Mr. Mason's office, its scientific

---

[15]Patterson to Cooper, 13 Oct., 18 Nov. 1845, 10 Feb., 10 Mar., 23 Oct. 1846; Cooper to Patterson, 15 Nov. 1845, 9 Nov., 16 Nov., 26 Nov. 1847; Farnum to Patterson, 29 Dec. 1845; Patterson to Farnum, 2 Feb., 17 Feb. 1846; N. P. Johnston & Co., London, to Patterson, 16 Sept. 1847, NA-c.

and mechanical requirements invest it with an armor, proof against political attacks." The move was accomplished with no apparent ill will. By the summer of 1846 Cooper was keeping house at the mint and inviting his political friends to visit him there when they made their forays into north Georgia.[16]

Cooper assessed mint politics correctly. The "Monster 're-form' " was always at work. Although he presided efficiently over mint activities during its most prosperous years and was probably its most popular superintendent, Cooper knew only too well that his was a political office entirely dependent upon Democratic success at the polls. He was unceasing in his efforts to get Democrats elected and was as sensitive to the political winds in Georgia as he was to serving the needs of the gold miners or responding to the commands of the Treasury Department.

During the six years Cooper was mint superintendent, someone was nearly always after his job. The most persistent applicant was Joseph J. Singleton, who seized upon the slightest shift in the political winds, or the hope of such a shift, to advance his claims. Cooper had been in office only eight months when Singleton suggested to Howell Cobb, a rising power in Georgia Democracy and representative of the Sixth District in Congress, that "a contingency exists that Mr. Tyler's nominations would be rejected generally and especially the collector of Customs at Savannah, and the Superintendent of the Br. Mint at this place. . . . if so, I had some hopes of being restored to an office which had been taken from me without cause." This modest effort came to nothing. Cooper and Todd, both of whom were appointed by Tyler while Congress was not in session, were confirmed by the Senate.[17]

Singleton's fight had only begun. The change of administrations in Washington from "His Accidency" John Tyler to Presi-

---

[16]Cooper to Patterson, 15 Apr. 1846; Cooper to Howell Cobb, 8 July 1846, Cobb Papers, University of Georgia Library, Athens.

[17]Singleton to Cobb, 17 Feb. 1844, Cobb Papers. Cooper's appointment was confirmed in 1844, but due to an oversight, Todd's nomination was not sent to the Senate that year, and his appointment was not confirmed until the following year.

dent James K. Polk, Democrat and heir to the legacy of Andrew Jackson, gave Singleton renewed hope. With a new occupant in the White House he had every reason to believe that this time his suit might be successful, so he made an all-out effort. He got his supporters to circulate a petition in his behalf. Through what must have been monumental exertions, they got 1,700 signatures.

This was an age when Americans took the right to petition the government very seriously. Hundreds of petitions were sent to Washington, the most celebrated being for the abolition of slavery, but there were many others to support the claims of aspirants to public office. The petition asking for the reinstatement of Dr. Singleton as mint superintendent called him "A warm and constant supporter of Gen. Jackson, his friends and measures; and more recently a warm friend and supporter of your Excellency. . . . [He] was turned out of office upon the accession of General Harrison, for no other cause than that of his candid and manly support of President Van Buren." The petition added that Singleton had been an efficient and obliging officer. "As an additional consideration perhaps worthy of our representation to your Excellency, the said ex-superintendent &c., repaired immediately after his appointment, to the Mint at Philadelphia at a sacrifice of absence from his business and family, for the purpose of preparing himself for entering upon the discharge of his official duties, which perhaps few would have done." The petitioners concluded that since Singleton's removal from office, there had been two superintendents at the mint, "which enables us to say that we prefer the original appointment to either." The petition was probably written by Singleton himself. The same convoluted sentence structure marks his letters.[18]

Singleton claimed that his support came entirely from Democrats, while Cooper's supporters were Whigs. "I will venture an assertion that $^{3}/_{4}$ if not $^{9}/_{10}$ of [my] petitioners . . . are Democrats of the 'first water.' . . . if there are half day whigs amongst that portion, I do not know them." His supporters included Hopkins Holsey of Athens, an ardent disciple of Andrew Jackson. Holsey

---

[18]Petition to James K. Polk, 1845, Copy in Cobb Papers.

recognized that this was not a Whig-Democrat struggle, but rather was a contest between two Democrats. It was a matter of "great delicacy" to remove one political friend to make way for another, he wrote to the president, but he suggested that between competitors of the same faith for an office, the principle of restoration was entitled to great consideration. Besides, he added, Singleton had been a great friend of Democracy far longer than the mint had been in Dahlonega.

Singleton also claimed that 1,000 of the 1,700 signers of his petition came from the immediate vicinity of Dahlonega, and that the others, like President Alonzo Church of Franklin College, were men of long acquaintance with him. Somewhat piously, he expressed the wish that his claims to the post be considered on their own merits and not in relationship to information on "the conduct of the present Incumbent." Only six months earlier Singleton had claimed that he was acting in Cooper's best interest as well as his own. About six weeks before Polk's inauguration, Singleton had sent a copy of the petition with a cover letter to Howell Cobb, explaining that he "hated to collide with Major Cooper," but simply wanted to procure another situation for him. "I hesitate not in saying that he is a gentleman, and one worthy of better office." He suggested that some place might be found for him at the Customs House in Philadelphia, where he mistakenly thought Cooper's father had a job, or perhaps there would be an opening in one of the departments in Washington. Now, six months later, Singleton thought that the situation called for a change in tactics.[19]

A separate petition that was circulated in Athens underscored his veiled reference to possible misconduct in office. After citing Singleton's sacrifice in abandoning a comfortable residence in "our neighborhood" to settle in Dahlonega, the petitioners concluded, "if statements made of the conduct of the Supt. *be true* . . . he ought to be promptly removed." The conduct to which they referred was the charge made by a dozen or so people in

---

[19]Singleton to Polk, 15 Apr., 17 July 1845; Hopkins Holsey to Polk, 14 July 1845, RG 56; Singleton to Cobb, 25 Jan. 1845, Cobb Papers.

Lumpkin County that Cooper kept a dram shop to which a gambling room was attached and in which the Holy Sabbath was often desecrated. What was worse, they charged, Cooper was guilty of drinking and gambling and Sabbath-breaking himself, conduct incomprehensible for a man with a salary of $2,000 per year. Among those making sworn testimony against Cooper was William E. Derrick, the clerk with the terrible handwriting who had worked at the mint with Rossignol. He said that he had seen Cooper playing cards on the Sabbath. The charges were sent to Washington, where the president left the decision of whether or not to make an inquiry into the charges up to the secretary of the treasury.[20]

These attacks on Cooper were not made until almost six months after Singleton began his campaign to be restored to office. His petition already had several hundred signatures before Cooper found out about it and launched a counter-campaign to save his job. He did not have to carry on the fight alone, for he got formidable support not only from Dahlonega, but from Democrats in his district and in Congress. Milton Gathright, the judge Farnum had dismissed as a "pettyfogging lawyer" and now editor of the *Dahlonega Watchman,* wrote to Howell Cobb as soon as he heard what Singleton was doing. In the unbridled language of the nineteenth-century frontier, he said exactly what he thought about "Soap-tail" Joe's maneuver.

> Singleton is making a powerful push for the office of Superintendent of the Branch Mint at this place. . . . I hope & trust our delegation in Congress will take it upon themselves to see the President elect (Mr. Polk) & defeat this movement. A removal of Majr. Cooper for Singleton would be inflicting a serious injury on those who have business transactions in the mint. Singleton . . . is not a man of business. The truth is . . . he is altogether too weak in the upper story for any kind of business that requires an effort of mind. If his claims were placed upon political grounds he would certainly be among the last to deserve it. For he exercises no in-

---

[20]Petition from Athens, 11 July 1845; Petition to President Polk from Dahlonega, 7 July 1845; Polk to secretary of the treasury, 8 Aug. 1845, RG 56.

fluence for his party either from argument & sound reasoning or personal influence. . . . Such is not the case with Majr. Cooper. He exercises an influence which counts & tells well. Our opponents know it & have felt it & it is they who are backing Singleton. Besides the business of the Mint has never been transacted so well and so promptly under any Superintendent as that of Majr. Cooper. Nor has any of them ever acquired the popularity he has & I must say deservedly so.[21]

George D. Phillips, a leading Democrat in the Sixth District, wrote to Cobb that extraordinary efforts were being made to remove Cooper and that Singleton had the support of the crowd for the post, but he dismissed petitions as meaningless. He compared Singleton and Cooper:

You know that the Dr. is a dull plodding man, and if he were again in office and remained there for half a century he would not be as well qualified for the office as Mr. Cooper was the first week he entered it. Under the Dr.'s administration depositors had to wait from two to four weeks for coin. Some improvement took place when Mr. Rossignol was in office, but since Mr. Cooper has been in depositors often get their coin as soon as an assay can be made. Mr. Rossignol was an efficient man but his manners rendered him unpopular and it was said, perhaps with some truth, he killed two birds with one stone, served a bank and Uncle Sam too; and for this I presume was removed. Mr. Cooper is easy and polite in his intercourse with all who have business at the Mint. If any charges of improper conduct have been brought against him I have not heard them. . . . I presume they dare not attack Mr. Cooper on the ground of want of qualification. No change could be made for the better on that score. . . . The truth is this: Dr. Singleton wants the office for the money. Harrison Riley, than whom the devil is not more artful, hates Mr. Cooper because he is a gentleman and a Democrat, and wishes to get him out of the county.[22]

---

[21]Milton H. Gathright to Cobb, 9 Feb. 1845, Cobb Papers.

[22]George D. Phillips to Cobb, 25 Feb. 1845, in U. B. Phillips, ed., *The Correspondence of Robert Toombs, Alexander H. Stephens, and Howell Cobb,* Annual Report of the American Historical Association (1911) 2:67.

Cooper went to Washington to fight for his job. He found support in high places. The week the presidency changed hands from Tyler to Polk, Cooper was in the capital city getting the Georgia congressional delegation to sign a solemn protest against his removal. He got the signatures of Walter Colquitt, Howell Cobb, John H. Lumpkin, William H. Stiles, and Hugh A. Haralson to a memorial that was presented to the new secretary of the treasury, Robert J. Walker. Mint Director Patterson agreed to speak personally to Walker in Cooper's behalf; later he wrote to Cooper that he came away from the interview convinced that "you will not be interfered with." Cobb wrote to President Polk that support for Cooper in his district "approached unanimity." The fact that no petition had been presented in Cooper's behalf, he assured the president, should not be wrongly construed. His friends did not deem a petition necessary. Cobb called Cooper "a true democrat, faithful officer and a worthy man." Cooper also wrote directly to the president to defend his position. Singleton labored for five months to get signatures to his petition, Cooper reported, and the number of refusals exceeded the number of signers. "By great perseverance, however & by sending his memorial to distant parts of the State, entirely uninterested in the welfare of the Mint and unacquainted with the manner of its management, he has procured a large array of names." He added that he had not wanted to trouble the president with petitions in his favor, but if that were necessary, he could get one that would "far outnumber the one presented by my antagonist."[23]

Cooper had support from within the mint family as well. Mason wrote to Patterson in glowing terms about Cooper. He praised him as an efficient man who not only pleased the depositors but was a peacemaker within the mint itself. "At present with the officers, and with the workmen in the Mint, there is quietness, peace and harmony, it was not so under [Singleton's] encumbency." He asked Patterson to use his influence so that J. J. Singleton will "never again be superintendent of this Branch Mint." Isaac Todd

---

[23]Cooper to Walker, 7 Mar. 1845, RG 56; Cobb to Polk, 24 Apr. 1845, RG 56; Cooper to Patterson, 13 Mar. 1845, NA-c; Patterson to Cooper, 20 Mar. 1845, NA-c; Cooper to Polk, 29 Mar. 1845, RG 104, "V," vol. 6.

and the new clerk, William Grisham, agreed. "We would deem it a public calamity to have Mr. Cooper removed and Dr. Singleton appointed in his stead."[24]

Cooper thought he had won his fight in the spring of 1845, but in the summer the Singleton forces filed charges of gambling, drinking, and Sabbath-breaking against him, and the struggle began anew. Cobb stepped into the breach once more. He appealed to Postmaster General Cave Johnson for support, and he wrote to President Polk imploring him not to remove Cooper. Congressman John Lumpkin of Rome also wrote to the president of his shock to learn of the possibility of Cooper's removal. "Mr. Cooper is and always has been a uniform and consistent Jacksonian democratic republican."[25]

James Cooper kept his job. He was the second member of his family to receive a favor from President Polk. His father, Thomas, the former actor, was rescued from his exile at the arsenal in Frankford and given a well-paying, not too taxing position as inspector of customs in New York City.[26]

Singleton was furious at Cobb's betrayal, for he had known the thirty-one-year-old representative since Cobb was a child.

> My dear sir, can you say that the young and flourishing Twig does not owe its prosperity to the source from which it sprang: or can you say that you never knew the like to wither and die. Then draw the comparison between a friend of twenty five years of undoubted standing, and one of not as many weeks at the time of your espousing the cause of the later and then divest yourself of all partiality whatever and say which is entitled to the greatest degree of respect.

The tirade continued. If Cooper, the reputed regulator of the Democratic party in north Georgia, had to have an office, then "some other might be found which would suit him better." Singleton called Cooper's efforts at political leadership a failure. The

---

[24]Mason to Patterson, 22 Mar. 1845, NA-c.

[25]Howell Cobb to C[ave] Johnson, 22 July 1845, RG 56; Cobb to Polk, 22 July 1845, RG 56; John H. Lumpkin to Polk, 2 Aug. 1845, RG 56.

[26]Coleman, *Priscilla Cooper Tyler,* 111-12.

Democratic candidates for clerk and sheriff whom Cooper espoused were both beaten. "Thus, you will at once perceive that his Dram shop and Gambling Rooms will not do, with all their displays of the U. S. Flag over his stew Pots, and deposits of cash in other Dram shops." He accused Cobb and Representative Colquitt of advising Cooper to establish a dram shop at Dahlonega as a rallying point for the Democratic party, a course Singleton predicted would fail. "Depend upon it, that James F. Cooper's course in this community cannot, nor will not be sustained." He charged that Cooper was away from his official post at least half the time.[27]

Almost two years later Singleton was still trying to get Cooper's job. "Remember the prayer of my 1728 petitioners," he wrote to President Polk. He had the number exactly now. His own memory was somewhat deficient, however, in recalling the more unpleasant details of his tenure in office. "If there ever was a murmur during my short official career, I have yet to learn of it," he wrote, adding, "but for . . . interference in behalf of the present incumbent, I would have been restored long since."[28]

His attempt to get his job back may be dismissed as inconsequential, but others also waited hopefully for their chance. One of these was E. H. Wingfield, the mint's first clerk, whose chief claim to the post was that he needed the job. He was aware that the name of General William B. Wofford, former speaker of the Georgia House of Representatives, would be offered. He was not disposed to detract from the claims of one who had served the party so well and so conspicuously. Nevertheless, Wingfield asked Howell Cobb to remember that "the Genl is amply provided with the good things of this life in the shape of property whilst I have been pursuing this ignis fatuus of Gold digging untill I am what Shakesper puts in the mouth of Othelo *poor indeed.*" That seemed reason enough to ask for consideration.[29]

Support for Wofford came from within the mint as well. The coiner Mason supported Wofford's appointment, in case Cooper

---

[27]Singleton to Cobb, 8 Jan. 1846, Cobb Papers.

[28]Singleton to Polk, 6 Nov. 1847, RG 56.

[29]Wingfield to Howell Cobb, 25 Jan. 1848, Cobb Papers.

left the mint to accept another post, because he hoped a new superintendent would be amenable to appointing his son Zelotes as a workman at the mint. Zelotes had held the post until 1845, when he resigned to take up the practice of medicine. He was not successful in his new profession, however, and now wanted to return to the mint. When Cooper did not resign, Mason's plans for Zelotes came to nothing.[30]

This was Mason's last attempt to promote members of his family for positions in the mint. Within six months he was dead. The clamor then began for his own job. Actually, the tussle began a full month before his death, in the tradition of Mason's own best efforts in mint politics. But because Mason was indeed dying, the struggle took on a ghoulish character.

Valentine Hodgson, who was more interested in politics than in his job as machinist, was the first to seize upon the obvious opportunity that Mason's demise would open for a man of talent. "In all probability the Chief Coinership of the Mint will soon be vacant, either by the mysterious hand of providence or resignation," Hodgson wrote to Patterson in late July 1848. "The present incumbent *Mr. Mason* is stricken with what his physician calls *Chronic affection* of the *Brain.*" His doctor thought he would never again be well enough to resume his mint duties. Hodgson believed that Mason was about to resign in favor of his son Zelotes, who since leaving the mint "has undertaken to read and practice medicine without much success." Happily Hodgson remembered that Patterson once told him that the coiner had to be a machinist, so he would like to be considered, but only, of course, "in the event of a vacancy, should there be no vacancy I am perfectly content, for I wish Mr. Mason to recover."[31]

Patterson assured Hodgson that he had done exactly the right thing, and he asked Cooper for his assessment of both Zelotes Mason and Hodgson as proper successors to Mason. But Cooper would not choose. Since Mason's condition was "hopelessly low," the su-

---

[30]Isaac Todd and D. H. Mason to Robert Walker, 22 Jan. 1848, RG 56; Valentine Hodgson to Cobb, 15 Feb. 1848, Cobb Papers.

[31]Hodgson to Patterson, 25 July 1848, NA-c.

perintendent appointed John D. Field to perform the duties of his father-in-law as coiner, melter, and refiner. He entrusted Field with the vault keys, but Cooper refused to state a preference. He believed Zelotes to be capable of performing his father's duties, since he had some knowledge of machinery and a smattering of chemistry, both of which were desirable accomplishments for the office. Besides, his appointment would greatly relieve the Mason family. "Mr. Mason's private affairs are in a very embarrassed condition, and it is believed that his death would leave the family quite destitute. The succession of the son to the emoluments of the office would greatly relieve this gloomy but perhaps not legitimate view of the question." As for Hodgson, he was "all that I could desire" in a "mechinician," and could perform the duties of coiner well. Cooper did not have the same confidence that he would do equally well as melter and refiner, tasks that required aptitude in calculation, the system and neatness of an accountant, and some acquaintance with chemical and metalurgic principles. In truth, Cooper concluded, the mint needed someone with qualifications possessed by neither Hodgson nor Dr. Zelotes Mason. The mint, he said, is "sadly in want of practical scientific knowledge in Chemistry, Mineralogy, and metallurgy." If the right man were found the mint could greatly expand its services to develop the resources of the country. Everything from iron ore to diamonds had been found in the region of Dahlonega, and it was embarrassing to Cooper to be unable to help those who brought in specimens for tests.[32]

Dr. Zelotes Mason advanced his own claim for his father's job while sitting at the dying man's bed.

> Sitting, as I now am, within a few feet of my father, who, I fear, is rapidly passing away from earth, the duty of writing this communication becomes exceedingly painful. . . . Nay! did not the circumstances of the case absolutely force me to it, affection would

---

[32]Patterson to Hodgson, 3 July 1848; Patterson to Cooper, 31 July 1848; Cooper to Patterson, 10 Aug. 1848, NA-c. Two small diamonds were found in north Georgia in 1845 and 1846. Sent to Philadelphia by mint officials, they were sold as cabinet specimens. One brought thirty dollars, the other fifty dollars.

hinder me from broaching *such* a subject at *such* a time. . . . During the early part of last March, father had a severe epileptic attack, remaining insensible for the space of one hour; and since then, has been gradually declining in health, but nevertheless able, until lately to perform his duties in the Mint. From his aversion to medicines of all kinds, he has depended almost entirely on dietetic means for his recovery.

Several weeks since, I was summoned in haste to see him. I found him suffering from passive congestion of the brain, afterwards producing complete paralysis of the left side, with aberrations of mind. He seems to be gradually sinking, and in all human probability, cannot long survive. . . .

Owing to the embarrassed condition of fathers monetary affairs (he having been connected with a large establishment for Tanning, where one of the company proved defaulter for a large amount, for which he is liable, and which will probably sweep a great portion of his property) he has often expressed a desire that I should fill his place, so as to be enabled to assist the family if he resigned or was called away by death: and owing besides, to the popular rumor that Mr. Hodgson has made, or is about to make, application for the office, I have felt it my duty immediately to address a letter to you upon the subject.[33]

Others aspired to the coiner's post as well. E. H. Wingfield, former clerk and would-be superintendent, applied for the job since Mason was "in Extremis and his dissolution may take place at any hour." He lined up some recommendations for the job, including one from former Congressman Dawson, whose wife was Wingfield's sister. A petition was sent from Dahlonega in his behalf. Other petitions supported John D. Field. Hodgson had a poor opinion of the value of petitions and quoted a local judge as saying that if necessary he could "get one with a thousand signatures to place a light house on Mount Yonah and make Dahlonega a port of entry." Hodgson's endorsers praised him as a man of gentlemanly character, useful in the community, talented, and

---

[33]Zelotes Mason to Patterson, 12 Aug. 1848, NA-c.

well liked. He himself thought his only serious shortcoming was that he was not a chemist.[34]

Mason died and the mint went into a respectful thirty-day mourning period, but the scramble for his position was stilled for only a single day at most. The day after the funeral Mason's widow wrote to Patterson urging that her son Zelotes be given his father's old job. Her reasons were simple enough. The family needed the money.

> In consequence of the embarrassed state of [Mason's] affairs, my youngest son David will not be able to pursue his collegiate education, which was his Father's particular wish. . . . [Zelotes] is a consistent member of the Presbyterian Church in this place. Should you see fit to appoint him to the office, he will aid his brother in obtaining an education. David has brought from college the most flattering testimonials of his progress in his studies, and of his moral character.[35]

Mason's death meant that operations of the coiner's department could not lawfully be conducted until a successor was named, but since all the metals and public property pertaining to his department were in the possession of Field, who had been performing the coiner's duties, the closing of Mason's account was expedited. All the principal applicants for the post stayed in the contest. Field circulated another petition, Hodgson wrote directly to President Polk, and Wingfield asked Singleton to recommend him for the job, but Singleton would not do it. Singleton was willing to suggest the name of someone else quite competent for the job "but for the recent scramble before the death of Mr. Mason, after death, and before burial, after burial & before the old man was cold." Cooper maintained his neutrality. "Indeed any other course on my part would falsify my pledges to them, and would be entirely inconsistent with my views as to the qualifications desirable in the officer to be appointed." He might have

---

[34]Wingfield to Cobb, 12 Aug. 1848, Cobb Papers; Dawson to Polk, 5 Sept. 1848, RG 56; Robert H. Moore to Patterson, 28 Aug. 1848; Hodgson to Patterson, 30 Aug. 1848, NA-c.

[35]E. A. Mason to Patterson, 31 Aug. 1848, NA-c.

added that he could not choose and still maintain harmony within the establishment.[36]

The appointment went to Field, who assumed his duties in early October 1848. Hodgson was in Philadelphia at the time the news came. He must have been disappointed, but he returned to Dahlonega to work. Dr. Zelotes Mason presumably resumed the practice of medicine, and the once more overlooked Wingfield turned with a vengeance on Howell Cobb, accusing him of not supporting him in his quest for office.[37] With Mason's death, the coiner's job became almost as much a political plum as that of superintendent. The assayer's post would be next, and it was an election year.

---

[36]Cooper to Patterson, 31 Aug., 12 Sept., 19 Sept., 1848; Singleton to Patterson, 5 Sept. 1848, NA-c; Hodgson to Polk, 6 Sept. 1848, RG 56.

[37]Patterson to Cooper, 20 Sept. 1848; Cooper to Patterson, 3 Oct. 1848, NA-c; A. M. Russell to Cobb, 18 Oct. 1848, Cobb Papers.

CHAPTER 7

For James Fairlie Cooper the Democratic party in Georgia's Sixth District was a stage, its voters an audience to be teased and entertained, cajoled and persuaded into voting for party favorites. For him a resounding victory at the polls gave the same heady satisfaction that prolonged applause once brought his father. Defeat for those he espoused was disappointing but not devastating. If Thomas Cooper in the last years of his stage career could minimize the importance of a certain lack of enthusiasm for him in urban audiences, so his son James could look philosophically on political losses. Thomas optimistically thought that time would remedy the growing indifference of his public; James, after the Democratic political disaster of 1848, could still look forward to a better day when the people would be more responsive to his and the Democratic party's charms.

Cooper did his best in that election year to carry the Sixth District for the Democrats. Act one of this political drama was securing the nomination of Howell Cobb for Congress. That staunchly reliable Democratic editor Milton H. Gathright had died and the editorship of the *Watchman* had been taken over by two mercurial men whose loyalties would shift with every political breeze. Cooper was surprised to hear Editor Billy Martin make an unfavorable remark on Cobb's nomination. "I fear that you have neglected our friend Billy Martin," he reminded Cobb a few months in advance of the Sixth District convention. "He is very vain & self-conceited and anything like neglect you know is the highest insult to such a character. You must nurse him up in

Some way. A few extra documents, a letter or so, and if you could get him a few names for his subscription list . . . you could win him quite entirely." Cooper suggested that if necessary he would pay for these subscriptions himself. It was not that Martin was a man of great influence, but he did occupy the editorial chair, and so he must be wooed. "It is difficult to make our people take any interest in the congressional election—they go, as a matter of course for the nominee—the point is to direct the nomination and our newspapers ought to be brought to agree in this particular if possible." He suggested also that Cobb should give a little notice to the other editor, George N. Lester, who was "quite green and a little soft corn would set well on his stomach."[1]

Cooper did not depend for success on persuading Martin and Lester, but rather determined in advance that Cobb had the support of the community. By the time delegates were selected to the nominating convention, "Every man whom I consulted was for you against the field," he reported to Cobb. "So strong was this feeling that the gentlemen of whom I spoke to you (M. & L.) not only withdrew all opposition, but went into the meeting and cooperated with us. They became ashamed of their opposition." Cobb won the nomination by unanimous acclamation and the election in October by 1,477 votes.

Much encouraged, the Democrats redoubled their efforts for the political finale in November, the presidential contest between the Whig Zachary Taylor, hero of the Mexican War, and the Democrat Lewis Cass of Michigan. It was a hard fight, the Georgia Whigs presenting Taylor simultaneously as a Southern slaveholder sympathetic to their wish to extend slavery into the territory recently acquired from Mexico, and as old "Rough and Ready," hero of Buena Vista. At Whig barbecues they belittled the Democrat Cass as the "Hero of Hull's Surrender," Cass having served with General William Hull in 1812 when Hull surrendered Detroit without firing a shot. Against such a colorful nonpartisan figure as Taylor the Southern Democrats had a difficult job, but Cooper hoped to win the Sixth District for the party.

---

[1]Cooper to Cobb, 19 Feb. 1848, Cobb Papers.

He worked hard, and Cobb's victory gave the Democrats a boost. Cooper thought the vote of Georgia for Cass was as sure as any future event. He wrote to Cobb,

> Never have I seen our Democracy more united and determined. Every hour since the October election has added new vigor and energy to our ranks. I could not have believed that one month could work such a change. The days of '44 are upon us here again, without perhaps as much excitement but with more organization and sterner determination to do our whole duty.[2]

But the Democrats did not win. They carried the two northern districts of Georgia for the nominee, including Cooper's own Sixth District, but they lost the rest of the state, and Taylor carried Georgia by a narrow margin. "The result is certainly as extraordinary as disastrous," Cooper wrote to Cobb four days after the election. "The rank and file have rebelled by regiments. . . . This wholesale defection is entirely unexpected and inexplicable," he continued. "I can not even console you with an explanation other than the indisputable truth that very many Democrats voted for Taylor."[3]

Whigs may have won their victory in Georgia by waging a nonpartisan campaign, but this did not mean that Whigs were disinterested in the spoils. Joseph J. Singleton, who was not averse to pressing his claim for a government position whenever his party was in power, said after Taylor's election that he had never seen such "agitation in the public mind . . . on account of the emolument of office." He described the Whigs as being distracted because there was not an office for every one who supported Taylor while the Democrats were amusing themselves at the scramble. All the officers' posts in the mint were being contested—even the "veriest scamp" feeling himself qualified for coiner or assayer—while it was generally believed that "anyboddy can fill" the office of superintendent and treasurer. Single-

---

[2]Cooper to Cobb, 20 Oct. 1848, in U. B. Phillips, ed., *The Correspondence of Robert Toombs, Alexander H. Stephens, and Howell Cobb,* Annual Report of the American Historical Association (1911) 2:131.

[3]Cooper to Cobb, 11 Nov. 1848, in Phillips, ed., *Correspondence,* 137.

ton confided to Cobb that dozens of aspirants for the latter office waited for final word "before they made their descent upon the present incumbents of the other two." The clerkship was also an object of consideration for many, "among whom is your Humble Servant, not for myself, I hope you will believe, but for a son in law of mine, who has been unfortunate in his mercantile business, and is now idle."[4]

For Cooper, it was just a matter of time before he would be replaced. Since he came to office by politics he had pledged not to murmur when politics took that office away, but it was harder to face the reality than the possibility. He at least toyed with the idea of resigning in favor of a successor, a Whig friend. Such a plan commended itself to him for two reasons: "it would thwart the designs of [William] Dawson, [Alexander H.] Stephens and other Federal leaders—and the other is the gratification of personal predilections by the appointment of a friend."[5] The friend was Robert H. Moore of Dahlonega. Other aspirants for the office were understandably upset at this prospect. John W. H. Underwood, of Clarkesville, who very much wanted the job for himself, considered this a fraud, while others accused Cooper of playing "Arnold's game, traytors to their country." When it was certain that Taylor was elected, "all his [Cooper's] pretended patriotism and Democracy left him," one disappointed man charged. On reflection, however, Cooper decided against the plan. As he explained to Cobb, some of his friends thought the Democratic party would benefit by his removal. "They believe that I have faithfully performed the duties of the office and they think that my decapitation would therefore furnish capital to be used in future campaigns under the old cry of 'proscription for opinion.' There are Whigs here who say that they are done with the party if Taylor removes me." Cooper wanted to be a martyr.[6]

---

[4]Singleton to Cobb, 21 Jan. 1849, Cobb Papers.

[5]Cooper to Cobb, 9 Jan. 1849, Cobb Papers.

[6]Underwood to Cobb, 14 Dec. 1848; W. Wyatt Charlton to Cobb, 16 Dec. 1848; Moore to Cobb, 26 Dec. 1848; Cooper to Cobb, 9 Jan. 1849, Cobb Papers; Samuel C. Elam to George W. Crawford, 27 Mar. 1849, RG 56.

Cooper, like his father, had a flair for the dramatic. When he learned that charges of neglect of duty were being prepared against him, he wrote to one of those involved in the scheme,

> How did you proceed with the *charges?* and what did they amount to? Lest you should have failed, I now place in your hands an acknowledgment that I am entitled to all the odium and penalties attached to the sin of being a zealous Democrat, and I have doubtless been indiscreet in advocating that cause as you would be in espousing the opposite direction were you in the occupancy of my office.[7]

Cooper explained to Cobb that this attempt to remove him from office was sheer duplicity. "I should glory in being removed for being a Democrat but I will not rest under charges of neglect of duty, when I know that the business of this mint was never half done until I was placed here." But neither his protest nor continued excellence in the performance of his duties at the mint kept some of Cooper's fellow citizens of Lumpkin County from sending a petition to the president of the United States protesting his extensive political activities: He interfered in elections by swaying the ignorant and unsuspecting. He was assiduous on the days of public elections on behalf of officials from constable to the president of the United States by letting people congregate in his dram shop, "disposing of the bane of life free of charge, all for the manifest purpose of accomplishing his political ends." He was "clamorous & indefatigable" in maintaining his political opinions in the late caucus. He got up political machines, organized mass meetings, left his office to attend them, and persuaded the indigent to attend by supplying them with money, clothing, and other articles. He even bet on elections.[8] If he was anything like his father, the last charge was probably true.

Cooper was such an active Democrat that he determined that even if Taylor retained him in office, he probably could not keep it long. He would never cease his exertions for the Democratic

---

[7]Cooper to John [Underwood?], 20 Feb. 1849, RG 56.

[8]Cooper to Cobb, 15 Feb. 1849, Cobb Papers; Petition of Citizens of Lumpkin County to President of the U. S., May 1849, RG 56.

party, and when the party called him, he would gladly leave his mint office because "I could not do my duty while holding this place by suffurance from the enemy." He had reason to hope that his party would call him soon. While the Whigs were filing charges against him, Cooper's fellow Democrats in Lumpkin County were pushing him for governor. "We are all alive in this Section for the nomination of Cooper believing . . . him to be the strongest man that can be started," one of them wrote to Cobb. Another promised that Cooper would "call to the polls the last fraction of a democrat in the mountains."[9]

Many Dahlonega citizens favored the appointment of Cooper's favorite, Robert Moore, as mint superintendent. A petition to the Georgia congressional delegation from Whig citizens of the town suggested that Moore should have the appointment because he was a good Whig and because "charity begins at home." They probably sent their petition to the wrong group. In 1849 the most effective channel for funneling requests for appointments to the authorities in Washington was through Georgia's George W. Crawford, whom Taylor appointed as secretary of war. "Political triumphs have their embarrassments, as well as exultations," one supplicant reminded him. "As the representative of Georgia in the Cabinet, all aspirants for office, look to you for *help*."[10]

Equally hopeful of getting the top job was John W. H. Underwood of Habersham County. He was untiring in his efforts to secure the position. He thought he deserved it. A Whig in a predominantly Democratic district, for six years he had battled Cooper's political influence. For him the opportunities for reward came but seldom, so it seemed unfair to import someone from a predominantly Whig district, where merit had ample opportunity to be appreciated. Underwood presented himself as honest, upright, and poor, a man who had made his way unaided by

---

[9]Cooper to Cobb, 9 Jan. 1849; William Woods to Cobb, 25 Mar. 1849, Cobb Papers; Thomas D. Harris to Cobb, in Phillips, ed., *Correspondence,* 137.

[10]Petition to Georgia congressional delegation, February 1849; C. Dougherty to George W. Crawford, 26 Mar. 1849, RG 56.

friends or fortune. A Clarkesville neighbor underscored this last point as being all too true. "He is *poor, very poor,* and has an amiable wife and four girl children and is consequently in great need of a salary." Underwood was anxious enough to go to Washington to pursue his chances even though it embarrassed him to be among the crowds there hunting for the office "loaves and fishes." He insisted that he was eager to undergo the scrutiny to which he thought applicants for office should submit, apparently confident that his position as an officer in the Clarkesville division of the Sons of Temperance would remove him from any former taint of barley corn. He tried to demolish the claims of his competitors. One lived in a Whig district a hundred miles away and had never known the service of fighting a Democratic majority. Another, Paul Rossignol, should not be considered since rotation in office was a republican principle. Besides, he added, "Mr. Rossignol is very objectionable to the people of our country. He followed John Tyler in his treason to the Whig Party. . . . He boldly insists that a monarchy is preferable to a Republic." Underwood thought that foreigners ought not to hold any appointive government office. Perhaps he tried too hard. A Dahlonega friend warned him against too much solicitude. "The office would suit you but you can live without it, and I do sincerely believe that constant application to your professional pursuits would be better for you in the end."[11]

Underwood's most important support came in half-hearted fashion from the state's two leading Whigs—Congressmen Alexander H. Stephens and Robert Toombs. Stephens said he would be pleased for Underwood to get the job, but he had no preference himself. "I have letters from a number of our choisest and most prominent men asking the same in behalf of themselves, I think not less than twenty. Under the circumstances I have thought it *proper* for me to put myself under no obligation to any one and to use no influence whatever to the prejudice of any."

---

[11]Underwood to Wm. Meredith (secretary of the treasury), 15 Mar., 17 Mar., 26 Mar. 1849; Reuben Nash to Crawford, 27 Mar. 1849; George D. Phillips to Crawford, 8 June 1849; William H. Underwood to John W. H. Underwood, 10 Mar. 1849, RG 56.

Toombs agreed that he would like for Underwood to have the job in the event of a change, but "from what I have heard from many sources, the Mint at Dahlonega is a crying abuse of official position and prostitution to partisan purposes."[12]

In fact, Washington was teeming with applicants for the superintendent's post. So many letters and petitions came into the Treasury Department about the job that a list of applicants was compiled. But neither the number of names on a petition and an avalanche of endorsing letters nor the qualifications of the applicant had much if anything to do with getting the appointment. It took just one word from the right man, and the appointment was secured. In 1849 the right man was Secretary of War Crawford. Samuel C. Elam, a Dahlonega citizen who was unknown to Secretary Crawford, suggested that Anderson W. Redding, keeper of the state penitentiary, be given the appointment. Crawford penciled a note on the letter and forwarded it to the secretary of the treasury. He did not know Elam, he said, but he was an intimate acquaintance of Redding. "He [Redding] is a self made man. He commenced life as a blacksmith—has often been a member of the State Legislature, and in the section of his residence, recommended as a candidate for the office of Governor of the State. I regard him as possessing every qualification for the office referred to."

Not until three weeks later did Redding himself apply for the superintendent's job, giving as his only "refference" George W. Crawford, who then amplified his earlier recommendation. When Crawford was governor of Georgia he appointed Redding as principal keeper of the penitentiary, an institution that had cost the state $10,000 per year for a quarter century. During the four years Redding was in charge, a net annual profit of $8,000 was realized. Crawford cited this as proof of the man's administrative capacity, but insisted that his mode of discipline was "paternal." Redding had a large and respectable family, Crawford said, and he possessed a moderate estate. More important, "his *moral* is

---

[12]Alexander H. Stephens to T[hompson] Allen, 20 Dec. 1848; R[obert] Toombs to [?], 24 Nov. 1848, RG 56.

unexceptionable. In that, he is a full-brained, round-headed, stout-built, kind-hearted, and high-mettled Christian man."[13] This was the new mint superintendent. Another "foreigner," he came to Dahlonega from more than two hundred miles away.

Cooper did not give way gladly. The very day he sent the first gold dollars to Philadelphia, he reported that a vacancy had been created in the office of superintendent "by a process familiar to politicians, other than death or resignation. No mention is made of my removal, but another officer is appointed, and as I cannot suppose that two are to occupy the station, it is not a strained presumption to infer that I am to give way. This I shall do with as good a grace as I can muster when my successor shall demand the keys."[14] He was not able to muster enough grace to satisfy the anxious Redding, who arrived in Dahlonega in early August, more than a month before his official commission came through. There were the usual difficulties with his oath and bond, so Redding had time to burn. Even after all the official papers were approved, however, Cooper refused to surrender his authority without a preemptory order from the Treasury Department. Redding was impatient, and his chief supporter in town, Samuel C. Elam, was beside himself. Elam charged that Cooper was trying to claim pay until the last hour of the last day, and added that he hoped that a "Whig administration will not pay two officers to do the business of half a man." Elam described himself as "a Henry Clay Whig, a full blooded coon not a ring missing on my tail" Whig, who had seen and heard enough of contempt and abuse of "monscratic incumbents" to make him extremely anxious that not one of them get a cent more than the law allowed. He thought Field and Todd ought to be ousted, too. "The Guiliton is too dull or works too slow. It ought to be ground or the machinery should be greased," he said.[15]

---

[13]Elam to Crawford, 27 Mar. 1849; Redding to Meredith, 24 Apr. 1849; Crawford to Meredith, 4 May 1849, RG 56.

[14]Cooper to Patterson, 12 July 1849, NA-c.

[15]Cooper to Patterson, 4 Aug. 1849; Redding to Patterson, 14 Sept. 1849, NA-c; Elam to Meredith, 15 Sept. 1849, RG 56.

The transfer was made from Cooper to Redding on 1 October 1849. Cooper had been in office for more than six years, only one of which—1846—was unscarred by some attempt to take his job away from him. The experience did not sour him on public service, however. Within ten days, he wrote to his political mentor Cobb about the possibility of an appointment as secretary of the Senate. "The office would suit me very well," he said. "I believe that I could fill it without discredit and it would give me a position & acquaintance quite desirable. Besides the pay is by 'no means inconsiderable' to a gentleman of leisure and out of soap."[16]

With Cooper's departure, the jobs of assayer and coiner were thrown open to the political wolves. Both Todd and Field were Democrats, and, as Cooper admitted, they followed his political example and overstepped the line of prudence. As long as he was superintendent of the mint, he provided them with a measure of protection, but he knew that as soon as he was withdrawn, both of them would be fully exposed to attack. Competition for their places began even before Cooper left the mint. One applicant for assayer requested help from Alexander H. Stephens, but again that Whig refused to be drawn into the contest.[17]

The first man to follow Cooper out of the mint was John D. Field, Jr., the coiner who never even had the satisfaction of having his appointment confirmed by the Senate. As soon as the Whigs came to power, a petition circulated in Dahlonega for Field's removal from office on the grounds that he was incompetent, that he interfered with the freedom of elections, and that during the most recent contest he was "clamerous, offensive and impertinent" in maintaining his political opinions. They charged him with being at the post office when the mails came in to read and "comment with all the fervour of a rabid partisan to promiscuous crowds of people." He often quit his office during a campaign to travel to distant counties to attend mass meetings. On the day of the presidential election he was at the polls by sunup

---

[16]Cooper to Cobb, 10 Oct. 1846, Cobb Papers.

[17]Cooper to Cobb, 9 Jan. 1849, Cobb Papers; Stephens to Meredith, 20 Mar. 1849, RG 56.

to challenge the votes of those whom he supposed disagreed with him. "However excusable such conduct may be in a private citizen we deem it altogether improper and unworthy of an office holder," the petition concluded. Among those who signed the petition was Harrison W. Riley, probably the richest man in town. He had the reputation of being as artful as the devil when it came to getting up charges against people. Other signers included former mint clerk W. E. Derrick and William Warwick, still a workman at the mint.[18]

Field's job was not safe even from his own brother, who happened to be a Whig. James J. Field applied for the position of coiner. He assured the secretary of the treasury that his brother would "cheerfully communicate the requisite information to enable him at once to enter on the discharge of the duties of the office."[19]

The successful applicant for the coiner's job was Robert H. Moore, who had hoped to be mint superintendent. Unlike James J. Field, however, Moore could not count on John D. Field to teach him anything about his new job. Instead, as soon as the coiner learned that he had been replaced, he left for the state capital, Milledgeville. He said he would be gone eight days, but stayed for seventeen. When he returned and found that Moore's official commission still had not come through, he stayed in town but a single day and left again. The mint was running out of money, and the new superintendent was worried. Redding wrote to Secretary of War Crawford,

> They [the Democrats] put every stumbling block in the way it is possible. Fields locked up his office before he left, I took out of his possession however the dies, and could coin the moment Moore can be authorized to act—you must know too that I am emphatically coiner as much as Superintendent—as Mr. Moore knows nothing about it only as I learn him, which I cannot do well until we come to the practice. Mr. Moore will learn after a while. He is a perfect gentleman, and one whom I shall take pleasure in helping out of and through his undertaking. Fields refuses to give him

---

[18]Petition to remove John D. Field, 1849, RG 56.

[19]James J. Field to Meredith, 31 July 1849, RG 56.

> the least information, even to speak to him, so having the Superintendency and coinage on my hands I could wish the appointment of Assayer was postponed for several months (the preferred one at the same time required to give the required evidence of qualification.)[20]

Redding's troubles did not bother Field. He considered both Redding and Moore to be incompetent and asked that their confirmation be denied by the Senate. Depositors were afraid to hazard their gold to Redding's management of the mint, he said, and Moore was entirely dependent on Redding's instructions. "If we must have Whigs do let us have compitent ones," he urged.[21]

Isaac Todd, the assayer, last of the Cooper staff still employed at the mint, must have felt uneasy. A petition requesting his removal, signed by Field's critics, accused Todd of the same political crimes as Field and described him as a "violent partisan of the Democratic faith" who left nothing undone to accomplish a political end. He would, for example, call on the Whig party to clear the way at the polls to let the mint vote. He once drew a weapon on a Whig who attempted to prevent an illegal vote. He would stand by and become a challenger at the polls. He left his office to go to Democratic mass meetings in distant counties. Todd's father-in-law, Alex Awtry, "a working Whig with five son-in-law who are Whigs," came to Todd's defense and asked that Todd not be removed. Todd was the "second best assayer in the U. S.," he said, and he and his Whig sons-in-law would feel they had been betrayed if Todd were removed. "You know that such a thing would sour the mind of any man." The town postmaster, J. H. Smith, also defended Todd. Smith, who happened to be one of Awtry's five Whig sons-in-law, said Todd was a good assayer and a quiet man in politics, but if he should leave, Smith wanted the job. Todd agreed to teach him to assay, quite an advantage for Smith.[22]

---

[20]John D. Field, Jr., to Patterson, 14 Nov. 1849, NA-c; Redding to Crawford, 9 Dec. 1849, RG 56.

[21]John D. Field, Jr., to Cobb, 24 Dec. 1849, Cobb Papers.

[22]Petition to Zachary Taylor, 1849, RG 56; Awtry to John M. Clayton, 18 Sept. 1849; Smith to Meredith, 11 Sept. 1849, RG 56.

Two other men, Dr. Matthew Stephenson and Francis V. Bulfinch, asked Redding's aid in securing the assayer's job. The new superintendent thought that either of them could do the work with a little practice, but they were both poor and could not afford to go anywhere to study and Todd would not let them use the equipment at the mint, thereby turning himself out of office. Todd, Redding said,

> is a perfect machine as an assayer—he was brought up a cabinet maker, but was employed by the Supt. of the Mint as assistant (waiting-man) to Dr. Farnum, one of the first assayers to this Branch. Dr. Farnum was master of his profession, and for the purpose of indulging in idleness and spending his summers North, he learned this man Todd, the manuel operations of it, and he can do it as well as any, but is totally unable to give the why and wherefore of it. Todd has had the place some 6 to 8 years and has secured himself a snug liveing.

Redding thought that he could probably do assaying on a first attempt as well as prepare acids and part gold and silver, but there was the matter of time. "If I can get my coiner fixed up and started, I can take the assayer along. I do not mean to brag, I am sure that I may not be vain upon these topics, but I am very sincere in what I say."[23] He was after all a "full-brained, round-headed" man.

Todd not only refused to teach Bulfinch or Stephenson how to assay, he also refused to teach his assistant. He would not even allow him to practice. Redding thought this essential, in case Todd should become sick or for any other reason be unable to perform his work. Fortunately, no such emergency arose. Todd purchased a store and a tavern in the village, but Redding could not complain that he was inattentive to duty.[24]

Bulfinch and Stephenson were both anxious to become mint assayer. Bulfinch, born and educated in Boston, had lived in Dahlonega for ten years. He had some experience in gold mining, but, like many other miners, he was not very successful. More than forty people in Dahlonega were willing to sign a petition for

---

[23]Redding to Crawford, 9 Dec. 1849, RG 56.

[24]Redding to Crawford, 14 Mar. 1850, RG 56.

him, and he had the support of the artful Harrison W. Riley, who called him "one of our most intelligent and thorough going Whigs, one worthy of public patronage." The Whigs of Lumpkin County were tired of seeing such a radical Democrat as Todd continued in office, "abuseing the administration while enjoying its favor." Bulfinch, despite his poverty, was willing to take the chance that he would be appointed assayer if only he knew how to do the work, so he went to Charleston to study with William Hume, the South Carolina state assayer. After eight days of instructions, he was certified as knowing a correct method of operations, "and his results, although not absolutely true, was as near to the truth, as his want of practice and familiarity with the instruments would justify."[25]

A more likely candidate for assayer was Dr. Matthew Stephenson, who had worked for twenty years to develop the mineral resources of Tennessee and Georgia. He was a Whig and, like the new coiner Moore, had also been an applicant for superintendent. Having failed to get the top position, he was willing to settle for something less. He, too, went to Charleston to study assaying with Hume. He stayed longer than Bulfinch—thirteen days to Bulfinch's eight—and he was a more apt student. Hume said that Dr. Stephenson had "acquired the proper method of operating and only required time and practice to be expert and exact." Privately, he told Stephenson that if he had to choose between him and Bulfinch, he would have no hesitation in voting for Stephenson. "Your acquirements and general information are superior, and in every respect, you have inspired me with greater hopes of your skill and care than your opponent. You possess the requisite knowledge to perform an exact assay, and if you fail by accident, I believe you have sufficient industry to repeat the operation."[26]

Before the end of the year 1850, Stephenson was named assayer and began his duties. Redding appointed one of his rela-

---

[25]Riley to Crawford, 2 Dec. 1849, 14 Mar. 1850, RG 56; Statement of Wm. Hume, 8 Mar. 1850, RG 56.

[26]Statement of Wm. Hume, 6 Mar. 1850; Hume to Stephenson, 9 Mar. 1858, RG 56.

tives as clerk, so at last the mint was completely staffed with Whigs. Zachary Taylor, whose election started it all, was already dead, and another election was less than two years away.

A mint officer's job was never secure for long, and Redding learned, just as Cooper had, that even if it was not an election year, someone would try to oust him from his post. Alexander Awtry, with his abundance of Whig sons-in-law, tried to get the superintendency for one of them, Postmaster Smith, before Redding had been in office a year. It was Awtry's opinion that only two people were pleased by Redding's appointment—George W. Crawford and Redding himself. The superintendent was a respectable man and a wealthy farmer who should have been left on the farm.[27]

The next year many believed the superintendent's job would be vacant again, for a well-founded rumor circulated that Redding would return to his job as keeper of the penitentiary. Governor-elect Cobb did offer him the job in October 1851, but Redding turned it down because the work required too much mental and physical effort. Besides, it did not pay enough. The job at the mint was better.

> My small fortune and large family compel me to look to pecuniary compensations. In my present position my salary is $2000 pr. anum the clerkship $1000 at my disposal which I give to one of my family making it actually equal to $3000 pr anum, the office is one of ease, and affords ample time to look after my other private interest. Indeed the only objection to this office is its inactivity.
>
> To discharge the duties of P. Keeper as they should be is to loose sight of every other pecuniary interest than its salary. . . . unless the Legislature will make the compensation equivolent to its responsibilities, and arduous duties . . . I must respectfully decline.[28]

This must have been a great disappointment to Dr. Singleton, who at the first hint that Redding might leave applied for his old job. "I want it, and from the orriginal troubles (and I may add sacrafices) in its organization, and sustaining it for the first 2 or 3 years in despite of Mr. Clay and others, I do think I am entitled to it,

---

[27]Awtry to Thomas Corwin, 8 Aug. 1850, RG 56.

[28]Redding to Cobb, 22 Nov. 1851, Cobb Papers.

independent of the prayer of 23 hundred petitioners."[29] The number of signers to what some called his "half-mile petition" had grown.

The struggle between rival Whig and Democratic factions to divide the spoils of mint offices ended in 1850. Stephenson was the last Whig named to a position at the mint. Ironically, he began his work as assayer the same week the state convention met in Milledgeville to determine the fate of the Compromise of 1850, that omnibus Whig bill put together by Henry Clay which proposed to settle forever the question of slavery in the territories and thereby save the Union. Though seemingly far removed from the squabbles over positions at the branch mint, the Compromise of 1850 was the backdrop for the biggest patronage fight in its history.

---

[29] Singleton to Cobb, 5 Nov. 1851, Cobb Papers.

CHAPTER 8

Support for the Compromise of 1850 crossed party lines in Georgia. Democrat Howell Cobb joined forces with Whigs Alexander H. Stephens and Robert Toombs to support it and the Union. Among their backers were delegates from the traditionally Democratic Cherokee country where the mint was located. Democratic opponents of the Whig measure were thus automatically branded as disunionists although they argued that to submit to the compromise meant abolition and ultimate disunion. At the meeting in the state capitol the pro-union forces won the day by adopting the famous Georgia Platform, which accepted the compromise as a permanent adjustment of the sectional controversy but with certain provisos. Congress must not interfere with the interstate slave trade or with slavery in the District of Columbia and New Mexico, and the fugitive slave law must be rigidly enforced. The Georgia Platform got credit for saving the Compromise of 1850, thus averting a national disaster. Both those who favored the compromise and those who opposed it at Milledgeville claimed victory. The followers of Stephens, Toombs, and Cobb congratulated themselves that the compromise and the Union had been saved; their opponents took satisfaction in the platform's bristling reservations.

Political repercussions from the Milledgeville meeting were momentous. A reshuffling of Georgia's political parties, already under way, was completed that week. Before the meeting adjourned, Georgia's Whig and Democratic parties no longer existed. They were replaced by the Constitutional Union and the

Southern Rights parties. The next year when Howell Cobb ran successfully for governor of Georgia it was as a member of the Constitutional Union party. Meanwhile, in Dahlonega, the good Whig assayer, Dr. Stephenson, was testing his newfound skill successfully, but his party and his job security had already vanished.

Throughout the nation the Whig party lost strength. So great was the opposition in the North to the fugitive slave law incorporated in the Compromise of 1850 that within four years the party that gave birth to the compromise paid for it with its life. By 1852 the Whig party was hopelessly weak, and the Democratic nominee for president, Franklin Pierce of New Hampshire, won an easy victory in the electoral college over his Whig opponent, General Winfield Scott.

The presidential contest as it was waged in Georgia in 1852, however, cannot be explained in so simple a fashion as a Democrat triumphing over a Whig. By then the Southern Rights party, established in 1850 in opposition to Cobb, Toombs, and Stephens, rejoined the national Democratic party, calling itself the Regular Democrats. Cobb's Constitutional Union party disintegrated into three parts: two Whig factions—one supporting General Scott, the other Daniel Webster—and a Unionist Democratic faction pledged to Pierce. With the demise of the party that fashioned the Compromise of 1850, Cobb, ever the astute politician, attempted a rapprochement with the Regular Democrats in order to maintain control of the state political machinery. When Regular Democrats refused to compromise on an electoral slate pledged to Pierce that included delegates from both factions, most but not all of the Constitutional Union Democrats capitulated. The dissenters were from the Cherokee country. Led by William B. Wofford, this "Tugalo" crowd, as they were called, put up a competing Pierce slate. Governor Cobb thought a separate Pierce slate was impolitic, and he took little part in the election. Five separate slates of electors appeared on the Georgia ballot in November: Regular Democrats, Tugalo Democrats, Scott Whigs, Tertium Quids (former Whig followers of Stephens who were pledged first to Daniel Webster, and after his death to Millard Fillmore), and Southern Rights advocates, an extremist group pledged to former

Governor George M. Troup. The Regular Democrats, dedicated to the states' rights philosophy of John C. Calhoun, carried the state with 33,400 votes. The Tugalo Democrats, dedicated to preserving the Union, gave Pierce 5,775 votes.[1]

Out of these complex political proceedings developed a new contest for the superintendent's job at the mint. The question was not whether the Whig Anderson Redding would leave the mint. Of course he would leave. The real struggle was over which group of Democrats who had voted for Pierce for president would get the spoils. The Tugalo faction had its strength in north Georgia, and if any credence were put in the oft stated premise that local people should be given preference, then the Tugalo group might win. But this was to reckon without the strength of Regular Democrats, who were determined that states' rights supporters, not union supporters, should be rewarded.

Superintendent Redding was among the first to acknowledge the inevitable consequences of a Democratic victory in the presidential contest. He knew that he would be replaced. Only "pecuniary want" made him request that he be allowed to keep his office until 1 October, when his four years expired. His request was denied because too many hopeful Democrats from both wings of the party were waiting for their reward. Among them was perennial applicant Dr. Singleton, who at the age of sixty-five made his last request to be restored to office. He implored Cobb to speak in his behalf, referring to the 1,700 petitioners who asked for his appointment during the Polk administration. A day later he wrote to President Pierce renewing his plea for a position. Again he mentioned his application under Polk and his petition of "2300 names and 1725 others which arrived too late to be sent on." The elasticity of his eight-year-old petition was remarkable. George Kellogg, a Regular Democrat from Forsyth County, was an ap-

---

[1]The complex political maneuvers in Georgia during the campaign of 1852 are traced in Horace Montgomery, *Cracker Parties* (Baton Rouge, 1950) 56-91.

plicant, while the Tugalo faction was represented by at least three others.[2]

At the center of the fight for office were two more representatives of rival factions of the Democratic party. Julius M. Patton, a Regular Democrat, was a staunch states' rights man, "efficient without being noisy." Representing the Tugalo faction was Jacob R. Davis, formerly of Augusta but a resident of the Dahlonega area for a half-dozen years. His chief supporter was Harrison W. Riley, one of Dahlonega's most colorful and wealthy citizens, a former Whig, a power broker, and first and always a promoter of Harrison W. Riley. He presented Davis's name to Howell Cobb as "a Democrat of the old school & in 1850 when distraction seemed to be abroad in the land he was found doing battle on the side of the union." Petitions for Davis were forwarded to Washington bearing the signatures of such strong Union supporters as John W. H. Underwood, former Whig applicant for mint superintendent, Cobb's close friend John H. Lumpkin, and William B. Wofford, the acknowledged leader of the Tugalo faction.[3]

The possibility of Davis's appointment provoked violent opposition in Dahlonega. Before the nomination was made by President Pierce and confirmed by the Senate on 7 April 1853, a strong anti-Davis movement emerged in the community. A merchant, W. C. Perry, who did not wish his name mentioned, and another citizen, W. M. Varnum, who asked that his letter be destroyed, wrote to Secretary of Treasury James Guthrie that if Davis were appointed citizens would rise up and have him turned out by petition. Davis, they said, was an advocate of the Tugalo faction "which done more to Defeat Genl. Pierce's Election than any thing could have happened," and he was backed by the area's most

---

[2]Redding to Cobb, 13 Jan. 1853, Cobb Papers; Singleton to Cobb, 11 Mar. 1853, Cobb Papers; Singleton to Pierce, 12 Mar. 1853, RG 56; Joe E. Brown to Pierce, 6 Feb. 1853, RG 56.

[3]Wm. H. Stiles to Jefferson Davis, 21 Mar. 1853; Stiles to Pierce, n.d., RG 56; Riley to Cobb, 10 Feb. 1853, Cobb Papers; Petitions for Jacob R. Davis as Superintendent, February 1853, RG 56.

"rabid Whigs." If he were made mint superintendent, all the other mint officers would surely be Whigs.[4]

Two weeks after Davis was confirmed by the Senate, a dozen citizens drew up a solemn protest and sent it to the secretary of the treasury. Five charges were made against the new appointee, the first two being somewhat shopworn accusations about gambling, drinking, and Sabbath-breaking, embellished with the revelation that Davis had left his wife in Augusta. The last three charges were more important, for they dealt with Davis's politics.

> Third it is universally known and understood that Mr. Davis has been and still is cheek by jowl with and under the influence of the notorious Harrison W. Riley who is an unscrupulous Whig demagogue of exceedingly bad moral character and it is generally understood that Mr. Davis will appoint a Whig his clerk and that the patronage and influence of the mint so far as he can wield it will be used against the democratic Party and against common morality.
>
> Fourth Mr. Davis belonged during the late canvass for President to what was called in Georgia the Tugalo party every energy of which was exerted to distract and divide the regular democratic Pierce and King party and to throw the choice of election in the Legislature where there was a majority of Whigs and where the vote of Georgia would likely been cast against Genl. Pierce we are all Pierce & King democrats and deeply regret the appointment of a man of Mr. Davis' moral and political character to a post of such importance and responsibility.
>
> Fifth, and last charge though . . . by no means the least—Mr. Davis is equally as objectionable to the democratic party as a Whig would be or more so if possible from the fact that he was trying to do the same thing that the whigs were trying to do which was to defeat the democratic party from giving the vote of Georgia to Pierce and King under the pretence all the while of friendship to the democratic party.

Give us a moral Democrat, they pleaded, in whose hands the treasury of the mint would be secure and whose influence would be exerted for the good of the country and the Democratic party.

---

[4]Varnum to Guthrie, 31 Mar. 1853; Perry to Guthrie, 2 Apr. 1853, RG 56.

The letter was signed by a dozen men, led by one J. B. Graham. Three of the signatories were justices of the peace.[5] Joseph E. Brown, a rising power among Georgia's Regular Democrats, sanctioned the charges. He told of attending two courts since the appointment and certified that he had met no "regular true democrat" who did not regret it. Davis, he said, had worked against the election of Pierce and King.[6]

The matter of whether Jacob R. Davis should or should not be appointed as mint superintendent was part of the huge patronage problem facing President Pierce in the early months of his administration. More than seven hundred appointments had to be made from thousands of applicants. To work at this task, the president and his seven cabinet members met daily for at least two hours. They considered the appointments to be made by state and position, keeping a file of applications and recommendations for each one. Opinions of the writers were weighed as well as their importance and standing in the Democratic party. It was the president's hope that through a skillful use of patronage he could reunite his badly split party—from the extreme Barnburners in New York, who bolted to form the Free Soil party in 1848, to the radical pro-slavery Southern Rights advocates in the cotton belt. It was probably an impossible job. Pierce complained that the pressure for office was so great that he had no leisure to examine credentials or to make mature decisions. He carefully composed his cabinet to include what he thought were representatives from each of the diverse segments of Democracy, but the two members from the South were both Southern Rights Democrats. The most conspicuous omission among Pierce's closest counselors was a representative from the Southern Unionists. Pierce pledged in his inaugural to resist any attempt to dissolve the Union, so the appointment of two Southern Rights men to the cabinet seemed an

---

[5]J. B. Graham, et al., to Guthrie, 20 Apr. 1853, RG 56. Other signers of the letter were Raymond Sanford, R. Moss, J. Payne, James Cantrell, James L. Barrett, B. M. Smith, W. M. Varnum, M. C. Healan, John Bruce, Allen Burns, and S. A. McDonald.

[6]Brown to Guthrie, 23 Apr. 1853, RG 56.

incongruity, but as Cobb's friend Philip Clayton, second auditor of the Treasury, explained, "we have the principles and the fire-eaters the offices."[7] It is possible that the appointment of Davis, a Tugalo Democrat, was an attempt to reunite Georgia Democracy, but if so it was an attempt quickly undone. On 11 May, not much more than a month after receiving the appointment, Davis was removed. He was notified by telegram.

Governor Cobb, ignored by Pierce in forming the cabinet, had recommended Davis for mint superintendent. He was astonished at Davis's removal, and refused to withdraw his recommendation. He said the charges against Davis were false, and at the very least the man was entitled to a hearing. "Before I abandon a friend he must at least have an opportunity of defending himself against the accusations of his enemies. This I call *simple justice.*" Cobb, anxious to reunite the divergent wings of the Democratic party, said that Davis's removal would have bad effects for the party.

> Mr. Davis belonged to a wing of the democratic party—which has received but few, if any, marks of favor and confidence from the administration. I speak of the Union democracy of Georgia. This appointment has given unalloyed pleasure to that numerous class of democrats in his section of the State who sympathized with him in feeling and principle. . . . *It gave more pleasure to a larger number of democrats than any appointment which you have yet made in your department.*

He added that a check of the Treasury Department records would show that the charges against Davis were of a stereotyped character.

> [These charges are] always on hand to be made against any thorough national democrat. . . . They were made against Major Cooper one of the predecessors of Mr. Davis but were examined in that instance and found—as they would be in this case—to amount to nothing. I will only add of Major Cooper that he was one of the most faithful officers ever connected with the Mint, and

---

[7]Quoted in Montgomery, *Cracker Parties,* 93-94. The procedure whereby President Pierce and his cabinet awarded the patronage is described in Roy Franklin Nichols, *Franklin Pierce: Young Hickory of the Granite Hills* (Philadelphia, 1958) 251-58.

> a man of the highest professional character. I mention this to show with what recklessness these charges are made.[8]

Davis, informed that a copy of the charges against him was in Governor Cobb's office in Milledgeville, went immediately to the state capital to read them. Rather that finding them "*so grave and so well established*" as not to admit of a doubt, he found them to consist of "gross and malicious falsehood," and he began at once to collect evidence to refute them.[9] The charges against Davis dealt with his personal life and his business activities in Dahlonega and the surrounding country over a period of a half-dozen years. He was accused of setting up a grocery store in Lumpkin County where liquor was sold on the Sabbath Day and where gambling was common. Later, his accusers said, Davis moved to Dahlonega, where he established a tailor's shop with a little "doggery" in one end where there was drinking and gambling.

In addition to running a tailor shop and grocery, Davis owned a small newspaper in Dahlonega, the *Mountain Signal,* which he purchased from J. R. Lawhorn. It was Lawhorn who told him the details of the charges filed against him.

> Your enemies seem confident. . . . I understand that the main charges against you are that H. W. Riley is one of your bondsmen or securities and that this will give him a fair opportunity of handling the effects of the concern. Another is that you . . . kept at one time an open tippling house on the Sabbath day, this foul false and damning charge has been sworn to in the motion of an affidavit and by one notorious Gavin Cochran, an individual you well know who would not be believed on his oath in a court of Justice by any individual in the town save old Jno. H. McCrosky. This I understand was administered by N. B. Hawkes in the presence of Varnum and A. Rudolph, Varnum paying him $2.50 to do so. Can it be that the President would sacrifice an individual upon the testimony of such characters as the one named.

A clue to the real difficulties confronting Davis was contained in a postscript.

---

[8]Cobb to Guthrie, 12 May 1853, RG 56.

[9]Davis to P[hillip] Clayton, 29 May 1853, RG 56.

> I learned that a letter was received sometime since (perhaps about the time you sent on your bond) by Wm. M. Varnum from his friend Stiles to this effect, to be certain that H. W. Riley was on your bond and thus wrote to James Gardner of Augusta who would give him your character in full Can't you learn something of Gardner I know you differ in politics but I was ever of impression that personally you were friends.[10]

Lawhorn advised Davis to go to Washington to see President Pierce before a commission was issued to his competitor, Regular Democrat Julius R. Patton, as mint superintendent. Davis took his advice.

Former Congressman William H. Stiles was involved in Davis's removal. In April he wrote to both the former coiner, J. D. Field, and the former assayer, Isaac Todd, for information about Davis. Todd repeated the gossip about Davis's tailor shop and "little doggery" where they probably gambled, and added that the appointment had astonished the community. Stiles's letter to John D. Field arrived when the latter was away, but his brother, James J. Field, answered it. He said the charges against Davis were filed by the leading Democrats of the county, that it was true that Davis was controlled by Harrison W. Riley, and that there was no point in turning a Whig out of office and replacing him with someone who was trying to do the same thing—to defeat Pierce. He continued,

> last week was court hear and I never have witnessed so much dissatisfaction among the democratic party in my life on no occasion as was manifested so soon as it was ascertained that Davis was appointed superintendent of the Mint[.] if you can have him ousted you will confer a greater favour on the democratic party hear than you ever have done in your life.[11]

Stiles sent along Todd's and Field's letters to Postmaster General James Campbell, who probably brought them to one of the morning patronage meetings of the president and his cabinet. Stiles's letter was blunt:

---

[10]Lawhorn to Davis, 25 May 1853, RG 56.

[11]Todd to Stiles, 26 Apr. 1853; Field to Stiles, 26 Apr. 1853, RG 56.

> The individual Harrison Riley mentioned in Fields letter, and who has become the security of Davis, is a man of notoriously the worst private character in Georgia. He has been implicated in more than one murder and robbing in this State.
>
> I also met accidentally on the Rail Road a few days since Major James Cooper. . . . after inquiring of me with much interest, by whose influence Davis could have received the appointment assured me that he had known Davis for years, that he was but a drunken tailor, and had kept a low grog shop and gambling house in Dahlonega for years, that he was entirely destitute of character or integrity, and utterly unfit to be entrusted with any charge whatever.

It was Cooper's opinion that if Governor Cobb had been in any way responsible for Davis's appointment that he had been "egregiously imposed upon."[12]

Stiles was also in touch with James Gardner of Augusta, editor of the Augusta *Constitutionalist,* staunch defender of Regular Democrats in Georgia. Gardner told Stiles that Davis had defaulted while secretary-treasurer of the Masonic lodge, and that while he was the agent of yet another society he had failed to give a satisfactory account of the money in his hands. It was after Stiles sent these reports to Washington that Davis's appointment was withdrawn.[13]

In defending himself, Davis retraced the steps of those who made the charges against him and got affidavits testifying to his good character. In Augusta he confronted Gardner with proof that there was no irregularity in the books of the Masonic lodge, and the editor retreated. Gardner wrote to Pierce that what he had told Stiles was simply a current report, that he knew nothing of the facts. After the confrontation with Davis, Gardner admitted that the facts did not sustain the accusation in either case. Another Augusta editor, James M. Smythe of the Augusta *Republic,* wrote to Pierce that "Many of us, who were members of the Southern Rights party, were gratified at his appointment be-

---

[12]Stiles to Campbell, 7 May 1853, RG 56.

[13]Gardiner referred to his contact with Stiles in a letter to President Pierce, 31 May 1853, RG 56.

cause we believed he would make a competent and faithful officer and it was calculated to suppress the murmurs of Union Democrats in reference to the distribution of offices."[14]

Davis's family stood by him, his mother, sisters, daughters, and brother-in-law swearing that it was a "gross and calumnious falsehood" that he had abandoned his wife. Others swore that he was simply a victim of hard times, that he left Augusta for Dahlonega in the hope of making a better living. In Dahlonega, James and William Burnside, his former partners in the grocery business, swore that there was no gambling at their store in Shoal Creek District and that the Sabbath Day was respected. When they moved to Dahlonega, the Burnsides put up a liquor establishment in a room adjoining those occupied by Davis, "but Davis had nothing to do with that business." Some of his friends swore that Davis was guilty only of poverty and that he was a man of "unimpeachable moral character." Many of them signed a petition in his favor. His fellow members of the Tugalo movement said that Davis's appointment gave them assurance that the president would not discriminate against those who "did battle for the integrity of the union." The head of the Tugalo forces, William B. Wofford, protested that he was mortified by Davis's removal, and speculated that the president had been "unduly influenced by some of the cabinet who were chagrined at . . . [Davis's] appointment." To the president himself, Wofford wrote that no appointment could have been made with a greater tendency to harmonize the Democratic party.[15]

---

[14]Gardner to Pierce, 31 May 1853; Smythe to Pierce, 2 June 1853, RG 56.

[15]Wofford to Davis, 25 May 1853; Wofford to Pierce, 1 June 1853, RG 56. The correspondence on the Davis case was so large that the Treasury Department prepared an abstract of papers in favor of Davis, and another abstract of those adverse to him. There were nine items relating to Davis's appointment and removal, twelve others in reply to charges against Davis, and sixteen more (lettered A through P) marked "Additional Papers." In the file, "Abstract of Papers Adverse to Jacob R. Davis as Superintendent of the Mint at Dahlonega," there are thirteen items.

Still, the charges against Davis continued. John D. Field, Jr., wrote to Stiles that Davis had a "bottle Dogery" in town where there was gaming. Not that he had seen it himself, he piously explained, as he did not go about such places. He also repeated the gossip that Davis had left his wife after exhausting her considerable means and spending the greater portion of her property. But he saved his greatest invective for Harrison W. Riley, the principal security on Davis's bond, whom Field described as "an infamous character." If there were defaulting on Davis's bond, Riley would never pay up. Not that he did not have the money, for he did, but "it is believed [that the property] would be transfered to some friend in due time to evade the payment of a defaulcation." Various citizens of the town swore that they had seen gambling, drinking, and dissipation in the back room of Davis's Tailor Shop and that Davis himself had bet money at a game of cards called bluff. Another man, who signed his affidavit with an X, swore that Davis kept three new decks of cards at his store for gambling and that the modes of gambling there by Davis and others included card playing, chicken fighting, pitching dollars, and rifle shooting. Gambling may or may not have taken place at the tailor shop, but Davis did have a liquor license. He paid five dollars for it in December 1851 for a twelve-month period.[16]

The charges against Davis were, as Cobb explained, so stereotyped that they lacked real substance. Davis's real sin was that he was a Union Democrat—that "miserable Tugalo Faction," one irate Dahlonegan called it. It was "Simon pure Democrats" who had saved the state for Pierce, and it was "preposterous" for Tugalos to claim anything for their efforts. John D. Field, Jr., heaped such abuse on the hapless Davis that even if Davis had been reinstated as superintendent, the two probably would have been unable to work together at the mint. He even accused the Whigs of being after the mint's money. Why else would they take such an interest in Democratic appointments, riding to remote parts of the

---

[16]Testimony Adverse to Davis (1853) in RG 56; Records of Inferior Court, Lumpkin County, 1851.

country hunting up men who really know nothing about Davis's gambling character and getting them to certify in his favor?[17]

Union Democrats claimed that opposition to Davis was confined to those who opposed the measures of the Compromise of 1850 and to the Winfield Scott Whigs currently in charge of the mint. They said that the charges against Davis never would have been filed if he had been a Southern Rights Democrat. An Augusta neighbor of Davis, whom he had known for twenty years, urged Pierce in the name of party harmony and justice to an honest man to restore Davis to his post. Unless the two wings of the Democratic party could be reunited in Georgia, he warned, the political destiny of the state "must fall into the polluting hands of Whiggery a consequence more to be dreaded perhaps than even the sacrifice of an individual." Another Augusta friend of Davis, this one a staunch States' Rights Democrat, insisted that President Pierce at least give Davis a hearing. E. Starnes, judge of the Superior Court in Augusta, said serious injuries would befall the "now united Democratic party in our State" unless the president gave Davis a chance to answer the "calumnies upon him."[18]

Davis went to Washington to defend his good name and to try to get his job back. He hand-delivered to the president a letter from Howell Cobb asking for a "full and calm hearing," citing the impeccable character references he brought with him.[19] It is doubtful if he did much more than meet Pierce. Hundreds of applicants sought interviews with the president, and he could not have talked with them all. Afterward, Davis went to the Treasury Department to see exactly what the charges against him were, and more important, who made them. Davis got a copy of the letter from J. B. Graham and the eleven others which had prompted the president to remove him from office, as well as Stiles's letter to Post-

---

[17]W. C. Perry to F. Burt (third auditor of Treasury), 7 June 1853; Field to Burt, 3 June 1853, RG 56.

[18]E. D. Chisholm and Wm. B. Wofford to Pierce, 28 May 1853; John H. Lumpkin to Davis, 30 May 1853; Benjamin Baird to Pierce, 30 May 1853; E. Starnes to Wm. L. Marcy, 31 May 1853, RG 56.

[19]Cobb to Pierce, 8 June 1853, RG 56.

master General Campbell, and brought them back to Dahlonega. On a July day when court was in session, he read the charges before the largest meeting of citizens of the county he had ever seen assembled. The *Cassville Standard,* whose editor was Davis's friend William B. Wofford, described what happened:

> On Wednesday of court, Mr. Davis the late Superintendent of the Branch Mint at Dahlonega made public the charges and by whom made, which were the cause of his removal. Among these was a letter of one Wm. H. Stiles, of vine and fig-tree memory, which abounded in wholesale abuse; among other things he calls Mr. Davis a drunken tailor, to which Mr. Davis's friends replied that Stiles drank more whiskey at Lumpkin, Union and Gilmer Courts, when Col. Chastain beat him 6,040 for Congress, than Davis ever drank in his whole life. The removal of Mr. Davis was a great mistake of the administration, for although he is warmly supporting Judge Johnson yet as Superintendent of the Mint, the position would have given him a larger field in which to exercise his talents as a sound and shrewd polititian. The whole matter between Mr. Davis and his accusers will undergo a local investigation. We will only add that we are creditably informed that many who had taken part against Mr. Davis, now deeply regret their course.[20]

Davis explained more fully to Howell Cobb just what happened. Graham, the first man on the list, declared that he had no intention of attacking Davis's character and was not aware that he had done so. "The truth is the greater number of them were imposed upon, while the balance was flattered with the belief that it never could be come at," Davis wrote to Cobb. The chief workers in the whole plot, he said, were John D. Field and his brother, James J. Field, "the most rabid Whigs in our state as you are well aware."[21]

Cobb thought that Patton would resign the superintendent's post as soon as he learned that Davis was removed on unjust and unfounded charges. He even got a personal interview with Pres-

---

[20]*Cassville Standard,* 30 July 1853, reprinted in Augusta *Constitutionalist and Republic,* undated clipping in RG 56.

[21]Davis to Cobb, 26 July 1853, Cobb Papers.

ident Pierce about Davis's appointment, but his efforts came to nothing. Cobb thought the interview went well and that the prospects of Davis being reinstated were good, but he probably misread the president's intentions. Pierce tried to be gracious and accommodating to all who sought favors, and sometimes this was misinterpreted as approval of their requests.

Cobb was at the nadir of his political popularity in 1853—indeed with his defeat for the Senate in the fall of that year he was without a post for the first time in his political career—and he did not have much influence. Eighty-six Democratic senators and representatives in the Georgia legislature even signed a petition asking the president not to remove Patton to reinstate Davis. No action "would be regarded as more unfortunate for the Democratic party in this state," they said. One Dahlonega constituent wrote to Cobb that the legislature refused him the senatorial nomination because he supported Davis. "We cautioned you we told you we beged you to desist from supporting such Scamps as Davis & Riley if you had not have done it, their is not a Doubt on Earth but you would Re'd the nomination in the caucus at Milledgeville for U. S. Senator but no you must be governed by your own & friends caprices & by that means got Defeated."[22]

Cobb certainly was no help in Davis's libel suit against his accusers which was on the docket for the October 1853 term of the Lumpkin Superior Court. Davis sued the defendants for $10,000, charging that they contrived to injure him, to bring him into public scandal, infamy, and disgrace, and to take away his office. The defendants pleaded truth as a defense. Depositions were taken for both the plaintiff and the defendants, the most important being that of President Franklin Pierce. He swore that he had been influenced to remove Davis by affidavits received from Dahlonega. He referred to charges preferred against Davis by a gentleman, "formerly a member of Congress," that one of the sureties on Davis's bond "is a man of notoriously the worst private character in Georgia, and that he has been implicated in more than one rob-

[22]Cobb to Pierce, 8 June 1853; Georgia Legislature's Petition against Davis's Reappointment, 15 Nov. 1853, RG 56; James Denton to Cobb, 26 Nov. 1853, Cobb Papers.

bery and murder in that state."[23] The decision in the case was not handed down until April 1855, when the jury found for the defendants. Davis was ordered to pay $169.55 for their court costs. He wanted to appeal, but he was too poor to pay the costs and give the security required by law in such cases.[24] For him the great fight was over.[25] Ironically, by that time the breach in the Democratic party that was responsible for his travail had healed.

Against this backdrop of constant political maneuvering, the work of the mint continued. But it was not Georgia gold that was coined there in those years. While Georgia politicians squabbled over patronage, Georgia miners heeded the cry of "GOLD!" that came from California. By the thousands they headed west.

---

[23]Deposition of Franklin Pierce taken 11 April 1854 before J. M. Carlisle and John F. Ennis, Records of Superior Court of Lumpkin County.

[24]Records of Superior Court of Lumpkin County, 1855.

[25]Both Davis and Riley lived many years after this. Riley died in 1874, shortly after his election to the legislature by a plurality of 63 votes. The *Mountain Signal,* announcing his election, said "the jug has been victorious." He died rich despite losses during the Civil War estimated to be at least $100,000. As befitting such a wealthy man, he was shown the utmost respect at his death. Dahlonega business houses were "all promptly closed and the citizens turned out *en masse* to attend his funeral." See *Mountain Signal,* 7 Nov. 1874. Davis left Dahlonega and returned to Augusta in 1857 or 1858. During the Civil War he was in the Quartermaster Corps. Afterward, when the state was under military rule, he was appointed judge of the City Court of Augusta. Later he moved to Washington, "where he held a lucrative position in one of the departments of the government, having outlived all of his traducers with the exception of probably one or two." He died in 1892. See *Mountain Signal,* 8 Jan. 1892.

CHAPTER 9

The California gold rush threatened to make a ghost town out of Dahlonega. Of course those with strong ties to the community hoped to prevent such a development. The area's chief booster was Dr. Matthew Stephenson, an amateur geologist and mineralogist, who later became assayer at the branch mint. Although poor himself, Stephenson seemed incapable of thinking of gold in sums of less than a million dollars. In 1849, when the miners in the Dahlonega area tried to decide whether to abandon the mines in Georgia for the brighter prospects of California, Stephenson mounted the courthouse steps and addressed a crowd of about two hundred miners. He pleaded with them to stay. Pointing toward Findlay Ridge about a half-mile toward the south, he cried, "Why go to California? In that ridge lies more gold than man ever dreamt of. There's millions in it."

The miners listened, but they did not stay. Instead they left in droves for the West, their heads ringing with Stephenson's promise, "There's millions in it." They repeated it so often that Mark Twain, visiting in the California gold fields, picked it up and made it famous in *The Gilded Age*. In Georgia, Stephenson's plea was soon corrupted to "Thar's gold in them thar hills," something miners in future years remembered when the easy riches of the West were stripped away while the desire for wealth remained as strong as ever.[1]

---

[1]Andrew W. Cain, *History of Lumpkin County for the First Hundred Years, 1832-1932* (Atlanta, 1932) 95; E. Merton Coulter, *Auraria* (Athens, 1956) 1.

If deposits at the branch mint may be taken as evidence of prosperity in the Georgia gold fields, times were never bleaker. In 1849 the mint coined less than a quarter of a million dollars in gold, less than in any year since 1841 when, after a slow start, business increased rapidly. A decline began in 1846 and reached its nadir in 1849.

Stephenson was not part of the mint staff when he begged the miners not to leave the state. Ironically, the exodus of miners from the Georgia hills meant a big increase in the amount of gold available in Georgia. In the next few years miners returning from California brought much gold home with them and took it to the mint for coining. Soon after Stephenson became assayer in September 1850, he was busy assaying California gold, enough of it to make the next two or three years among the most prosperous in the mint's history.

California gold began to filter into Dahlonega by February 1850, but Superintendent Redding did not anticipate large amounts of it because of the great distance from the West Coast. By the middle of 1851, however, he changed his mind about the prospects for the mint "from the great number of Miners that have gone from this section of Georgia."[2] That year, the mint coined far more gold from California than it did from Georgia. While slightly less than $155,000 came from Georgia deposits, more than $214,000 came from California. By 1853 the amount of Georgia gold deposited at the mint was a negligible $18,293.94, while that from California was valued at $269,617.78. That year more gold came to Dahlonega from South Carolina than from Georgia.[3]

In Philadelphia the new mint director, George W. Eckert, who assumed his duties in July 1851, was fascinated by the influx of so much California gold into north Georgia. Was the diminished production from Georgia due to the emigration of the mining pop-

---

[2]Redding to Patterson, 1 Feb. 1850, 2 July 1851, NA-c.

[3]Redding to George W. Eckert, 3 Dec. 1851; "Amt. of Gold Received from Different States," *1851 Rept.*, NA-c; Statement of Amt. of Gold Deposited of Domestic Origin at Mint & Branches, Jan.-Sept. 1853, RG 104, "V," vol. 9.

ulation? "I should wish to learn, also whether, if your miners have gone to California, do they generally remain there, or return. And if they return, what is the nature of the reports they make as to the *net* profit of digging there as compared with that in your region: in other words do they come back sanguine, and with the intention to return; or dissatisfied with the desire to remain at home?"[4]

Redding estimated that 1,800 miners left the Georgia gold belt for California, but not more than ten of them planned to remain there for more than a year or so. Some who went out were quite successful, came home and got hands and went back again, and returned a second time "abundantly remunerated." They purchased farms and abandoned mining. Redding added that eight-tenths of the *practical* miners made money, from $1,000 to $12,000 in fifteen months.

> Out of the 100 miners that have returned to this county but one single company of three, have gone to mining here & these will abandon it at the end of the present year or verry soon thereafter. . . . our absent miners [advise] their friends and families . . . to abandon all idea of emigrating to [California]—saying the time is past for success in any short period and that all the Georgians will return in the course of 1853.

Practical miners found California mining more profitable than Georgia mining, Redding said, but the amount of money brought back into the state was still less than that carried out.

> My observations lead me to the fixed conclusion, that few, if any of the pursuits in labor, pay so little, as Gold mining, in Georgia, and as a whole it has not paid anything in California. The Gold Mines in this section will not average more than 50 cents a day to the hand with the best skill and industry. And there is not more than 500 operators now in the whole Gold Belt of Georgia—there is not believed to be 100 in this county of all classes. It is not to be denied but that the mines are exhausted here. . . . that will reduce the receipts of this Branch (of Georgia Gold) below Fifty thousands annually without some new impetous.[5]

---

[4]Eckert to Redding, 19 Oct. 1852, NA-c.

[5]Redding to Eckert, 8 Nov. 1852, NA-c.

Gold mined in California was quite different from that mined in Georgia, so Redding and his fellow inexperienced officers at the mint had to cope with problems unknown to previous mint employees. Gold from California was liberally laced with silver, so much of it that all deposits had to be parted, a process little used in Dahlonega before 1850. Special supplies needed for the process included parting matrasses which were easily broken, either in transit or in use. "The cast matrasses . . . have proved so worthless that we are compelled to order again, they appear to be too thin in their bottoms; some of them have broken whilst boiling on the sand bath, others have dropped their bottoms & contents in transfering them from one place to another," Redding reported in some distress during his busiest year as mint superintendent. The breaking of the glass matrasses caused bookkeeping problems, too. When the matrasses broke, their contents of mixed silver and gold were irretrievably lost, and thus the books would not balance.[6]

From the beginning Redding had trouble with bookkeeping. Accounting for the relatively large amounts of silver separated from the gold taxed his clerical abilities. He had been on the job but a week when he complained that the former superintendent, Mr. Cooper, had failed to furnish him with any quarterly accounts and had not given him any instructions on his duties. The director of the mint in Philadelphia was exasperated. Could Redding not read the laws governing the mint and the correspondence in his office and figure out what he was supposed to do?[7] Knowing little himself, Redding blamed others. The "singular manner" in which the books were kept and entries made during

---

[6]Redding to Eckert, 6 Aug. 1852; James Ross Snowden to G. S. Smith, 12 July 1853, NA-c.

[7]Redding to Patterson, 8 Oct. 1849; Patterson to Elisha Whittlesay, 17 Oct. 1849, NA-c. Redding served under three directors of the U. S. Mint: Robert Patterson until June 1851; George W. Eckert, July 1851-15 April 1853; and Thomas M. Pettit, 15 April-1 July 1853. Pettit died in office and was succeeded by James Ross Snowden, who assumed his duties 1 July 1853. On that date Redding left his post in Dahlonega.

the first three years of the mint's operations—while Singleton was superintendent—made it difficult to get the accounts together. Before Redding left office in 1853, the auditors in the Treasurer's office in Washington would have equally harsh criticism of his "informal and inaccurate manner" of filing reports.[8]

The mint charged twelve cents per ounce to part gold and silver, and in 1853 the Congress required that one-half of one percent of the gross value of gold deposits be charged for coinage. For a few months the silver parted from a gold deposit was paid to the depositor in gold dollars, but it was not long before the director of the mint determined that the expense of parting was so great that all the silver recovered in this way should go to the mint to cover expenditures.[9] The complications in bookkeeping that these changes entailed, especially in the amount allowed for the wastage account, were so numerous that Redding was constantly confused, and his successor, Julius Patton, could keep matters straight only by steady correspondence with the mother mint in Philadelphia.

The fineness of California gold, never as high as that from Georgia, dropped steadily after the first years of the gold rush. In 1848 it was 945 parts gold in a thousand, but by 1850 it was down to 934 parts. As a result the Dahlonega Mint began to accumulate a surplus of silver that from time to time was shipped to Philadelphia in return for dimes and half-dimes, for which there was always a demand in the South. "We are beginning to experience much inconvenience for want of small coins," Redding noted in 1851, a condition that still prevailed five years later when his successor commented that the community was "greatly troubled for silver change."[10]

The sweeps of the Dahlonega Mint piled up in the basement after 1846, when they were last sold, until 1853, when Patton, in

---

[8]Redding to Patterson, 29 Oct. 1850, NA-c; G. S. Smith to Thomas M. Pettit, 5 May 1853, NA-c.

[9]Eckert to Redding, 24 Mar. 1853; Snowden to Patton, 29 Nov. 1853, 18 Jan. 1854, NA-c.

[10]Redding to Patterson, 21 Feb. 1851; Patton to Snowden, 5 Jan. 1856, NA-c.

one of his first acts as mint superintendent, inquired about selling them. An assay of sweep samples showed them to be quite rich—as much as $42^1/_2$ cents per pound. Patton was anxious to sell the sweeps, for he needed money to repair the building. After a delay of many weeks because of the "dreadful condition" of the roads and a shortage of barrels, the sweeps left Dahlonega in the spring of 1854. The shipment was made in stages: by wagon to Athens, then by rail to Augusta, and by barge to Savannah. Eighteen barrels weighing 7,230 pounds made the journey. Like those sold earlier, these were shipped to London, where Dr. Farnum handled their sale. When all expenses were deducted, the sweeps netted $2,140.57. This was the last time that sweeps accumulated over a period of years. For the remainder of the mint's life they were shipped to Philadelphia about once a year, usually two to four barrels at a time, where they were sold and the funds paid to the mint's credit.[11]

Both Redding and Patton had difficulty with coining. Dies were often delayed in shipping, and they broke easily when they were put into use. With the addition of the gold dollar to the mint's production in 1849 and the three-dollar gold piece for a single year, 1854, the die problem became more complicated. Dies for the three-dollar piece were shipped to Dahlonega in June 1854 with the instruction to "Strike such number as will meet demand there may be for them."[12] There was little demand, and only 1,120 of the coins were minted. The gold dollar was never popular. "[It] is loosing its novelty and it is believed, will not be called for but seldom (by few if any) by the end of the present year," Redding wrote to his superior officer in Philadelphia not long after he assumed his duties as superintendent. The coin was too small to be practical. Only two-thirds the size of a half-dime, the gold dollars never had Mint Director Patterson's approval. He thought the coin was "too diminutive" and if counterfeited could not be easily detected

---

[11]Patton to Snowden, 2 Sept., 2 Nov. 1853, 4 Mar., 23 May 1854, 3 Aug. 1855, 3 Aug. 1857, 1 Sept. 1858; Snowden to Patton, 26 Oct. 1853, 6 July 1858; Statement of Sale of Sweeps, 15 Dec. 1854, NA-c.

[12]Snowden to Dahlonega and Charlotte Mints, 1 June 1854, NA-c.

by weight. Congressman Joseph Ingersoll objected to the coins on the basis that they were but toys, useful only as playthings, a counter for a card table. They could be hidden under the seal of a letter.[13] While a few gold dollars were coined at Dahlonega every year from 1849 to 1860, officials there always preferred to coin half eagles. They were in more demand and their larger size made them easier to handle.

As long as Dr. Farnum or his successor Todd served as assayers at the mint, the fineness of the coins was quite high, but when Redding took over with his new staff, the fineness of the coins diminished. It may have been because the California gold contained so much silver, or perhaps it was because Redding, Stephenson, and Moore had so little expertise. Whatever the reason, the low quality of the Dahlonega coins for the early years of the 1850s became a point of contention. They remained within the margin of error allowed by law, but for the first time the Dahlonega coins varied more from the exact standard than any of the others. The annual assay for 1851 coins showed that the fineness of coins from the various mints was Dahlonega, 899.3; New Orleans, 899.5; Charlotte, 899.8; and Philadelphia, exactly 900. Redding tried to blame the low fineness on the "old copper that the coiner was compelled to use during the pressure for Coin during Nov. & Decr. past . . . the old copper owing to its corrosion and oxidized surface has caused the Coiner to miss his calculation to an extent." The coiner was Moore, who by Redding's earlier admission knew nothing of the business only "as I learn him." The mint director would not accept old copper as a proper excuse, but he was never able to get a better performance out of Redding and his men at Dahlonega. Again in 1853 he urged Redding to correct the tendency to low fineness exhibited in the coinage of 1851 and 1852, which Redding again promised to do, "provided I do not too soon sail & stay, too long, up '*Salt River.*' "[14]

---

[13]Redding to Patterson, 3 Jan. 1850, NA-c; Don Taxay, *The U. S. Mint and Coinage: An Illustrated History from 1776 to the Present* (New York, 1966) 201-204.

[14]Eckert to Redding, 19 Feb., 10 May 1852, 24 Mar. 1853; Redding to Eckert, 1 Apr. 1852, 4 Apr. 1853, NA-c.

Redding was indeed about to sail up Salt River to be succeeded by Julius R. Patton, who discovered almost at once that his predecessor had a poor concept of the composition of a coin. Redding told Patton that coins should have not less than 74 parts of silver, far more than mint regulations allowed. Patton's instructions from the new mint director at Philadelphia, James Ross Snowden, called for coins of 900 parts gold, 8 parts silver and 92 parts copper.[15]

Patton did not have trouble with the fineness of coins, but he did have difficulty maintaining their proper weight. The scales and rolls in use at the mint when he took over in 1853 were badly worn. Within a year they were replaced by new ones sent from Philadelphia. Unfortunately, the new rolls again proved to be too soft, so more were sent the following year. In 1858 another requisition came for still more rolls for the Dahlonega Mint. Patton explained to Snowden that the "last pair obtained, made at Pittsburgh, are pronounced by the machinist to be very hard and excellent rolls, but he says they were not made true on the face & that he cannot grind them thus on the lathe here—which was bought twenty years since, and seems to be a very imperfect machine. The strips, when rolled out, have to be put through the drawbench some *twenty* times, and even then they are not regular and of uniform thickness." As a consequence, Patton had great difficulty keeping the weight of coins within legal limits. To prevent error, for more than a year he personally selected every tenth piece and weighed it himself; if a piece was found to be out of limits, he required the whole number to be weighed again.[16]

Patton's extreme caution in weighing coins was necessitated by the adverse report at the annual weighing of coins in February 1857. One half eagle was $^{3}/_{16}$ of a grain above and another $^{3}/_{16}$ below the legal limit. One gold dollar was $^{1}/_{16}$ grain above the legal limit and another $^{1}/_{16}$ grain below that limit. The mistakes

---

[15]Snowden to Patton, 29 Sept. 1853; Patton to Snowden, 8 Oct. 1853, NA-c.

[16]Patton to Snowden, 23 Sept. 1853, 2 June 1854, 25 Dec. 1855, 15 Mar. 1858; Snowden to Patton, 29 Mar. 1854, NA-c.

canceled each other out, but Secretary of Treasury James Guthrie demanded an explanation from Snowden, who in turned pressed Patton for an answer.[17] Patton was shocked. The weight of Dahlonega coins had always been satisfactory before. "The hand who adjusted the coins last year, is the same one, who has performed that service since the organization of the Branch in 1838," Patton explained. "He seemed to be very skilful, and the correctness of his adjustments heretofore, shows that he is entitled to be so considered." Because the bulk weight was always within the limits allowed by law, the mint had not weighed coins separately.[18] It was a year later, after personally weighing every tenth coin, that Patton concluded that new rolls were a necessity. Snowden ordered them from Blake and Johnson in Waterbury, Connecticut, and directed the manufacturers to be very careful. Within a matter of weeks the rolls were completed. The only defect was a pinhole on the face of one of them "so very small we do not think it will do any damage," officials of the Connecticut firm explained. "If this is not satisfactory we will replace at no cost to the mint." The rolls cost $100.[19]

Patton had taken over his duties as mint superintendent in July 1853. A States' Rights Democrat, he was chosen to succeed the hapless Jacob R. Davis, who never served a single day in office. Patton, a man about thirty-five years old, came to Dahlonega from Cassville, where he practiced law. Earlier, he served during Georgia Governor George W. Towns's term as financial secretary in the executive department and as state treasurer. Governor Howell Cobb dismissed him from that position in 1851 because of Patton's states' rights tendencies.

When Patton came to Dahlonega he faced many challenges. Within a year the amount of bond required of him was increased

---

[17]Snowden to president of U. S., 12 Feb. 1857; Guthrie to Snowden, 16 Feb. 1857; Snowden to Patton, 17 Feb. 1857, NA-c.

[18]Patton to Snowden, 24 Feb. 1857, NA-c.

[19] Snowden to Blake and Johnson, 22 Mar. 1858; Blake and Johnson to Snowden, 15 Apr. 1858, NA-c.

from $10,000 to $25,000.[20] He also found the mint to be in poor condition. The fencing around the building sagged; the steps, balustrades, and stairways were dilapidated. There was no water on the premises except the well inside the building that supplied the engine. A new well was dug outside, but it was no sooner finished than it went dry. "It has occurred to me that this last well ought to be sunk deeper & a chain pump placed in it—to use in case of fire," Patton wrote to Snowden. "Otherwise we are almost powerless in the event of fire as the well in the building has a pump worked by the engine & we could not obtain any water from it until steam could be got up and consequently would be useless in case of fire." The cistern to collect rain water failed, and the engine well was so low that barely enough water was available to carry on the mint's work. Maintenance continued to be a problem. By early 1857 worn-out wooden gutters had to be replaced with tin ones and the outbuildings needed repair.[21]

In 1854 the Dahlonega Mint, like all the nation's mints, was put under a new set of rules and regulations that Patton was required to enforce. Workmen were to be on the job ten hours a day—from 7:00 A.M. to 5:00 P.M.—with an hour for dinner to be taken at the mint. At the end of every month, the superintendent was to report to Philadelphia on the "habits of attention, skill, sobriety, and fidelity of each workman, or the reverse." Extra time worked by employees was paid for at the regular rate, and pay was reduced for absences. Holidays were Christmas, the Fourth of July, and general election day. Doors were closed at 2:00 P.M. on Saturdays. Watchmen and messengers must be "middle-aged, able bodied, men of good character and steady habits," and no newspapers, books, or pamphlets were to be received at the mint so that "workmen would not thus misapply time during working hours by reading such." Further, "visits to the Mint for casual observation or amusement are to be discouraged as tending to the interruption of the Officers and Workmen, and to the exposure of

[20]Patton to Snowden, 3 Aug. 1854, NA-c.

[21]Patton to Snowden, 21 July 1853, 25 Dec. 1854, NA-c; Patton to Guthrie, 1 Jan. 1857, RG 104, "V," vol. 16.

the metals and coin. Ordinary visits will be restricted to one day, say Saturday of each week, and no other visits admitted on any other day except by express permission of the Director."[22]

By the time these regulations were put into effect at Dahlonega, the business boom caused by the California gold rush was over. Coinage at Dahlonega was but $292,760 in 1854, and it dropped by more than half to only $116,778 in 1855. In succeeding years coinage continued to decline. Under those conditions, Patton thought that the mint regulations, if followed to the letter, would increase the expense of running the establishment. "As our receipts are not very heavy or regular," he explained, "it will occur to you that we frequently, for several days together, have no work for the hands; and it seems to me, when this is the case, that a more economical practice will be to require the workmen to report themselves every morning, and if there is no work for them to do, to permit them to return to their homes, than to keep them in attendance during working hours, doing nothing but (in the present season) burning wood." Several other points in the regulations apparently did not apply to the Dahlonega branch, and Patton expressed the belief that he should not be required "to enforce regulations which did not promote the public interest." Snowden agreed that Patton must use his discretion as to the attendance of workmen at the mint when there was no work for them, but he urged that in "all other particulars you will please enforce the regulations with as much strictness as may be convenient."[23]

Appropriations to run the Dahlonega Mint remained stable until 1858 despite periodic threats to dismantle the operation and turn it into an assay office. Speculation along these lines was advanced in 1852 when new mints at New York and San Francisco were opened, making the need for the branch mints at Dahlonega and Charlotte questionable. The mint director at the time, George

---

[22]Regulation for the Government of the Mint of the United States, August 1854, RG 104, "V," vol. 2.

[23]Patton to Snowden, 1 Dec. 1854; Snowden to Patton, 11 Dec. 1854, NA-c.

Eckert, advised the secretary of the treasury that if these branches were converted to assay offices, manned by an assayer and two workmen, expenses could be cut by a total of $14,600, but the change was not made. When Patton sent in his estimate of expenses for the fiscal year ending 30 June 1855, which totaled $12,100, few questions were asked and Congress appropriated the money. By 1858, however, business at the branch mint was so drastically reduced that Congress appropriated only $6,500 for its operation, $4,380 less than was requested.[24]

Patton served more than seven years as superintendent of the mint at Dahlonega. He came to office at the end of the great furor occasioned by the earlier appointment of Jacob Davis to the post, but his tenure in office was serene. Not even in the election year of 1856 was there much competition for his job. The fact that there was no change of party when James Buchanan succeeded Franklin Pierce as president of the United States may be largely responsible for this, but Patton himself must be given some credit. He managed the declining fortunes of the mint quietly, and he was never the center of political controversy. With the change of administrations in 1857, a few letters were sent to the new secretary of the treasury, Howell Cobb, from hopeful aspirants to the superintendent's post, but none of these really anticipated success. Most of them paid tribute to Patton as an able man, but they wrote just in case the president should desire a change. The reasons for wanting the job were familiar: they needed the money; four years in office was enough for any man; rotation was a sound principle. Patton wrote but a single letter in his own behalf. He said he was content to serve, and there was no popular demand for a change of officers at the mint.[25] The contest for position was so tame that it hardly seemed possible that only four years had

---

[24]Eckert to Thos. Corwin, 30 Jan. 1852, RG 104, "V," vol. 9; Patton to Snowden, 23 Sept. 1853; Snowden to Patton, [?] Aug. 1854; Patton to Snowden, 18 June 1858, NA-c.

[25]H. Barker to Cobb, 18 Dec. 1856; Philip Martin to Cobb, 15 Nov. 1856, Cobb Papers; M. J. Camden to Cobb, 12 Mar. 1857; Patton to Cobb, 10 Feb. 1857, RG 56.

passed since the whole region was in turmoil over who should have the mint post.

Not much gold came to Dahlonega from California after 1853, and mining in the Dahlonega area declined in the mid-1850s. Patton blamed the slight interest in mining on bad weather and the high price of labor. A severe winter in 1855 and drought both that year and the next hampered mining efforts. Every New Year's Day for three years Patton wrote to the secretary of the treasury that prospects were good for increased mining in the area, but those reports were always followed twelve months later with an explanation of why things had not worked out as expected. In 1857 Patton explained that new steam mills were being put up, and efforts were being made to supply water for the purpose of sluice washing the hills and high grounds of the gold region. Everyone anticipated success. But the next year he reported that "the high price of cotton, provisions and labor have had a tendency to depress mining operations." He hoped, however, that 1858 would be a better year. Again, he was disappointed, and his New Year's Day letter to Secretary Cobb in 1859 had a now familiar ring. "The gross amount of receipts of bullion for the year just closed is smaller than for any previous year, but the amount of Georgia gold received is greater than has been deposited in any one year since 1852. This fact shows that mining interests in this section are reviving."[26]

In 1857 two major discoveries of gold were made, boosting hopes that the area would once again be the scene of major mining. One of these was the Findlay Chute, on the east end of the ridge towards which Stephenson had gestured almost a decade before saying "there's millions in it." The vein of gold was discovered on lot number 1048 by a man named Duncan who said he dreamed where the gold was located. Duncan was hired by J. J. Findlay, whose claim to the land was so dubious that he made Harrison W. Riley his confidant and partner. Findlay and Riley sank a shaft, and until they struck a stream of water that forced

---

[26]Patton to Guthrie, 31 Mar. 1855, 1 Jan. 1857; Patton to Cobb, 1 Jan. 1858, 1 Jan. 1859, RG 104, "V," vol. 16-18.

them to abandon operations, they took out legendary amounts of gold. At one time, it was said that Findlay brought to Dahlonega a ten-pound string of rock and gold, eight pounds of it pure gold. Estimates of the amount of gold taken from the Findlay Chute before water filled the shaft were as high as a quarter of a million dollars. That same year a top pocket of gold was found in the bed of the Chestatee River by Boling W. Fields. Crowds flocked to see the rich Boley Fields Pocket where, according to one eyewitness observer, gold glittered in the sunlight "like stars set in the rock."[27]

Miners returning from California thought that if hydraulic means were used for mining, astonishing results might be expected. The Yahoola River and Cane Creek Hydraulic Mining Company had already begun digging the ditch to bring water to the mines when Patton wrote his optimistic New Year's Day report in 1859. Financed by New England money, the company sent Charles T. Jackson, assayer for the state of Massachusetts, to Dahlonega in December 1858 to make a report. He found work already well advanced. J. J. Singleton, son of the late superintendent of the mint, was civil engineer for the project. He leveled the whole route of the water works from a quarter mile above the fall of the Yahoola River to Dahlonega, a distance of 14 miles, 208 rods. By the time of Jackson's visit, one-fifth of the ditch had been dug, and work was beginning on the high trestle aqueduct, a structure 240 feet high and a thousand feet long. "It has to be strong," Jackson reported in a bit of understatement. The ditch would cost $32,600 and the trestles another $50,000. But when completed, vast amounts of water from the Yahoola River would be available, flowing under great pressure to wash the ridges of the Georgia mountains free of soil and gravel to get at the precious gold. He reported that the Georgia Gold Company was about to resume operations, and its properties would be reached by the waters of the ditch. "The auriferous rocks there are decomposed and disintegrated to a depth of 80 feet. It would wash with great ease and leave the gold behind," he reported. "With energy, econ-

---

[27]Cain, *History of Lumpkin County,* 112-14.

omy, and honesty, the Dahlonega mines cannot fail to richly repay any company that will so work them by hydraulic means."[28] According to engineer Singleton's calculations, when the canal was completed, the water in it would be three feet above the public square in Dahlonega. The ditching had a fall of four feet to the mile; the trestles, cuts, flumes and acute angles a fall of eight feet per mile. On the high trestle that would span the Yahoola River less than two miles from Dahlonega, the fall would be ten feet per mile "so that the water would pass more rapidly and in smaller volume."[29]

Hopes for the project were high in May 1859 when mining engineer John H. Blake visited Dahlonega to report to the Yahoola Company on prospects for hydraulic mining. He described the gold-bearing quartz veins as crumbly and not requiring much work. The country was so broken with hills and ravines that extensive excavations could be made. Gold veins could be reduced to powder with only simple machinery. Using the crudest methods miners had taken $16 million in gold from the area since the 1820s, Blake noted. When he thought of the hundreds of tons of gravel that could be removed by a single hose in a day, he found himself "sanguine as to the results to be obtained by turning the waters of the thriftless Yahoola into the virgin hills." He had every reason to think that profitable results might be expected by substituting the waters of the Yahoola for "bone and muscle, picks, shovels, and wheelbarrows, pens, longtoms, and rockers." He found the whole country excited about the prospects. He warned officials of the Yahoola River and Cane Creek Hydraulic Mining Company in Boston, however, not to expect gold to flow in upon them without care. "When the canal is completed your work begins," he said. Men were already at work sawing lumber for the trestles and flumes. He reported that only white labor was

---

[28]Charles T. Jackson, *Report Upon the Gold Placers in the Vicinity of Dahlonega, Georgia Which were Reported Upon by William P. Blake in August 1858* (n.p., n.d.) 50-55.

[29]J. J. Singleton to H. H. Van Dyke, 1 Dec. 1858, in Jackson, *Report Upon Gold Placers,* 62-63.

used, but that plenty was available, and the country was healthy, not unlike western Massachusetts. "A New Englander may as safely venture here in the summer as go to the New England States."[30]

In February 1859 officials of the Yahoola River and Cane Creek Mining Company asked Mint Superintendent Patton to be the company treasurer so that he could keep the company funds in the mint vaults, an idea vetoed by Secretary of the Treasury Cobb. But Patton maintained a lively interest in the prospects of the company. He invited Governor Joseph E. Brown to visit the area and see for himself the efforts being made to "bring out the golden treasury now buried in our hills and mountains." Patton also used the bright prospects of the future to excuse the failures of the present. Since nearly all the labor in the region was engaged in building the Yahoola ditch and the giant trestle, receipts at the mint remained light throughout 1859 and the first quarter of 1860.[31]

These vast efforts to increase the amount of gold mined in Georgia, plus the possibility of ore being brought back to the state by Georgia miners who had gone to the Rocky Mountains in the Pike's Peak gold rush of 1859, encouraged the Georgia legislature to pass a resolution in December 1859 urging Georgia's congressional representatives to use their influence to get the usual appropriations for the mint continued. The resolution noted that serious efforts were made by the last Congress to withhold appropriations for the mint and thus to abolish it even though the "Mint at Dahlonega is almost the only one which directly benefits the actual laborer, the gold digger himself, and one of the few establishments of the Federal Government of any sort wherein a pittance of Federal money is expended at the South."[32]

---

[30]Blake to C. A. Dexter, 17 May 1859, in Jackson, *Report Upon Gold Placers,* 57-61.

[31]Patton to Cobb, 28 Feb., 1 July 1859, 31 Mar. 1860; Cobb to Patton, 7 Mar. 1859, RG 104, "V," vol. 18; Patton to Gov. J. E. Brown, 10 June 1859, Joseph E. Brown Papers, Georgia State Archives, Atlanta.

[32]Acts of General Assembly of the State of Georgia, November-December 1859, 402-403.

Nothing came of the Yahoola River and Cane Creek Hydraulic Mining Company's project immediately, and the mint itself was closed within a year's time for far more serious reasons than the diminished supply of gold. It may have been that Patton was not an acute observer of the political scene—his letters were the dullest written by any mint superintendent—or it may have been that he had the same myopia that afflicted many Americans in the late 1850s, but he saw no sign of impending civil war. The big mining ditch was abandoned with the outbreak of war, and the partly finished trestles were left to rot and decay for four years. The mint itself was seized by a "foreign" government. But Patton was not at the mint for this denouement. For reasons unknown he resigned as superintendent on the first day of October 1860.[33] His undistinguished career as the mint's chief officer was marked only by the fact that he served longer than anyone else, and he was the only one not forced from office by politics.

---

[33]Patton to Cobb, 7 July 1860, RG 56.

CHAPTER 10

Just weeks before Abraham Lincoln was elected president of the United States the last superintendent of the branch mint at Dahlonega assumed his duties. He was George Kellogg, a successful businessman from Forsyth County and a former member of the Georgia legislature. Joseph E. Brown, who in 1860 was serving his second term as the state's governor, had touted Kellogg for the position of mint superintendent in 1853 when the contest for the post was so lively. Governor Brown described him as "a Christian, a moralist, a man worthy of imitation."[1] Kellogg was also a dedicated States' Rights Democrat, a persuasion that probably made the decisions he had to make as mint superintendent easier than if he had been a supporter of the Union.

The declining fortunes of the mint took a slight upturn in late 1860, bolstered by the new enthusiasm for mining in the Georgia gold belt. Kellogg busied himself with the mint routine during the three months that remained before the state seceded from the Union, and in the best tradition of mint politics he installed his son Henry as clerk.[2]

In January 1861, when Georgia summoned its convention to consider an ordinance of secession, Kellogg was far more interested in the "present excitement of the country" than in gold.

---

[1]Brown to Franklin Pierce, 6 Feb. 1853, RG 56.

[2]Henry Kellogg's bond as clerk was received at the Treasury Department 22 Oct. 1860.

Dahlonega was alive with rumors that Union supporters wanted to take possession of the mint and hold it for the government, saying "they had as good right to do so as the governor to take Fort Pulaski." Kellogg viewed these reports as "idle talk," but he did not want to take any chances. He believed the time had come for the South to act, since all hope for peaceful settlement to the problems had faded, but he did have his position as mint superintendent to consider. "I have only been here a short time & in case Ga. secedes and takes the Mint I would like to be continued. At the same time, being a government officer I think I should act prudent. I do not desire to make too many confidents," he wrote to Governor Brown.[3]

Bluff, eccentric, wealthy Harrison Riley led the Dahlonega forces who wanted to seize the mint and hold it for the United States. The extent of Union feeling in north Georgia, however, was not well known, so Governor Brown was cautious. A frequent visitor to Dahlonega, Brown knew Riley well. He suspected, probably correctly, that the Dahlonega merchant was more interested in notoriety than rebellion. He also knew that Riley was a popular man and would have community support if the governor made trouble for him. So Brown made no show of military force in the mountains. Instead, he wrote to several people in Dahlonega that he knew of Riley's plan, but that he "had known him too long and had too high an appreciation of his good sense and patriotism to believe he would attempt such a thing and that as old, personal friends he and Riley must have no collision." The ploy worked. Riley was soothed and the state of Georgia assumed control of the mint.[4]

Georgia seceded from the Union on 19 January 1861. Superintendent Kellogg warmly approved the state's action. In early February he noted that the "excitement has all subsided on the subject of taking possession of the Mint." He was, however, per-

---

[3]Kellogg to Brown, 12 Jan. 1861, Teleman Cuyler Collection, University of Georgia Library, Athens GA.

[4]Isaac W. Avery, *History of the State of Georgia for 1850 to 1881* (New York, 1881) 186-87.

sonally confused about his own duties. The state revoked title to property ceded to the United States along with the machinery, but Kellogg did not know what to do with the gold bullion he had ready for coinage. Did the governor think "there would be any impropriety in continuing to coin with the present dies until there is further action [on] the subject?" The Governor gave his assent, but he reminded Kellogg that he was responsible to the authorities of the state of Georgia and "not at all to the U. S. government."[5] So coining continued. Georgia was no longer part of the Union, and the mint at Dahlonega was under state control, but the 1,597 half eagles coined there in 1861 bore the imprint of the United States of America.

After the ordinance of secession was passed Kellogg heard nothing from his former superiors in the United States Treasury Department, so he looked to Governor Brown for all his instructions. Should he continue to make monthly reports on deposits and coinage to the mint at Philadelphia? "I see no impropriety in sending this statement if things remain as they are now," he wrote to the governor in February. Do as you think best about making reports, the governor advised him, but hold the bullion and the property. Kellogg, operating in a state of limbo, assured Brown that he would not turn over the bullion to the United States even if officials asked for it, but he continued to report regularly to Philadelphia. As the end of the quarter approached he even sent along a requisition to Mint Director Snowden for salaries for the first quarter of 1861 which Snowden approved! Secretary of the Treasury Salmon P. Chase balked at this. "Notwithstanding this requisition is approved by you," he wrote to Snowden, "the Department before issuing a warrant for such purpose must be fully satisfied that the branch Mint in question is legally conducted under the authority of the United States, of which there are doubts."[6]

---

[5]Kellogg to Brown, 4 Feb. 1861, Cuyler Collection; Brown to Kellogg, 9 Feb. 1861, Governor's Letter Books, 1847-1861, Georgia State Archives, 777.

[6]Kellogg to Brown, 18 Feb. 1861, Cuyler Collection; Kellogg to C. G. Memminger, 21 Mar. 1861, RG 56; S. P. Chase to Snowden, 22 Mar. 1861, RG 104, "V," vol. 3.

Meanwhile, to make sure he would not be forgotten in case the mint was continued in operation either by the state or by the Confederacy, Kellogg wrote to Governor Brown, Confederate Secretary of the Treasury C. G. Memminger, and Howell Cobb, who had resigned as secretary of the treasury of the United States to join the Southern cause, that he wished to be continued as mint superintendent under the Southern Confederacy.[7] The status of the mint at Dahlonega, as well as the branch at New Orleans, was uncertain. The Confederate Congress passed a resolution on 9 March to continue the mints in both places and asked the secretary of the treasury to get an estimate of the lowest amount of appropriation that would be needed to keep them open. The superintendent at New Orleans indicated that the cost of operating the mint there would probably surpass its income. Kellogg thought a liberal reduction could be made in the expenses at Dahlonega, but he could not positively say how much. He would still need at least $6,000 per year for salaries.[8]

The uncertain future of the mint and his own responsibilities weighed heavily on Kellogg. His bond was in the possession of the United States government. Could he later be held responsible? What about the United States funds in his possession? He held a U. S. Treasury draft for $2,300, and another $3,000 was credited to him in the assistant treasurer's office in Charleston. In mid-March, with the fate of the mint still uncertain, Kellogg learned that the assistant treasurer in Charleston had resigned, so he decided to make the long trip to the coast to get the mint's money.[9]

As always, eager applicants stood ready to take over as mint superintendent, whatever government should be in charge of

---

[7]Kellogg to Brown, 18 Feb. 1861, Cuyler Collection; Kellogg to Cobb, 22 Feb. 1861, RG 56, Correspondence Confederate States of America; Kellogg to Memminger, 21 Mar. 1861, RG 56.

[8]Richard Cecil Todd, *Confederate Finance* (Athens, 1954) 12; Kellogg to Cobb, 19 Mar. 1861, Cobb Papers.

[9]Hardy Strickland and William Philipps to Cobb, 19 Feb. 1861; Kellogg to Cobb, 19 Mar. 1861, Cobb Papers; Kellogg to secretary of the treasury of the U. S., 9 Jan. 1861; John A. Dix to Kellogg, 22 Jan. 1861, RG 104, "V," vol. 20.

running it. "Times is squally in Georgia," a Union supporter in Fannin County wrote to Abraham Lincoln in January, offering his support to defend the mint from the "grasps of cecessioners" and at the same time asking for appointment as its superintendent. Two days after Lincoln's inauguration another Union supporter in Tennessee reminded the president that "the time had arrived for a general change of officers and managers of the different offices &c. of this government," and he would like the Dahlonega post. A Northern supporter of the Confederacy, equally eager for appointment, appealed to Howell Cobb and asked for a job. A former superintendent of the United States Assay Office in New York, he had "a serious notion of uniting my fortunes with your Republic if I can be in any way useful. . . . if you want a Director for yr Mint send for me."[10]

Pursuit of office was pointless because the mint did not long survive. Kellogg received deposits through April—300 ounces of gold—all of it from Georgia. He dutifully made his report for the first quarter of 1861, but he submitted it to Confederate Treasury Secretary Memminger rather than to United States Treasury Secretary Chase. The mint held almost $17,000 in coins and about $10,000 in bullion, two-thirds of it in silver.[11] Two weeks after the beginning of hostilities with the attack on Fort Sumter, Kellogg and the assayer, Isaac Todd, submitted their resignations to Abraham Lincoln, Kellogg's to become effective on 15 May and Todd's whenever he could be relieved by a successor. Kellogg explained that he was instructed to make his reports to the government of the Confederate States of America, but that as soon as his successor was appointed by that government, he would take the proper vouchers and "remit to the United States Government a full exhibit of everything connected with this Branch Mint."[12]

---

[10]Andrew H. Kee to Lincoln, 15 Jan. 1861; A. D. H. P. Beborn to Lincoln, 6 Mar. 1861, RG 104, "V," vol. 20; Samuel Butterworth to Cobb, 13 Mar. 1861, Cobb Papers.

[11]Register of Gold Bullion Deposited and Coins Paid at the Mint, April 1861, RG 56; Kellogg to Memminger, 17 Apr. 1861, RG 56.

[12]Kellogg to Lincoln, 25 Apr. 1861; Todd to Lincoln, April 1861, RG 56.

The Confederate government named no successor of Kellogg, and on 14 May the Confederate Congress voted that the mints at New Orleans and Dahlonega be closed on 1 June. The Confederacy would take all bullion and coins, and the other mint assets were to be sold. Kellogg's last days at the mint were busy ones. He closed down operations, balanced the books, shipped the bullion and coins to Charleston, sold what supplies he could, and made a complete inventory of mint property. The most valuable item as far as the Confederacy was concerned was 1,200 pounds of nitric acid.[13] Then he locked the mint records in the vault, kept the key, and on 28 June turned the building over to a caretaker. The Dahlonega Branch Mint was no more. It had been 23 years, 2 months, and 11 days exactly since the first beautiful coin was minted there.

---

[13]Inventory of the Branch Mint at Dahlonega, Georgia Together With Machinery Attached, &c., 14 June 1861, RG 56; Kellogg to [Memminger?], 26 June 1861, RG 56; Receipt of George Gordon of Mint Property, 28 June 1861, RG 56.

EPILOGUE

During the four years of the Civil War the mint building, like its counterparts at New Orleans and Charlotte, was used as a private assay office. Lewis W. Quillian, one of the men who had been a laborer at the mint, lived there throughout the war, kept watch over the building, and assayed the small amounts of gold brought to him. Only once was he busy. In late summer 1862 the Confederate States of America made a deposit large enough to cast 17 gold bars, 196 silver ones, and 3 others of mixed silver and gold.

Shipping the 1,800 pounds of bullion, however, proved more difficult than melting it. It left Dahlonega in a wagon drawn by two spans of horses and guarded by troops. More than two months passed before it reached its destination. At other times the caretaker-assayer was challenged by the job of shipping the mint's supply of nitric acid wherever it was needed for manufacturing ammunition. If it was difficult to get nitric acid to Dahlonega—and many accounts attest to that—it was even more difficult to ship it out again. The roads were in worse shape in wartime than they had been earlier, so a delay of six months was not unusual.[1]

Although the war itself did not come to Dahlonega, it was not always peaceful there. At least once the Confederate government dispatched troops to maintain order. They must have stayed in the mint building, for the Lumpkin County Grand Jury protested that for the first time in the history of the county the roads were

[1]Quillian to Memminger, 3 June, 23 Aug., 15 Sept., 1 Oct., 22 Nov. 1862; Kellogg to Memminger, 22 Nov. 1861, RG 56.

patrolled by a military force with headquarters within sight of the courthouse.[2]

If Confederate troops did occupy the mint, they did little damage. The same cannot be said of the Federal troops who occupied it later. Just a few months after the South surrendered at Appomattox, an inspector from the mint in Philadelphia arrived in Dahlonega to assess the damage of the wartime years to the building. Federal cavalry troops, which roved unmolested over much of the building, were still there when he arrived. The mint could have been in much worse shape. The machinery was rusty but salvageable, and the building itself, except for the chimneys and a shingle roof so thick fire was an imminent possibility, needed few repairs. The mint was sturdily built, the inspector observed.

He must have gone outside town to look at the ditch that the Yahoola River and Cane Creek Hydraulic Mining Company had started digging before the war, because the inspector was favorably impressed by the prospects for renewed gold mining in the area, prospects good enough to warrant opening a government mint or assay office there. He was especially impressed by a single ditch with aqueducts twelve miles long.[3]

The possibility of mining in north Georgia did not bring the mint back, however. Instead, it brought more Federal troops to the area to keep order. They arrived in January 1867 and stayed until mid-May 1869. Their mission was to keep the peace so that capital investment needed for mining would not be frightened away. The troops lived at the mint, but they made daily forays into the countryside to put down any civil unrest. As a sideline, they registered new voters in the northeast Georgia district.[4]

---

[2]Grand Jury Presentments, Lumpkin County Superior Court, February Term, 1863.

[3]James Booth to James Pollock, 19 Sept. 1865, RG 104, Records of the Bureau of the Mint.

[4]Capt. S. C. Green to Bvt. Lt. Col. John D. Wilkins, 16 Jan. 1867, National Archives, RG 107, Records of the War Department, Letters Received; Wilkins to Maj. Gen. S. Thomas, 8 Feb. 1867; Wilkins to Gen. Thos. Swords, 8 Feb. 1867, National Archives, Records of the War Department of the South, RG 98, vol. 196.

In late 1869 the Treasury Department decided to sell the branch mints at Charlotte and Dahlonega. On the day of the sale, 11 January 1870, the highest bid for the Dahlonega Mint was but $1,525, which the government declined. A year later Congressman W. P. Price of Georgia's Sixth Congressional District introduced a resolution in Congress that authorized the secretary of the treasury to convey the mint property to the trustees of North Georgia Agricultural College. He noted that the building, abused or neglected for a decade, could be put to better use. "The people are poor," Congressman Price said, "but are deeply impressed with the importance of education."[5]

So it was done. The transfer of the property was made on 20 April 1871. Unfortunately, the old building had less than eight years left. It burned to its rock foundation on 19 December 1878. Not long afterward another building was erected on the site. The new building had the same outline as the old one and the same hand-hewn granite block walls in the basement rooms. Used as the main administration building of North Georgia College, it still stands more than a century later. The college building is topped by a steeple leafed with Lumpkin County gold from the same mines that once were the sources of gold that was minted into coins bearing the mint mark "D."

That mint mark has become a collector's item in the twentieth century. Numismatists treasure the coins bearing it and are willing to pay thousands of dollars for them. Dr. Joseph Farnum, the mint's first assayer, who was exacting to the point of paranoia about his work, would be pleased about this, although perhaps a little bitter because others—doubtless unworthy—have received more benefit from his skill than he did himself. The practical coiner, David Mason, who took in stride such mishaps as cracked dies and soft rollers, would probably marvel at the value of his handiwork. And Dr. Joseph J. Singleton, who always had a ready explanation for everything, would remind collectors that this inflated value was to be expected. He always maintained that the Dahlonega Branch Mint coined "the best of money."

---

[5]Notice of Sale, 14 Dec. 1869, by George Boutwell, secretary of the treasury; Cong. W. P. Price to Boutwell, 16 Mar. 1871, RG 46.

APPENDIX

Roster of Employees
Dahlonega Branch Mint, 1837-1861

Superintendents

Joseph J. Singleton	1837-1841
Paul Rossignol	1841-1843
James F. Cooper	1843-1849
A. W. Redding	1849-1853
Julius M. Patton	1853-1860
George Kellogg	1860-1861

Other employees

Edward H. Wingfield	1837-1841
Joseph W. Farnum	1837-1843
David Hastings Mason	1837-1848
Isaac L. Todd	1837-1850, 1853-1861
Charles Gilbert	1837
Frederick D. Boartfield	1837-1861
Charles Matlock	1837-1840
Charles Thomas	1837-1839
William Warwick	1838-1851
Zelotes H. Mason	1840-1845, 1853-1860
Samuel S. Blair	1841-1842
William E. Derrick	1842-1843
Augustus M. Russell	1843-1844
Henry S. Autry	1843
Albert C. Adams	1843-1848
William Grisham	1844-1849
John D. Field	1845-1849, 1853-1861

Valentine M. Hodgson	1845-1850
William G. Lawrence	1848-1852
Hardin Perkins	1848
James L. Howell	1848-1854
Henry B. Williams	1849-1853
Robert H. Moore	1849-1853
Matthew Stephenson	1850-1853
William M. Rodes	1850-1853
John C. C. Lawrence	1852-1855
Lewis W. Quillian	1852-1861[1]
Robert B. Patton	1853-1860
Thomas Henley Wimpy	1855-1861
Henry C. Kellogg	1860-1861
William H. Bell	1860-1861

[1]Quillian also served as caretaker-assayer during the Civil War.

GLOSSARY

Mining Terms

Flume An inclined channel, usually of wood and often supported by a trestle, for conveying water from a distance to be utilized for various purposes including placer mining.

Hydraulic Mining A method of mining by washing the ore out of the ground with a powerful jet of water as from a hose.

Long Tom An inclined trough in which gold-bearing earth is crudely washed; usually called long tom because it is longer than a rocker.

Nugget A native lump of precious metal like gold.

Panning Washing sand or gravel in a pan to separate heavy metal from it, especially gold.

Placer A glacial or alluvial deposit of sand or gravel where gold is obtained by washing the deposit; the place where such deposits are found.

Rocker A rocking device used in rocking out auriferous earth by hand, leaving the heavier gold behind, usually made from a gum log.

Shaft A vertical or inclined opening of uniform and limited cross section made for finding or mining ore, raising water, or ventilating mines.

Tunnel A level or nearly level subterranean passage driven across or at right angles to the veins of metal desired to be reached.

Vein A fissure in a rock filled by mineral matter, usually that deposited by solution of underground water, as a vein of gold.

Minting Terms

Alloy A baser metal mixed with a finer one to give durability or some other desired quality, as to a coin.

Assayer A man of science who analyzes ores, bullion, alloys, etc. to determine the proportions of pure or precious metals present, refines base metals, toughens brittle metals such as gold, parts gold and silver, etc.

Assay Balance A very sensitive balance used in assaying gold or silver. It usually has magnifying lenses for reading the gradations.

Bullion Uncoined gold or silver considered merely as so much metal without regard to value imparted to it by its form.

Chilled To become surface-hardened by sudden cooling while solidifying, as cast iron.

Clippings The metal remaining after the edges of coins have been clipped.

Coiner A mechanic who stamps the impress of money bearing the important design and date on the obverse and reverse sides of the coin.

Collar A ring to confine a planchet while being stamped, often adapted to impress letters or milling on the rim.

Cornet A metal bead flattened out and made into a roll for treatment with acid. In assaying, a bead is the globule of precious metal obtained by the cupellation process.

Crucible A vessel or melting pot of clay or graphite used for melting and calcining substances requiring a high degree of heat as metals, ores, etc.

Cupel A small cup, shallow and porous (such as burned bones) used in assaying gold and silver.

Cupellation Refinement of gold or silver in a cupel by exposure to a high temperature in a draft or blast of air, by which the lead, copper, tin, etc., are oxidized and sink into the porous cupel.

Die A metal block or plate, often one of a pair, so cut or shaped to give a certain desired form, or impress any desired device on an object or surface by pressure or a blow, used in forging metals, coining, etc.

Eagle A $10 gold piece.

Fineness Indicated proportion of pure metal in gold or silver. Fineness is usually expressed in thousandths; that is, pure metal is 1.000; U. S. gold is .900 fine.

Fluxer One who fuses metals and minerals.

Half Eagle A $5 gold piece.

Ingot A mass of metal such as gold cast into a mold to get a convenient shape for storage or transportation to be later remelted for casting or rolling.

Lathe A machine used for shaping an article.

Mattrass A round-bottomed glass flask having a long neck used in assaying metals.

Melt To melt or fuse ore, usually to separate the metals.

Milling Cutter A tool-steel cutter used for shaping and dressing metal surfaces.

Milling Press A machine used to smooth metals by pressure.

Mint Mark A letter on the coin designating the mint in which it was struck. "D" was the mint mark for Dahlonega.

Mould A form for shaping and molding ingots.

Parting The separation of gold and silver when the two metals compose an alloy, either native or artificial, for the purpose of obtaining the metals respectively, in the form of fine bars. (Bars containing 90 percent of pure metal are generally considered as fine bars.)

Planchet A flat piece of metal, especially a disk of metal ready to be stamped, as a coin.

Quarter Eagle A $2.50 gold piece.

Refine To reduce to a fine, unmixed, or pure state; to free from impurities, as to refine gold or silver.

Retort A vessel with a bent shape in which substances are subjected to distillation or decomposition by heat.

Smelter One who melts or fuses ore, usually to separate the metal.

Steam Chest A compartment in a steam engine through which steam passes from the boiler to the cylinder.

Sweeps The ashes, fluxes, crucibles, sweepings, and all other refuse from rooms in which the metals are worked, containing a small amount of gold or silver.

Wastage The amount of gold and silver lost in the process that these metals undergo preparatory to striking the coins. The wastage by law must not exceed a certain percentage of the gross amount of metals worked.

Bibliographical Note

This study is based primarily on the hundreds of letters between officials of the United States Mint in Philadelphia, the branch mint in Dahlonega, and the Treasury Department in Washington. These are preserved in the National Archives. The most important of these collections are "Correspondence of the Mint of the United States at Philadelphia with the Branch Mint at Dahlonega, Georgia, 1835-61," RG 104 (Microcopy T-646, Rolls 1, 2, 3); "Records of the Bureau of the Mint," RG 104, "V" series, 20 vols.; "Letters from United States Mints and Branches to Secretary of Treasury, 1834-1861," RG 104; and "General Records of Secretary of Treasury," RG 56.

Several manuscript collections were useful, especially the Howell Cobb Papers and the Teleman Cuyler Collection, University of Georgia, Athens; the Thomas Green Clemson Papers, Special Collections, Clemson University, Clemson SC; and Dugas Family Papers, Georgia Historical Society, Savannah. The Governor's Letter Books, 1847-1861, in the Georgia State Archives, Atlanta, were also valuable.

For local history of the Dahlonega area see Andrew W. Cain, *History of Lumpkin County for the First Hundred Years, 1832-1932* (Atlanta: Stein Printing Co., 1932) and E. Merton Coulter, *Auraria: The Story of a Georgia Gold Mining Town* (Athens: University of Georgia Press, 1956). A good description of Dahlonega by a foreigner who visited there shortly after it was settled is George W. Featherstonhough, *A Canoe Voyage up the Minnay*

Sotor (London: Richard Bentley, 1847) vol. 2. A complete accounting of the amount of bullion received at the Dahlonega Mint and of the coins minted there, their number and denomination is in C. M. Birdsall, *The United States Mint at Dahlonega, Georgia. Its History and Coinage* (Easley SC: Southern Historical Press, 1984).

Index

Adams, Albert C., 191
American Journal of Science, 10, 15
Appomattox VA, 188
Athens GA, 17, 26, 27, 30, 33, 76, 168
Athens Whig, 33
Augusta GA, 5, 24, 26, 35, 36, 64, 83, 88, 89, 97, 107
Augusta *Constitutionalist,* 156
Augusta *Republic,* 156
Augusta *Sentinel,* 33
Auraria GA, 4
  post office, 56-57
Autry, Henry S., 191
Awtry, Alexander (Alex), 142, 145
Baker, Mr.: installs mint machinery, 37
Baltimore MD, 38
Bank of Augusta, 98
Barrett, [?], 49
Bell, William H., 192
Benton, Thomas Hart, 13-14, 15
Bimetal system, debate on, 12-14
Blair, Samuel S., 89, 91, 94, 95, 101, 191
Blake, John H., 177
Blake and Johnson: make new rolls for mint, 171
Boartfield, Frederick, 49, 70, 191
Boley Fields Pocket: gold strike at, 176
Brown, Joseph E., 152, 178, 181, 182, 183, 184
Buchanan, James, 174
Bulfinch, Francis V., 143-44
Burnside, James, 157
Burnside, William, 157
Cabarrus County NC: gold strike in, 9
Calhoun, John C., 15, 93, 94, 149
California: gold rush in, 162, 163, 165
  gold brought to Dahlonega, 164, 175
  gold, quality of, 166, 167
  end of gold rush, 173
Campbell, James, 155, 160
Cane Creek, 6
Cass, Lewis, 132
Cassidy, Mr., 18, 19, 20, 23
Cassville Standard, The, 160
Cessna, G. K., 21n, 56, 57, 74
Charleston SC, 47, 88, 107, 112, 113, 115, 184, 186
Charlotte NC: gold discovered, 7
  branch mint at. *See* U. S. Branch Mint at Charlotte

diminished mining prospects, 45
Chase, Salmon P., 183, 185
Cherokee County GA, 3
Cherokee Indians, 2, 3, 8
removal of, viii, 16, 45-46, 83
Cherokee Nation, 1, 2-3, 15, 16
gold discovered in, 9
invaded by whites, 11
Chestatee River, 4, 9, 93, 176
Choice, John, 21n, 98, 99, 100
Church, Alonzo, 119
Civil War, 179, 187
Clay, Henry, 15, 146
Clay, Henry M., 21n
Clayton, Ephriam, 5
Clayton, Philip, 153
Clemson, Thomas Green, 93, 94
Cobb, Howell, 117, 119, 120, 121, 122, 123, 124, 129, 131, 133, 145, 147, 148, 149, 150, 153, 156, 158, 159, 160, 161, 171, 174, 178, 184, 185
Cobb, John A., 27
Cochran, Gavin, 154
Coins, gold. *See* U. S. Branch Mint, Dahlonega
Coins, silver, viii
Branch Mint allowed to coin, 80
shortage of in Dahlonega, 167
Colquitt, Walter, 122, 124
Columbus GA, 26, 30, 33, 35, 36
Compromise of 1850, 146, 147, 148, 159
Confederate States of America, Congress of: continues branch mints, 184
closes branch mints, 186
deposits bullion at Dahlonega, 187
quarters troops at mint, 187
Constitutional Union Democrats, 148
Constitutional Union Party, 147, 148
Cooper, James F., 112, 113, 116, 117, 119, 121, 122, 126, 128, 131-33, 134-35, 136, 140, 153, 156, 166, 191
appointed branch mint superintendent, 104
background and personality, 111-12
begins mint operations, 107-108
establishes regular coin delivery, 109-10
charges against, 120
job challenged, 117-18, 120-23
replaced as mint superintendent, 139-40
Cooper, Mark A., 103
Cooper, Mary Fairlie, 110
Cooper, Thomas A., 110, 111, 123, 131
Cotton: relation to gold mining, 95
Covington GA, 27, 30
Crawford, George W., 136, 138-39, 141, 145
Creek Indians: war, 30
Customs House, Philadelphia, 119
Dahlonega GA: early names of, 2, 4
description of, ix, 1-2, 4, 16, 38
gold rush in, vii. *See also* Gold mining
life style in, 5
people of, 2, 189
tippling shops in, 6, 120, 124, 154, 158
home of Branch Mint, viii, 5
condition of roads to, ix, 168, 187
courthouse in, 1, 4, 5
jail in, 6
during Civil War, 187-88

Dahlonega Recorder, 36
Dahlonega Watchman, 115, 120, 131
Davis, Jacob R., 152-53, 154, 156, 157, 159, 161-62, 171, 174
  appointed branch mint superintendent, 150
  charges against, 151, 154, 158
  removed from office, 153
Dawson, William, 89, 127, 134
Democratic party, ix, 16, 85, 117, 124, 131, 132, 133, 134, 136, 142, 146, 149, 151
  Regular Democrats, 148, 149, 152, 156, 157
  Barnburners, 152
  Southern Rights Democrats, 152, 156, 181
  Southern Unionist Democrats, 152, 157, 158, 159. *See also* Tugalo Democrats
Derrick, William E., 95, 96, 97, 101, 120, 141, 191
Dugas Family, 88
Duke's Creek, 8-9

Echfeldt, Adam, 61
Eckert, George W., 164, 174
Elam, Samuel C., 138, 139
Emerson, Ralph Waldo, 45
Emory College, 21, 27
Etowah River, 4
Extra Globe, 85

Fannin County GA, 185
Farnum, Joseph W., 34, 47, 51, 52, 53, 54, 55, 56, 57, 59, 62, 63, 64, 65, 66, 68-69, 73, 78, 80, 83, 84, 85, 91, 99, 100, 102, 106, 107, 109, 143, 169, 189, 191
  background, 33
  appointed assayer at branch mint, 33
  arrives in Dahlonega, 48
  complaints of, 49, 50, 53
  work habits of, 60-61, 101, 103
  personality of, 67, 68
  resigns, 104, 105
  bids on sweeps, 115-16
  handles sale of sweeps, 168
Featherstonhough, George, 1-2, 5, 6, 7, 8, 16
Few, Ignatius, 18, 20, 21, 22, 23, 24, 25, 27, 29, 30, 31, 35, 36, 37, 38, 41, 42, 43, 58, 68, 75, 76-77
  appointed branch mint commissioner, 17
  criticized, 19-20, 40
  character of, 21
Field, James J., 91, 98, 100, 101, 141, 155, 160
Field, John D., 97, 98, 99, 100, 126, 127, 128, 139, 141, 142, 155, 158, 160, 191
  appointed coiner at branch mint, 129
  removed from office, 140
Fields, Boling W., 176
Fillmore, Millard, 148
Findlay, J. J., 175, 176
Findlay Ridge (Chute), 163, 175, 176
Forsyth County GA, 181
Forsyth, John, 43, 77
Fort Pulaski, 182
Fort Sumter, 185
Forward, Walter, 101, 102
Franklin College, 28, 119
Free Soil party, 152
Freud, Sigmund, 67

Gainesville GA, 20, 23, 27, 40
Gathright, Milton H., 100, 120-21, 131
Gardner, James, 155, 156

Gilbert, Charles, 49, 50, 191
Globe, The, 13, 14, 26
Georgia Gold Company, 176
Georgia Platform (1850), 147
Georgia, State of: wants Cherokees removed, 3
secedes from Union, 182
revokes title to mint property and machinery, 183
Gold: discovered in Georgia, 9
found in South, 7-11
amount found in United States, 83
diminishing supply of in Georgia, 16, 36, 45, 65, 83, 84
from Georgia used on North Georgia College tower, 189
Gold mining: methods, 10
near Dahlonega, 6-7, 9, 16
increased activity in Georgia, 93-95, 175-76
unprofitability of, 165
decline of, 175
by hydraulic means, 176-77
post-war prospects, 188
Graham, J. B., 152, 159, 160
Grisham, William, 123, 191
Guthrie, James, 150, 171

Habersham County GA, 87, 88, 89, 136
Hall County GA: jail as model, 6
Haralson, Hugh A., 122
Harrison, William Henry, 85, 118
Hawkes, N. B., 154
Hodgson, Valentine, 112, 125, 126, 127, 128, 129, 192
Holsey, Hopkins, 118
Holt, A. B., 21n
Howell, James L., 192
Hull, William, 132
Hume, William, 144
Humphries, John, 5

Ingersoll, Joseph, 169
Ingham, Samuel D., 13
Insurance and Banking Company of Augusta, 96
Irving, Washington, 110

Jackson, Andrew, vii, viii, ix, 13, 17, 20, 21, 118
Jackson, Jabez, 32
Jackson, James, 32
Johnson, Cave, 123
Jones, William E., 33

Kellogg, George, 149, 182, 183, 184, 186, 191
appointed branch mint superintendent, 181
resigns, 185
Kellogg, Henry C., 181, 192
Kendall, Amos, 57, 85
King, William R., 151, 152

Land lottery, 11-12
Lanman, Charles, 12, 16
Laudonnière, René de, 8
Lawhorn, J. R., 154, 155
Lawrence, John C. C., 192
Lawrence, William G., 192
Lester, George N., 132
Lincoln, Abraham, 181, 185
Lumpkin County GA, viii, 5, 89
carved from Cherokee County, 4
gold discovered in, 9, 94
home of branch mint, 15
Lumpkin County Grand Jury: on removal of Cherokees, 46
vindicates Singleton, 86
protests presence of CSA troops, 187
Lumpkin, John H., 122, 123, 150
Lumpkin, Wilson, 76

McComb, Samuel, commissioner of Charlotte Branch Mint, 40, 43n
McCrosky, Jno. H., 154
Macon GA, 30, 33
Martin, Billy, 131, 132
Mason, David Hastings, 34, 39, 48, 49, 51, 52, 53-54, 55, 56, 63, 64, 69-70, 72, 74, 81, 82, 91, 92, 99, 103, 106, 116, 122, 124, 189, 191
  appointed coiner at branch mint, 33
  describes Dahlonega, 38
  begins tanning business, 95
  personality of, 67, 69-70
  final illness and death, 125-128
Mason, David, Jr., 128
Mason, E. A. (widow of D. H. Mason), 128
Mason, Zelotes, 70, 71, 82, 125, 126, 128, 129, 191
Matlock, Charles, 49, 191
Memminger, C. G., 184, 185
Milledgeville GA, 26, 33, 141, 147
Milledgeville Journal, 11
Montgomery AL, 7
Moore, Robert H., 134, 136, 142, 169, 192
  appointed coiner at branch mint, 141
Moore, Samuel, 22, 23, 24
Mount Yonah, 127
Mountain Signal, 154, 162n

Nacoochee Valley, 2, 8, 9
Narvaez, Panfilo de, 8
New Echota Treaty, 45
New Hanover (brig), 35
New Orleans LA: branch mint at. *See* U. S. Branch Mint at New Orleans
New York City, 83
New York Journal of Commerce, 26
Niles Weekly Register, 14
North Georgia Agricultural College, 189
Nuckolls, Nathaniel, 4
Nuckollsville GA, 4

O'Bar Mine, 93

Parks, Benjamin (Benny), 3, 4, 9
Patterson, Robert, viii, 20, 22, 24, 25, 26, 29, 33, 34, 37, 38, 42, 44, 52, 53, 62, 64, 74, 75, 78, 81, 82, 83, 90, 94, 95, 103, 105, 107, 112, 115, 116, 122, 125, 168
Patton, Julius M., 150, 160, 161, 167, 168, 170, 171, 172, 173, 174, 175, 176, 178, 179, 191
  becomes branch mint superintendent, 155, 170
Patton, Robert B., 192
Peale, Franklin, 37, 45, 49
  describes Dahlonega Branch Mint, 39-40
Peck, Adam, 97, 98, 99, 100
Perkins, Hardin, 192
Perry, W. C., 150
Persse, Richard, 18, 20
Phillips, George D., 121
Philadelphia PA, 12, 14, 15, 18, 24, 35, 48, 64, 69, 116
Pierce, Franklin, 148, 149, 150, 151, 152, 156, 158, 159, 161, 174
Pigeon Creek, 6
Pigeon Roost, 6, 9
Pike's Peak: gold rush, 178
Pinchback gold, 79
Pittsburgh PA, 170
Polk, James K., 118, 119, 120, 122, 123, 124, 128
Ponce de Leon, Juan, 8
Pond, Asa, 32-33

Presidential elections: of 1844, 118; of 1848, 132-33; of 1852, 148-49; of 1856, 174
Price, W. P., 189
Quillian, Lewis W., 187, 192
Redding, Anderson W., 139, 141-42, 143, 145, 164, 165, 166, 167-69, 170, 191
  proposed as branch mint superintendent, 138
  background, 138-39
  assumes superintendent's duties, 140
  leaves mint, 149
Reed, Conrad, 9
Reid, Templeton, 14
Riley, Harrison, 4, 99, 141, 144, 150, 151, 154, 155, 156, 158, 161, 175, 182
  described, 121
  biography of, 162n
Rodes, William M., 192
Rossignol, Adrienne, 99
Rossignol, Emily, 99
Rossignol, Paul, 89, 91, 95, 99, 100, 101, 109, 120, 137, 191
  appointed branch mint superintendent, 86, 87
  background, 88
  charges against, 97
  character, 98
  replaced, 104, 105
Rudolph, A., 154
Russell, Augustus M., 108, 109, 113, 121, 191
Savannah GA, 18, 24, 26, 33, 34, 63, 88, 108, 168
Savannah River, 24
Scott, Winfield, 46, 148
Second Bank of the United States, viii, ix, 13, 56, 67
Shaw, Josiah, 20, 21n, 32
Sellers, Messrs., 51, 52, 64
Shinplasters, viii, x, 80, 109
Singleton, Joseph J., 20, 34, 35, 36, 37, 38, 40, 41, 46, 49, 50, 51, 52, 53, 55, 56-57, 59, 60, 62, 64, 65, 67, 69, 70, 71, 72, 76, 77-78, 79, 80, 82, 83, 85, 86, 87, 106, 122, 123, 124, 128, 133-34, 167, 189, 191
  appointed branch mint superintendent, 33
  assumes duties at mint, 44
  charges against, 73-74, 85-86
  replaced as superintendent, 86
  applies for superintendent's job, 117-19, 124, 145, 149
  described, 120-121
Singleton, J. J., Jr., 176, 177
Smith, J. H., 142, 145
Smythe, James M., 156
Snowden, James Ross, 170, 171, 183
Soquee River, 88
Soto, Hernando de, 8
South Mountain NC, 7, 11
Southern Banner, 95
Southern Cultivator, 28
Southern Rights party, 148. *See also* Democratic party
Spencer, John A., 104, 109
Spoils system, ix
Starnes, E., 159
Stephens, Alexander H., 134, 137, 140, 147, 148
Stephenson, Matthew, 143, 148, 164, 169, 175, 192
  background, 144
  named assayer, 144
  urges Georgia miners not to leave, 163

Stiles, William A., 122, 155, 156, 159
Taylor, Zachary, 132, 133, 135, 145
Tertium Quids. *See* Whig party
Thomas, Charles, 49, 70-71, 82, 191
Tinsley James, 27, 29, 31, 36, 75, 76
  background, 28-29
Tocqueville, Alexis de, vii, x, 2
Todd, Isaac, 49, 69, 103, 104, 105, 106, 107, 117, 122, 139, 140, 143, 155, 169, 191
  appointed assayer at branch mint, 108
  removal urged, 142
  description of, 143
  resigns, 185
Toombs, Robert, 137, 138, 147, 148
Towns, Benjamin, 27, 28, 29, 31, 74, 75, 76
Towns, George W., 171
Trollope, Mrs. Frances, vii
Troup, George M., 149
Tugalo Democrats, 148, 149, 150, 151, 157, 158. *See also* Democratic party
Twain, Mark, 33
  The Gilded Age, 163
Tyler, John, 101, 104, 117, 122, 137
Tyler, Priscilla Cooper, 111
Underwood, John W. H., 134, 136-37, 138, 150
United States Branch Mint at Dahlonega
  the building: selection of site, 18-19; construction delayed, 21-22; bid let, 26-27; plans for, 22, 24-26; construction of, 5, 29-31, 36-37, 38, 42; difficulty in obtaining materials for, 40; payments to contractor, 29, 30, 42, 75-76; description of, 1, 5, 25-26, 58; quality of construction, 37, 39-40; security of, 58; machinery for, 24, 35-36, 37, 38-39; cornice, 39, 75; roof, 36, 38, 42, 58, 77-78; well and pump, 36, 51, 172; vaults and safes, 44, 92-93; value of, 84; enclosure of, 59, 74; danger of fire, 172; deteriorating condition, 172; threatened with takeover by Union supporters, 182; used as assay office, 187; occupied by CSA troops, 187-88; occupied by Federal troops, 188; pronounced salvageable, 188; bid for purchase rejected, 189; given to North Georgia Agricultural College, 189; destroyed by fire, 189
  the institution: begins, 44; appropriations for, 173, 174, 178; deposits at, 57, 78, 82, 92, 93, 105, 107, 108, 164, 185; equipment, 64, 80, 166, 171; supplies for, 62-63, 80, 92, 112, 113, 166; assay operations, 57-58, 80, 107, 167; coining operations, 47-48, 52, 63-65, 80, 81-83, 92, 109, 112, 168, 173, 183; defacement of dies, 113-14; dies missing, 114; sweeps, 115-16, 167-68; bullion account, 61-62, 78-79, 89-90, 101, 102; staff of, 44; staff arrives, 48-49; staff housing, 44; staff duties, 91, 102-103; salaries and wages, 44, 49; lack of harmony among staff, 53-

55, 67, 90; fear of dismissal, 64, 85; job hunting at, ix, 31-33, 117, 127, 128, 133-34, 136, 145, 174, 184, 185; petitions for jobs in, 88, 106, 118-20, 124, 127, 135, 136, 138, 149, 150; jobs become political, 128-29, 140-41, 142-44; workmen at, 49-50, 51; rules for workmen, 49-50, 172, 173; as neighborhood mint, viii, 67; possibility of closing, 74-75, 89, 91; closed, 186
Coins: half eagles, 48, 52, 65, 80, 82, 83, 169, 183; quarter eagles, 64, 80-81, 82, 109; dollars, 114-15, 139, 168-69; $3 pieces, 168; quality of, 52, 169, 170-71; irregular, 82; demand for, 107; clippings from, 115; counterfeited, 114; delivery of, 96, 109-10; Mint Mark "D," 16, 189
United States Branch Mint at Charlotte, 15, 24, 29, 39, 52, 59, 61, 63, 83, 169, 173, 187
United States Branch Mint at New Orleans, 15, 63, 169, 184, 186, 187
United States Branch Mints: advocated, 15
bill to create passed, 15
regulations for, 172
at New York and San Francisco, 173
CSA continues New Orleans, Dahlonega mints, 184
Dahlonega, Charlotte buildings to be sold, 189
United States Mint at Philadelphia, 12-13, 17, 26, 37, 65, 79, 81, 103, 118, 169, 183, 188
United States Treasury Department, 17, 60, 76, 77, 117, 138, 139, 159, 167, 183, 189
Ure's *Dictionary of Arts and Manufactures,* 92

Van Buren, Martin, 34, 45-46, 65, 67, 75, 85, 86, 110, 118
Varnum, William M., 97, 98, 99, 100, 150, 154, 155
Vigne, George T., 11
Virginia, University of, 38

Waggamon, George A., 15
Walker, Robert J., 122
Ward's Creek, 9
Warwick, William, 50, 51, 53, 69, 71, 95, 141, 191
Washington College, 33
Webster, Daniel, 148
Western and Atlantic Railroad, 84, 111
Western Herald (Auraria), 4
Whig party, ix, 16, 88, 118, 132, 133, 134, 135-36, 137, 142, 146, 148
Scott Whigs, 148, 159
Tertium Quids, 148
Williams, Henry B., 192
Wimpy, Thomas Henley, 192
Wingfield, Edward, 34, 47, 54, 55, 98, 124, 127, 128, 129, 191
Wofford, William B., 124, 148, 150, 157, 160
Woodbury, Levi, 17, 19, 20, 21, 22, 26, 27, 43, 76
Worcester, Samuel, 3
Worcester vs. Georgia, 3
Worley, William, 18, 19

Yahoola River, 12
Yahoola River & Cane Creek Mining Co., 176-78, 179, 188